T0294002

A Poet's Journal & Other Writings 1934–1974

A Poet's Journal &
Other Writings 1934–1974

PADRAIC FALLON

edited by Brian Fallon

THE LILLIPUT PRESS
DUBLIN

First published 2005 by
THE LILLIPUT PRESS
62–63 Sitric Road, Arbour Hill,
Dublin 7, Ireland
www.lilliputpress.ie

A CIP record for this title is available from
The British Library.

ISBN 1 84351 074 X

1 3 5 7 9 10 8 6 4 2

Set in 10.5pt on 12.5pt Sabon with Centaur titling
Printed by MPG Books, Bodmin, Cornwall

Contents

Introduction   VII

I   *A Poet's Journal 1951–2*
     I–X   5

II   *Memories and Essays*
     The Unique Genius   71
     The Native Roots   83
     The Poet in the New Ireland   91
     Raftery: Poet of the People   95
     Athenry: Childhood Memories   102

III   *Ireland's Poets and Playwrights*
     Five Aspects of Yeats   111
     W.B. Yeats: Man and Poet   122
     W.B. Yeats and Tradition   126
     Yeats the Playwright   130
     Yeats' Vision and the Later Plays   134
     Æ, Poet and Visionary   138
     Letters from Æ   144
     Austin Clarke: Poet, Playwright,
         Prose Writer   150
     Elsewhere in Time   162
     F.R. Higgins: The Poet as Folksinger   166
     F.R. Higgins Reassessed   179
     James Stephens as Wonderchild   186
     James Stephens: A Selection   189

Contents

Sean O'Casey on Himself   193
Synge to Kinsella   199
Ibsen and Synge   207
George Bernard Shaw's Dublin Roots   211
A Batch of Poets, Mostly Minor   214
Graves and Pound   219
Graves and the Muse: Oxford Addresses
    on Poetry   223

IV   *General Book Reviews*
A Half-Day's Ride   231
Taurine Province   235
Poems by T.S. Eliot and Edith Sitwell   237
The Green Fool   241
Old Galway. The History of a Norman
    Colony in Ireland   244
As the Crow Flies   247
Lucky Poet. A Self-Study in Literature
    and Political Ideas   251
The Hungry Grass   255
The Life of the Virgin Mary   258
The Man Who Was Shakespeare   261
The Little Monasteries   264
Plays by Giraudoux and Ionesco   266
New Poems, Rainer Maria Rilke   269
The Esdaile Notebook   272
Poetic Love   275
Nationalism in Modern Anglo-Irish Poetry   279

V   *Verse Chronicles 1956–8*
I–VIII   287

Introduction

P ADRAIC FALLON would not have described himself as a professional critic; he was a poet, dramatist and occasional short-story writer, who also produced a sizeable body of journalism and miscellaneous writings (including radio scripts). Obviously, a good deal of this prose output—articles, reviews, essays, memorabilia—belongs to its time and place. Nevertheless, from such a heterogeneous mass of material a solid core remains that is of far more than period interest. It becomes plain that Fallon had an inborn critical faculty and it grew steadily over the years as his reading, working experience and insight expanded or deepened. In fact, it is quite striking how relevant many of his judgments and intuitions seem today, and how fresh his language still reads and sounds.

Nothing that Fallon wrote was mere hackwork, and his poet's personality and outlook are stamped indelibly on even his most casual-seeming article or book review. He lived and wrote in an era in which relatively few creative writers drew any hard and firm line between journalism and literature, with the result that it was a considerable age of literary journalism. Almost all the leading Irish writers of the time—indeed most writers everywhere—wrote prolifically for newspapers and/or magazines, not merely for money but because they had opinions and viewpoints that they needed to communicate to the reading public.

It was, after all, the golden age of the literary magazine,

and Ireland had *The Bell*, the *Dublin Magazine*, *Envoy* and *Irish Writing*—an impressive quartet, which has no obvious equivalent today. National newspapers also welcomed contributions from the literary intelligentsia, which varied from Austin Clarke's donnish, acerbic pieces in the weekly book pages of *The Irish Times*, to Brendan Behan's racy, demotic articles in the *Irish Press*. Literary men had their 'columns': Patrick Kavanagh wrote regularly for John Ryan's *Envoy*; Fallon himself contributed a 'Poet's Journal' to *The Bell*; and Brian O'Nolan's 'Cruiskeen Lawn' column in *The Irish Times*, written under the pseudonym Myles na gCopaleen, has of course gained canonical status. Benedict Kiely wrote prolifically for the *Irish Press* and also became a virtuoso performer on radio—another medium much favoured by the literati. (It goes without saying that much of the material I have mentioned eventually appeared in book form.) Frank O'Connor, in his later years, wrote regularly for the *Sunday Independent* and in recent years literary men as varied as Anthony Cronin and Hugh Leonard have followed him ably.[1]

As we all know, literary criticism has since moved more and more into the domain of the specialist scholar at the expense of the professional writer. In our day the academic critic has tended to dominate the field and criticism has become increasingly a province of the universities. It has acquired a specialized vocabulary and a quasi-scientific approach, making it primarily an area of research and study rather than a branch of *belles-lettres*—let alone a form of journalism whose chief function is to stimulate and entertain literate but non-specialist readers. It often smells of the university reading-room and not of the small, book-strewn studies, literary pubs and newspaper or magazine offices in which a whole generation of Irish writers produced their work—often with an eye fastened on the clock or on their wristwatches. Though the gain in accurate scholarship may be considerable, so is the—quite inescapable— loss of sheer readability and style. While the best academic critics have many virtues and in terms of sheer book-knowledge can often make the old-style essayist–critic sound dilettantish, the ability to handle words sensitively and economically is not as a rule one of these virtues. Their approach is primarily abstract and conceptual, often with a leaden-footed historicist bias, whereas the typical criticism of a poet or novelist is more concerned with evoking and analysing creative personalities, their unique psychological or cultural ambience, and their qualities of style and sensibility. And as well as the intuitive sense that is a genuine writer's birthright—what Hemingway called his 'inbuilt shit-detector'—he has the hard-earned right and ability to sum up and analyse a fellow-writer's technical equipment.

Padraic Fallon was a practising writer for roughly half a century, from his late teens to his death at sixty-nine. His prose and verse appeared in many publications, a number of which are long defunct, but two long-term outlets in particular should be mentioned: the *Dublin Magazine* and *The Irish Times*. Both were largely the result of personal friendships—in the first case with Seumus O'Sullivan (James Sullivan Starkey), the magazine's scholarly founder–editor, and in the second with R.M. Smyllie, not only a famous newspaper editor but an outsize personality in the Dublin of his time. Fallon contributed to both publications over several decades and this is reflected in the choice of material I have selected here. (It should be borne in mind, however, that a number of *The Irish Times* pieces included here appeared later than Smyllie's death in 1954.)

Perhaps the most important of his critical and quasi-polemical writings, however, is the 'Journal' he wrote for *The Bell*—ten instalments in all, running from September 1951 to November 1952. Though he had more than twenty years still to live and obviously changed his views on a number of points, they represent the core thinking on his art and can be taken as a kind of poet's testament. (Incidentally, I have been surprised on several occasions by the interest and enthusiasm with which a number of younger writers spoke to me about this 'Journal' and the formative effect it had on them.)

In a sense, Fallon was a child or grandchild of the Literary Revival and remained faithful to many of its sources and affinities—French Symbolism, Oriental philosophy, classical and Celtic mythology, folk and historical themes. Partly these were inherited from Yeats, the commanding literary figure of his youth, and partly from his mentor Æ (George William

Russell). He also had an enduring love of the Elizabethans and the Metaphysical Poets, and he was soaked in the English Romantics, though generally selective in his literary likes and dislikes. Among his Irish poet–contemporaries or immediate elders he was closest to Austin Clarke and (for a time) F.R. Higgins; with Patrick Kavanagh he admired the early to middle-period verse and prose, but disliked most of the later work as well as the persona Kavanagh had gradually acquired.[2] He blew hot and cold about Auden, was resolutely hostile in his later years to Eliot, and regarded Pound as a central though maverick figure whose talents had flowered again late in life with the 'Pisan Cantos'. MacNeice—whom he knew personally—he only came to appreciate after his death. He also perfected the work of another Northerner, John Hewitt.

Fallon also praised Robert Graves selectively and regarded his prose work *The White Goddess* as a seminal one in its time and context. But as a lifelong poetry reviewer he showed a wide-awake discernment of the quality of younger writers and was probably among the earliest to single out the work of Philip Larkin, Ted Hughes and Thomas Kinsella. (He was also stimulated by the poetry of Sylvia Plath when he first encountered it in the mid-sixties, though he had no opportunity of reviewing it.) Among poets of the younger generation he was interested in the early work of Seamus Heaney, Michael Longley and Eavan Boland, among others; however, by this stage he was no longer an active reviewer.

Though Fallon relished a great deal of American literature as a whole—from Melville and Emily Dickinson down to Hemingway and Ogden Nash—he tended to stand back from the wave of Americanization that grew like a tsunami in the decades after World War II. Leaving aside the expatriates Pound and Eliot, he was indifferent to William Carlos Williams, regarded Robert Frost as a slightly bogus figure and was lukewarm about Wallace Stevens. Robert Lowell he respected but without real enthusiasm; so far as I can establish, he never reviewed any book of his. He was impressed by Richard Wilbur's early poems but lost interest in him later. French literature—particularly French Symbolism—always meant far more to him, but though he produced outstanding translations from Baudelaire, Rimbaud and Mallarmé he left behind no important critical writings on any of them. By contrast, there are two acute pieces included here on Rilke, another major influence of his middle years.[3] He was also cognizant of contemporary French theatre—then intellectually fashionable in Dublin—from Cocteau down to Anouilh and Montherlant.

From his intellectual godfather, Æ, Fallon acquired much of his intellectual culture, but it was Yeats who became his touchstone as a poet. This is hardly surprising for a young writer growing up in a milieu where Yeats was not only a massive, dominating literary presence, but a flesh-and-blood individual who could be seen in person hieratically walking the streets of Dublin.[4] The early (1934) essay reprinted from the *Dublin Magazine* is an act of considered homage by a young poet to a Grand Old Man. In his middle years Fallon reacted strongly against the more histrionic, declamatory aspect of Yeats' verse and his review of A. Norman Jeffares' 1949 biography shows a degree of disillusionment that is partly to be explained as a reaction against his former discipleship. However in the final decade of his life he swung round again to a more positive position, though he always preferred the Yeats of *The Tower* and *The Winding Stair* to the poetry of his final years, which he maintained was often self-conscious and mannered. Joyce he regarded as the initiator of an entirely new cycle of Irish literature, though without feeling any special affinity with his work or mentality. He was, incidentally, friendly with a number of people who had known Joyce well and who sometimes reminisced intimately and revealingly about him.

Fallon was of course a dramatist as well as a poet, though his finest plays were written for radio while those created for the professional stage did not achieve much more than a short-lived, coterie success.[5] Shakespeare and the other Elizabethans—particularly Ben Jonson—were lifelong addictions, and the striking essay on Tourneur shows that his knowledge of the period was far more than a peripheral or semi-amateur one. (He had in fact intensively studied Elizabethan blank verse, whose legacy can be seen in certain of his own plays.) In his middle years he came greatly to admire Ibsen, against whom he had previously been prejudiced through Yeats' rather dogmatic and ill-considered rejection of him. Synge was an enthusiasm of his youth and he became increasingly critical of him as he grew older—as, indeed, he grew increasingly sceptical about much of the Literary Revival in general. His attitude towards Sean O'Casey was ambivalent and though he greatly respected George Bernard Shaw as a public personality and a courageous, *engagé* figure of major intellectual calibre, he did not think highly of his plays and predicted that Shaw's standing as a dramatist would diminish quite rapidly after his death. He was much impressed by Beckett's *Waiting for Godot* when he saw it first—either in London or in the tiny (and long-vanished) Pike Theatre in Dublin, though he found the later plays repetitive. However, there seem to be no more than a few tangential references to Beckett—whom he met personally at least once—in his published criticism.

During the late 1950s Fallon wrote a quarterly 'Verse Chronicle' for the *Dublin Magazine*, sometimes reviewing as many as seven or eight volumes of new or recent verse at a time. Inevitably a certain amount of this is now dated, or more accurately, many of the poets he wrote about have faded from view. However, the 'Chronicle' contains too much good, intelligent and sometimes prescient material to ignore it—for instance, the singling out of Ted Hughes and Philip Larkin (then relatively little known) as important figures of the future. And if certain other judgments of his now seem dubious or less relevant, in the light of what has happened since, that is only to be expected. Criticism written in the heat of the moment, with the battle-smoke of topical controversy billowing about almost blindingly, is a very different thing from criticism written in a university library with the benefit of accumulated hindsight.

At any rate, I have given a selection of these 'Verse Chronicles', some in full and others unavoidably truncated. They show at the very least that Padraic Fallon was consistent and honest in his stances, that he was always closely interested in other men's literary craft, and that his views were always entirely—sometimes idiosyncratically—his own, not mere careerist sailing and tacking with the variable winds of fashion.[6] At the moment he is still somewhat out of fashion himself, but the literary climate appears to be changing as it always does in the long run. Increasing familiarity with his work—verse, plays, prose—will surely reveal his central role in the Irish literature of his time.

One recurring theme through many of his reviews and essays is the aspiration of he himself and various of his contemporaries to encourage the development of an independent Irish literature in the English language. (Though Fallon was undogmatically in favour of his compatriots being taught Gaelic, he did not consider it feasible to base a modern literature on it.) Today this view is often derided as cultural chauvinism, but that is a facile or even cheap misjudgment, since Fallon was the reverse of a chauvinist, let alone an isolationist. There is, after all, a flourishing American literature in English, not to mention Canada, Australia, etc.—or for that matter, various flourishing schools of Latin American writing that are quite independent of Spain. In insisting on the same privilege—or rather the same right—for Ireland, Fallon was merely implying that many or most Irish writers would profit from greater historico-cultural awareness and an alert, firmly established, tradition to buoy them up. Has time proved him wrong in this? Personally I doubt it.

Poetic Doctrines and Definitions

The ten think-pieces that Fallon contributed successively to *The Bell* magazine in the early 1950s are unique in his critical writings. In general the latter have rather an ad hoc character, whereas *The Bell* 'Journal' is something like a sustained manifesto, or at times a sustained self-inquisition. These essay/articles more or less form a declaration of his poetic (and dramatic) principles and are also partly a guide to younger, fledgeling Irish writers. The tone at times is consciously topical and colloquial, almost popular—perhaps a little uneasily so in fact.

The 'Journal' also represents a considered challenge to some of the literary gods and fashions of the day. For instance, T.S. Eliot's plays such as *The Cocktail Party* were then the subject of uncritical adulation, though today they seem stilted and dated; unfashionably Fallon dared to point this out. Other cults and idols are treated with similar disrespect on occasion. Basically, Fallon's allegiance was to an imagistic type of poetry, with its roots in Symbolism but also in the Elizabethans and Metaphysicals; the type of quasi-journalistic verse that became popular from the thirties onwards seemed to him to compromise fatally with prose thinking and prose logic. (This largely explains his ambivalent attitude to W.H. Auden, for example.) However, he does not dogmatize over his personal stances and indeed seems more interested in reaching some constructive synthesis, not in mere polemics or in fostering literary controversy for the sake of a little easy publicity.

Since Fallon had become an unfashionable figure at the time of his death, it should be pointed out that in the fifties he was one of the most respected Irish writers of the middle generation, whose verse plays for radio, in particular, were widely praised. (Apart from their initial productions on Radio Éireann, these were performed on the now-defunct BBC Third Programme and also in Germany.) So the 'Journal' does not represent the thoughts-out-of-season of a disgruntled or sidelined literary figure, but the credo of a writer with an acknowledged position and reputation. Fallon's failure to publish his poetry in book form, until the last months of his life, no doubt told against him heavily, but he was also the victim of a swing in taste and attitudes that swept aside many of his generation in favour of the new Anglo–American literary orthodoxy. In drama, too, Beckett had brought about a major change in taste.

It scarcely seems necessary to introduce *The Bell* itself at this stage, but it is more than half-a-century dead and almost two generations have grown up without its intellectual presence or influence. It ran from 1940 to 1954 and consciously sought controversy on urgent, topical issues—such as literary censorship and Irish neutrality during World War II—as well as dealing with purely literary topics. Until 1946 it was edited by Sean O'Faolain, who was succeeded by Peadar O'Donnell; Anthony Cronin and Hubert Butler were also closely associated with it. *The Bell* was published as a monthly, in an extremely plain, functional format, and normally it carried no illustrations or graphic material.

It is one of the features—curiosities, almost—of Irish writing since independence that so much of the burden of criticism has been shouldered by the poets. Sean O'Faolain is one outstanding prose exception and there have been others, but broadly I think the generalization holds true. Louis MacNeice, Austin Clarke, Thomas Kinsella and Anthony Cronin are all obvious examples, while more recently we had Seamus Heaney, Derek Mahon, Eavan Boland *et alii*. (Patrick Kavanagh stands rather outside this argument, since he was a polemicist and troubleshooter more than a critic, but he still took part in all the leading cultural debates of his time.) It seems overdue to add Padraic Fallon to their number.

Finally, I must acknowledge the vital support of my brothers, the helpfulness of my wife, and the patient aid of Jane Miller. And due acknowledgment should be made to *The Irish Times*, which carried many of the poet's reviews and poems. (*The Bell* and the *Dublin Magazine*, alas, no longer exist.)

Notes

1. Fallon himself wrote a series of articles for the *Irish Press* during the 1950s. He did so, however, mainly as a kind of honorary farmer (he did in fact farm twenty acres in Co. Wexford at this time, as well as working in the Customs and Excise) and the articles are rarely about literary or cultural topics.
2. He was one of the first to praise Kavanagh's novel *Tarry Flynn*, a book that received a cold or puzzled reaction from most Irish critics on publication. Kavanagh thanked him when they met in a Dublin street shortly afterwards.
3. Fallon read Rilke in the translations of the late J.B. Leishman. He knew little or no German.
4. He met Yeats in person two or three times, probably in company with Æ.
5. A selection of the radio plays was published recently by the Carcanet Press.
6. Fallon himself felt that fashion was 'the merest commonplace'. While discussing the various literary coteries of his time, he said to me: 'The clique always stands for a cliché.'

A Poet's Journal & Other Writings 1934–1974

I
A Poet's Journal 1951-2

A Poet's Journal I

WHAT KIND of a mind is it that can keep a journal? The Gides and the Joyces, the notemakers, the lest-we-forget people who wish to remember things in tranquillity, and the people who will hot things up later in a pot of myth? You will have always the novelist to whom the happening is more than an event, and you will have the novelist to whom it is so much local legerdemain, and you will have people like myself who are not as interested as they should be and leave it to something inside them to substitute for what happens—another kind of reality. I am ashamed of my own lack of interest so often that I have ceased to be ashamed of it. But as this doesn't stop me from excusing myself in the small hours, I suppose I have a social conscience somewhere, even if I haven't grief enough for everything.

I sin against everything, not so much in being light-hearted as in playing at being light-hearted, making a mask of merriment while the funeral's next door, avoiding the night-mare even in thought; and if I face it in art it is only to make a song about it, get rid of the load in the easiest way possible. And yet, and yet, a long face is an insult to the life that is in you; and a sad face won't prevent the Koreans from being shuttlecocked from one side of the Parallel to the other. Then, too, I haven't much belief in the people who have grief for everything. I remember that the women of Egypt wailed while the corn god was being reaped and ground by the men, but that their grief didn't prevent them from making their griddle cakes and their stirabout out of the poor deity. There was also, I believe, a similar bit of camouflage when the totem animal had to be slaughtered, they murmured sweet nothings into his ear while they put the knife through his gizzard. Forgive us our trespasses for they are so necessary to us. In the same way, we murmur the litany of democracy and grudge the housemaid her evenings off.

But I must really sort myself out one of these days and find opinions in myself about everything. As it is, I never know what I think about anything until I come to write about it; and then I get such a shock at my lack of detailed knowledge that I keep inside my own current. An article like that of Hubert Butler's on Sean O'Faolain's Autoantiamericanism (for the love of Mike!) makes me envious of all downright efficiency. And yet the informed comment has as much influence nowadays as a paper cracker at a Christmas table. History is getting too large for us, and even if we specialise, it is only a specialist world that will listen to us. The scholar is as lost as the poet. And all men of liberal feeling! They are under a constant siege from warring opposites, a siege that is growing daily as the propaganda war moves hysterically towards the atom bomb; soon they will be as isolated as the conscientious objector is in wartime; and what then? A gaol for the poet? Well, hardly, he hasn't enough of influence, no one reads him. He is too unsure of his facts and figures to blazon himself as a publicist. He is truly only in himself, the Narcissus of arts. But still one of the gang, one who knows, one who evaluates things by intuition, one who can be dangerous.

I am giving myself away. I think I will be shot within the next few hours if I do not cozen the local Gauleiter. But it does hurt a liberal when a liberal seems to defect. The prospect of sudden death is appalling enough, but our bodies have the good sense never to contemplate it with that kind of assiduity that comprehends; the prospect of having one's mouth shut comes in a more palpable form and I feel choked already and stuffed with anger. Not that I want to speak very much while others can do my kind of speaking better, the Hubert Butlers, *et cetera*, but I like the opening to be there just in case. We must have our soapbox even if we trundle it around ourselves. At rock bottom, we do not speak for ourselves but for all the people.

So if a liberal does achieve a soapbox, he must talk for the people, not at them. But if he is an artist he will talk for himself. That is the trouble. In spite of his opinions and all the headlines of things, the common good, democracy, the communal soul, the artist must always talk about himself. He is his own material and medium, and the most illiberal of liberals. That is the way he's built. He evolves a world out of himself and never rests on Sunday. And so he is lopsided, outside the limits of his art he is lopsided, he is a structure that is building afresh with every day, but unlike the banker and the businessman and the politician he lives in the present and not in the yesterday. He is definer of that amorphous and chaotic ghost, to-day, and I don't wonder that Plato planted his boot on his hinder parts, since to define anything nowadays is to despair of it.

Any kind of artist in any kind of art is nowadays speaking a foreign language; his public is so small that he is practically talking to himself. He is in the position, indeed, of the specialist, so when he takes it on himself to popularise the art-world, he takes on something of the nature of a special representative reporting to the people's newspaper on proceedings abroad. This is a rotten way to live, really, and if a poet hadn't his round dozen of other poets to take an interest in him, he'd develop a belief in metempsychosis and return out of spite as an animal that makes the loudest noise, a bull-elephant, say, or an Orange Order drummer. That's how the despised coteries begin and that's how there are two pubs instead of one. And that's why the younger tribe are always taking the socks off their elders. We all want a hearing and by gosh we're going to have it. And why not? And if the elders are impatient of the youngers, why, tear them off their clay feet. All very natural, and Christy is as good a man as his Da. But what the older and younger do not realise is that they speak the same language and that all together they count no more heads than two hands can count fingers. There are not more than a dozen remarkable poets in Ireland to-day; but in spite of our prose critics—who never know anything about poetry anyway—there are a dozen remarkable poets in Ireland; and every one of those seems at loggerheads with his fellow. I don't think I have ever agreed with nearly all the poets about the general merits of a particular poet, any one particular poet. All of us sense quality, and most of us have the grace to admit it. We don't like to, but we do. If we don't, it is a fall from grace for which there is no redemption.

So we, the poets, have to be minutely careful when we come to criticism. No pontificating. No act. No GROSS intrusion of the self. No personal plumes through the denigration of one's fellow. We are bad critics of each other, but we are the best. And in spite of ourselves a family has been thrust upon us, with all its family feelings and family failings.

They seem to manage things better in England, but there the elder men have the political nature of the elder statesmen; they give the kid something to shut his mouth. And in return, the great man has his table of Knights who eat out of his hand rather than bite it. It's a good insurance for one's old (poetic) age, and when I retire with all my savings, I'll buy a directorship in some publishing house and print every boy with a mouth on him. In the meantime, however, my reputation is in the hands of the noble Twelve who will carve me up quite coldly to see how my heart so beats. That's the penalty of initiation; no favours.

But just to know they are there is a heartening thing, to know that they get you, to know they have the patience to find their way into the cloak, to know that not a sound goes astray and that your syllables are counted. To know that twelve people can really become your poem for a matter of moments is enough to keep any poet writing and to keep him experimenting and to keep him searching all the time for that different and surprising self he finds in every poem. It is enough alright; and yet—be honest, my friend, it is not enough. For if you write one short story, you touch 100 people for every one you touch through a poem. It is a prose age, alas, and the prose boys have it each way, the cash and the cachet. It only remains for us to starve grandly on our few hundreds a year.

And why, anyway, am I writing this journal? I haven't said a thing I didn't know before and I am more anxious to be clever than I am to be honest. A bad failing, that.

To-morrow, I will examine my conscience. To-night, as usual, it is too late and I am too sleepy.

—*The Bell,* September 6th, 1951

Editor's note: Sean O'Faolain and Hubert Butler had recently been involved in an exchange of politico-cultural polemics in *The Bell* under the blanket title 'Autoantiamericanism'. Fallon was writing at the height of the Korean War, which to many people—including himself—seemed then to be a major step towards World War III. In 1945, after the defeat of the Japanese, Korea had been divided along the 38th Parallel into two nations, North and South, the former under Soviet tutelage and the latter under American. The North Koreans invaded the South in June 1950 and UN forces—predominantly American—became heavily involved in the fighting, provoking in turn large-scale Chinese intervention. An armistice was signed in July 1953 though the two Koreas remained bitter enemies. Latter-day estimates put their war losses at over three million dead, wounded and missing, with another five million people left homeless.

A Poet's Journal II

WHAT IS poetry anyway? A display of personality or a vision of reality? Can it be both in one poem? Examples, please.

Yeats, of course, comes into mind first. Romantic speech, sonorous rhetoric, master of the perfect stanza and the dove-tailed line, who has, as my friend Don MacDonagh says, put certain parts of the dictionary out of action for all his juniors, meaning the lovely and long Latinity that prolonged the plain Saxon of everyday idiom. Let us see what side of the G.O.M. comes down on personality or vision. I feel it is important to distinguish between them, but I really can't say why. Perhaps it is that personality builds the stage for a one-man show, and could be merely a glorification of the ego; no, not glorification, expansion would be the more accurate, a kind of living by proxy.

The first poem that comes to mind is one I could quote by heart at one time, the poem to Eva and Constance Gore-Booth. This is a genuine poem. And while it serves the poet emotionally in two ways or on two planes, i.e., releases him from the contemplation of two girls as they grow old, and allows him at the same time to develop in a startling image certain beliefs he held regarding the nature of eternity—while it serves him emotionally, I say, on these different planes, he does not intrude on the poem, he is not striving to live through it.

Example of 'living through a poem', i.e. living by proxy, just to make things plain to myself. Well, 'Words for Music' is ballad stuff, the proxy-life is permitted. There is that poem, almost in the same convention, and almost, too, a reminiscence of Fred Higgins, which he calls 'The Delphic Oracle'.

> There all the golden codgers lay,
> There the silver dew,
> And the great water sighed for love
> And the wind sighed too.
> Manpicker Niamh leant and sighed
> By Oisin on the grass,
> There sighed amid his choir of love
> Tall Pythagoras ...

This Tennysonian lotus-land is built up to contrast with a Pan-world of copulation which is equally unreal. It is ineffective because of a poetic vocabulary which he sought to strengthen by an occasional strong word, but which he only vulgarised by contrast; it is the world of the dreamer and is called up only to satisfy a certain lack of life in the poet himself.

But is that a poetry of personality? Take a younger poem that does not bleed phantasy. Go back into the middle period, his ripening August, take him when his verbal and rhythmic craft could do what he wanted them to do, take the poem 'In Memory of Major Robert Gregory'. Here, I think, personality is dominant, it is cut and sculptured into stanzas, and the separate sections glitter in their separation. Every stanza is a wonder of rhythm and imagery, but the poet takes six steps from diamond to diamond before he reaches the dead man for whom he writes. And when he does reach him, it is only to gaze into the background admiringly. And the ending stanza, word-perfect as it is, makes me think of a child hurrying to the end of his recitation-piece.

Yeats, indeed, spread so much scenery around him that his poetry in general leaves me with the final impression of an actor fitting himself with a part—not as he would have us think, a man in search of his soul.

And after I say this, I remember the thunderous bell-sound of a poem that seems to repeat the theme of the Gregory poem, 'All Souls' Night'. He calls it an Epilogue to *A Vision*, but I cannot help thinking of it as a prologue, the tall magician on the stage-edge waving our attention to the starry curtains that never lift. Does the personality, after all, transcend the vision?

That brings me back again to the need the poet felt for the ballad-stuff, the 'Crazy Jane' inconsequences that only dovetailed now and again with the straight work. What sticks out here is that the straight work could not be the full expression of the poetic person, since it left such a large hangover of material to express itself separately. The 'Crazy Jane' poems and their familiars are merry and bawdy and somewhat surrealist, but they are all secondary to the main stream into which they should have flowed if the poem was an organic whole. What prevented this meeting of the waters?

Could it be the poet's elaborate stanza-making?

Analogy again. Pound? Eliot?

Pound's *Cantos* were built to express the whole vision of the poet by using all his material. In that they were successful. He uses an art-form in which he can be mythic and moronic in the same space of a line. He can be stately and slummy, cryptic, gnomic and diffusive on the one page. Pound found an art-form for the whole man by chucking his early love of the stanzaic form for a medium that gave him any freedom he required in dealing with any kind of material. *Il miglior fabbro*? I think so.

What then about yourself? Find a medium that is the good old medium? Will you chuck the stanza-trunks and walk naked?

Well, wait a bit. Pound was never happy inside a stanza. The buffalo plains of Idaho do not fit into the convent garden. He was nothing but a reflection of an older poetry when he rhymed his lines, Provençal in fact. But when he started eating up continents, from Chicago to Cathay, Marc Apollo circling the globe, well, he needed a way to disgorge his giant eating, something so formless that it must be a form in itself, a book that has eaten up all the books.

You're not a book, nor a bookman, nor a historian. And when you write free verse it slows up your feet, you cannot take those little flying dives on a rhythm that the finch takes when he nips from one tree to another, shutting and opening his wings, wayward but keeping the direction. That's why you dislike Eliot, the cumbersome, the lumbersome, trundling his portentous yeas and nays from one heap of garden rubbish to another. Eagle, indeed. He had never a feather to fly or moult.

Let us look at Eliot, the younger Eliot, the New Englander he was before he shored up a pew somewhere in Little Gidding, Ford and W.H. Auden. Let us take *Prufrock*. And above all, let us forget the things that have been written about it. Read it again with a fresh mind.

Language first. The talk-tongue of everyday. To elevate it, as the professors say, there is constant but irregular use of rhyme and simile that has not reached the depth of imagery. '... The evening is spread out against the sky / Like a patient etherised upon a table.' And '... streets that follow like a tedious argument / On insidious intent / To lead you to an overwhelming question.' All the usual tones of description elaborating a scene as if it were a psychology. The film technique of the smarter producer. After it, in many lines, as if the poet were tapping with his fingers on the coffee-table, are some remarks on the portentous nature of time. Then the faintly comic entrance of Monsieur Prufrock.

> And I have known the eyes already, known them all—
> The eyes that fix you in a formulated phrase,
> And when I am formulated, sprawling on a pin.
> When I am pinned and wriggling on the wall,
> Then how should I begin
> To spit out all the butt-ends of my days and ways?
> And how should I presume?

The pain of the adolescent is real enough, God knows, but this, I think, is the rhetoric of a qualm. It has been asserted—I am bringing in the critics in spite of myself—that Mr Eliot resignedly keeps his language flat and his imagery flatulent so as to keep them consonant with his vision of life, so that they drag him down into the everyday reality, the useless and neurotic time-spending. This is what the professors call 'entering into the character'. Is it effective?

It is the mode of the dramatist.

Is it effective?

Yes.

You agree with me. I agree with you. In taking on a character, the poet takes on the limitations of the character. Would you agree with that?

Not altogether. The poet is not a dramatist but a poet. In some part of his scenario, slyly or wildly, in character or out of it, he will throw his (character's) limitations to the wind and be himself.

Then you value personality rather than the vision?

Again, not altogether. But no poet ever limits himself to *all* of his work. If high jinks are in him, out they must come. If he possesses verbal richness, he will pick themes or treat themes in a way that will allow him to spend it. Austin Clarke does that of necessity. And Auden when he is not cataloguing.

Still, your subconscious responds to:

> Defunctive music undersea
> Passed seaward with the passing bell
> Slowly; the God Hercules
> Had left him, that had loved him well.

I accept the response. I will not define it. But I feel tricked. I feel he is using my subconscious unfairly. He decks himself out with the God-plume, speaks largely and comprehensively as the most incorrigible Romantic, and drops bits of coloured glass into my well, green flames and blue-veined hands of highbred vampires—

Is it a poem?

It is a most impressive poem. Fragments I store amid my ruins. But it is almost alone, and not important in the order of his work.

It is a facet of his image of the world. If it is fragmentary, it still gets together in one piece somewhere inside you. Surrealist technique of the kind you like. Do you still think he makes a virtue of his limitations?

Certainly. One or two swallows, you know. And I am thinking inevitably of *The Waste Land* and the *Quartets*. He knows not the image, the everyday bit of glass that connects the sunlight and becomes an odd diamond. The 'Burbank' poem is a collection of out-of-the-world things, smoky candle-ends of time-axles in Istria, Gods and princesses and cigars all together on the Rialto. But does he make an image see as—say—Rilke makes it see? After all, he may be the poet of a thousand hesitations, but surely even hesitation must find the divining image—

Teresias?

C.I.F. from nowhere with a pocketful of currents to pick the bones of Phlebas the Phoenician, undersea, a long time dead. Look, these figures, as in the 'Burbank' poem, are the statements of an outworn romance, the kind that died when geography became available to everybody. What is this Teresias but a dressed-up Prufrockian? And what is *The Waste Land* but a change of Prufrockian scenery? Having written *Prufrock*, why change the covers and bring it out in a new edition? Obvious, he had in the meantime collected a romantic paraphernalia of Tarot Cards and Holy Grails and had seen a typist somewhere hanging out her unmentionables, plus a Bradford Millionaire in a top hat, all quite permissible and all quite unimportant except they definitely turn into symbol and are pointed and starred with meaning. Why, the notes are almost as long as the poem, the notes are necessary background, and he might just as well give us the notes and never print the poem. No. The technique is a falsity in itself, he is romantic in picture and in the desire of the picture, and to give them in dead language is due either to a lack of language or to the destructive quality in him, the nihilist desire of castration. He touches nothing that he does not dehorn.

Ecce homo.

Yeats, then?

Yeats never discovered himself through a poem. He had made his mind up before he wrote it down. Result, he could concentrate on the things in a poem, but the thing itself was dead from the start. Final result, a startling and beautiful performance, a marvellous rhetorician on the rostrum.

Eliot and Yeats?

You have read them, you have absorbed them, they are part of your bloodstream. Go thou and do not likewise.

—*The Bell*, December 8th, 1951

A Poet's Journal III

WORDS. Poems are written with them. Not with soul, not with spirit. With words. Mallarmé.

Two ways of using them. Three, if we combine the two in one, which we usually do. The poetic, the prosaic, becoming the poetic-prosaic.

Define the difference between the poetic and the prosaic. Let Robert Graves define it.

The prosaic method was invested by the Greeks of the classical age as an insurance against the swamping of reason by the mythographic fancy. It has now become the only legitimate means of transmitting useful knowledge. And in England, as in most other mercantile countries, the current popular view is that 'music' and old-fashioned diction are the only characteristics of poetry which distinguish it from prose, that every poem has, or should have, a precise single-strand prose equivalent. As a result the poetic fancy is atrophied in every educated person who does not privately struggle to cultivate it. And from the inability to think poetically—to resolve speech into its original images and thought into multiple sense—derives the failure to think clearly in prose. In prose one thinks on only one level at a time, and no combination of words needs to contain more than a single sense; nevertheless the images resident in words must be securely related if the passage is to have any bits. This simple need is forgotten; what passes for simple prose nowadays is a mechanical stringing together of stereotyped word groups without regard for the images contained in them ... The joke is that the more prose-minded the scholar, the more capable he is supposed to be of interpreting ancient poetic meaning.

Where does this lead us?

I am thinking of the thirties; no, I suppose it began earlier with the war-poets, the revolution Yeats couldn't see, couldn't appreciate. The prosaic method. Letting the theme state itself in the flat language of everyday.

It has never been effectively done in flat language alone. Wilfred Owen stands out as the poet of the 1914–18 War. Why? Because he used language poetically. Take the poem 'Exposure'. Or 'Futility', or 'Anthem for Doomed Youth'. No writing down, deliberate flatness. Lucid exposures of the poet's attitude to things.

But in the thirties?

Well, the thirties are a kind of composite Eliot-Auden portrait, composed by their imitators. I have difficulty in seeing either Eliot of Auden clearly because of a cumbered landscape, because of the steamrolling criticism of the time. Eliot and Auden used language to define the poet's attitude in relation to the world around them; Eliot was 'an old man in a dry month', he delivered the myth in a mouthful of dust; Auden, on the other hand, being a poet of lyrical calibre, could see the dissolving language of the myth efficiently enough, but to define the poetic attitude, he took on the livery of the hour, the jacket of old man *Zeitgeist*, and used postcard words in combination with the Freudian idiom, trick-writing as Salvador Dali trick-draws. He solved all his equations too easily.

Explain postcard words.

The snapshots of the journalist, the coloured catalogue. Let us allow him his stature in this English landscape. A revolution was necessary. It was a time for the satiric poet. The satiric attitude needed to be redefined. Eliot's method was personal to Eliot—or to Eliot–Pound, and a more immediate method was a necessity.

Why?

Because the age demanded that it be lived in. The balloon had burst, the bread-queues began. The poet developed a social conscience. To every poet his Aristophanes.

War around the corner, crowding the little hour. A two-strata society, the rich and the poor, and the difference becoming more emphatic. At the head of things more than inefficiency and vague graft, a cosmic drift into chaos, Christ internationally sepulchred. And no man to blame, but all men. Therefore the structure of society of which all men are guilty; this man-guilt forcing the poet to see himself in social terms. Witness the flight of the undergraduates to the Communist camp, the social survey, the art of the manifesto, the poet limping down side-streets losing himself in generalities.

The vast and prosaic English social conscience dominating the poetic methods of speech. Labour intellectuals, engineers of a materialist Utopia, insisting on the importance of the merely physical scene—as if, when a man has enough to eat, he will find heaven in his backyard—poetry a propaganda tool, a journalistic interpretation of a situation, needing journalistic language if it was to be of any current use.

Not only the poetasters were sucked in.

Herr Freud harrowing the underworld.

The prosaic dominant. The single strand.

Despair, disillusion, have their arts, but theirs is not the art of writing down, or the art of the aside. This latter is the art of the mime, of the stage play to which an actor contributes his personality and presence, where words can be cut to the flattest essentials of speech because the actor is there to elaborate. A poem is not a play. The unit of feeling is different. In a poem a word is the unit, in a play the scene; one is the poetry of words, the other of situation, the latter to be defined only on the stage, by actors before an audience.

Which does not rule out the verse-play. (I will return to this, God willing.)

The effect of all this social propaganda was to confine the poet in the straitjacket of his time. He threw it off, of course. Read any journal of the past ten years and note how the mystic way of speech is returning, the art of double and treble meanings, the concentration on the image, the variety and individuality of theme, good writing.

And the theme doesn't matter now. It may be of any time or all time, and of social or merely private importance. The individual has come back to his own.

Which is the way that I, personally, want it. A free-for-all, in which the thing that is in you can make its own way out to its public, using its own personal language.

Poetry is made of words, said Mallarmé. But a poem is a series of continuous and immediate inspirations, one word borrowing another, and the poet has not very much choice about them. He will use the words that strike matches in his Unconscious, when he has them; he will use others disdainfully to plug holes when he hasn't, going back again to find the right ones later, the misfires.

But to go back to the thirties, Ireland in the thirties.

I think young men nowadays completely misunderstand the climate of that time, young Irish poets, I mean, and the overwhelming sense of frustration we had in being steamrolled out of existence in Ireland. What I had to say was bound up with life in this country, not with life in England. It is not a matter of nationality, it is more a matter of idiom and different life-experience. In England the usual poet has an urban upbringing and is secluded within the distinctions of class, and forever afterwards he misses the common life he should have had shared with people in his childhood. So that virile thing, the people's common tongue, never becomes his speech, as it become the Irishman's and the Welshman's. Behind us, a powerful ghost, engaging our rhythms to some hereditary and ancient wheel, is the Irish language. I am not particularly Irish. I do not demand that we restate old themes or confine ourselves to Irish subjects, but I do think that it is necessary that we express our own particular problems in our own way. And that means using all our resources, just to be ourselves. Our own idiom.

But in the thirties nothing was so difficult. The Faber booklets lifted their hindlegs at you from every bookshop. English magazines closed down on Irish work under the impression that it was Georgian stuff, reflections from the minor shires, and the great propaganda machine moved amongst us. If you didn't write the English way, you were out.

Outs for me, for the first thing I had to do was to get this country into perspective. I had to treat the country as if it was in my mind, that is, as it had come to me through folksong and folktale, and as I had lived it in fair and market, in town and country, a boy amongst his own people, who was lucky enough to have contacted the last remnants of the old Gaelic-speaking life and felt it reflected in the attitude of the community. Why, I used to holiday in houses where one man would recite Raftery's poems to another, where a boycotted landlord used to pass by under the protection of sweating policemen, where the Land War was still a real thing, where men working in a field would run a mile to see a horse gallop, where eighteenth-century recklessness lasted well into my time at fairs and race-meetings, where beggars talked John Millington Synge, and every man was an individual, the big house in the background dying into inanition. The Ireland of my youth connected me historically with the eighteenth century, but it was an emotional connection too, a joy in just living, in delighting in active things, in kicking up, like a young colt, one hell of a dust.

There is more to life than despair of life. There is this body-joy in its own energies, the thing that makes trees grow and men marry, ebullient stuff the masters of the thirties ruled out. Let despair come later. Having lived his joys, he will cope with that, too. There is measure and number in all things, but you discover them through excess.

The communal despair of English poetry was something outside of us at the time. We were only ten years a nation once again and in the act of building. But already the colder poetry, the parade of the conscience through the confession-box, was appearing in Austin Clarke. In my ebullience I used to dub it the middleaged spread. Nothing communal about this stuff, the chilled articulation of a man beset by eternity, and all alone as man is always alone. And the language! Words used till all the meanings were doubled and treble. Rhythm stopped as if there were unseen hobbles.

In Ireland, for too long, there has been no criticism, no adequate criticism, and the poets are grouped roughly into those who have foreign leanings and those who have Irish leanings. This is sheer nonsense. In those short lyrics of Clarke's, the art is more French than Gaelic. I do not agree with the sternness of the technique, I do not agree that a large problem should be hammered into a miniature, that it should be pared till only the kernel fits a small shell, but this was definitely a new and poetic expression of an innate Catholic attitude of feeling, and because it was quiet and still and difficult it can be ignored by those prose praetors, men of the single-strand meaning who praise poetry for its prose qualities.

Irony. Eliot lecturing at University College, Dublin, when this little booklet appeared from the Tower Press. Delight in the lost sheep. So pleased to meet one who has found Christianity, even that Anglican—hum—divergence, the—er—sustaining, the—haw—creative thing.

Mock me with Matins. The dovecote should have known better. Is poetry of the canon and not of the Apocrypha? Isn't it obvious that a Church creates a psychology? Once in, never out again, the struggle for reconciliation being the real poetry, the bitter soul-making stuff that a man drags out of his God-experience. If the poet substitutes the struggle for the piety, that is his vocation; he is not ordained with oils and a whip.

A man takes his body from his parents, but his psyche is all man's. He is the history of the world. All times in all men.

Tall. Bring this down to the workshop.

He can set a poem, play, story in any time, but in writing it must take all times into account.

Meaning that he can place a play in the early civilisations, but not attempt to write it as a man of the time would write it?

Yes.

But is the setting necessary if the psychology is twentieth century?

I speak of poetry, not psychology. I talk of myth, of myths, old tales that are explanations of forgotten rituals. Man's relations with the Gods are never out of date. They have the inner relevance of a neurosis. Complexes of urge and energy. Mark the large names in recent poetic history: Yeats, Eliot, Pound, Clarke.

Clarke goes for the plain story.

To find the mystery of the monks he returns to source, humanising because he sees to-day in yesterday. His abbots and nuns face both ways, weighing God and the poet in the twin scales of faith and unfaith. He likes the twin horns of his friend Dilemma. He has never decided between doubt and miracle.

Reservations about plays.

Elaborateness in the making. He mistakes a play for a lyric. We can ponder a lyric but we listen to a play. And the mysteries of assonance and dissonance bypass us. Rhythmic writing is enough.

His drama-speech.

I would apprentice him to a Chicago gangster for twelve months. He besets me with sonorities, phrases mantillaed like señoritas, that keep me looking over my shoulder. That is to watch a procession rather than to take part in it.

The cure.

A Dáil debate three times daily after meals.

I will see him there.

—*The Bell,* December 9th, 1951

Editor's note: T.S. Eliot visited Dublin in the 1930s and lectured at University College Dublin. The reference to Freud 'harrowing the underworld' presumably alludes to the motto he took from Virgil: *Flectere si nequeo superos, Acheronta movebo.*

A Poet's Journal IV

ONE THING I can say about the young writers who contributed to the recent discussion in *The Bell* is that they made their case with astonishing maturity. But what is a young writer? And what is an old writer?

At the wisest, I'd define a young writer as a man who wants to write; an old writer as a man who can't write. In between times, and by times, he is just a writer. It is repetition and not age that makes a writer old. Yeats was a young man at seventy, Higgins was old at forty.

And how old was Joyce when he became a real writer? That pamphlet of his, 'The Day of the Rabblement', was written when he was twenty-two. It was no better as a piece of writing than John Montague's contribution to *The Bell*. I don't know how old Montague is, and I have seen none of his creative work, but there was nothing in his article with which I could quarrel, and I am not in the greys of middle age. It is a question, however, if a young man should be so poised. As a critic, yes; but as a creative talent where there must be extremes of bias, I have my doubts. Still, there was Joyce of the pamphlet and the Joyce of *Stephen Hero*, the dated Joyce of *Portrait of the Artist*, and the gigantic Joyce of *Ulysses*. It took the creative Joyce a long time to catch up with the maturity of the young critic.

Take Yeats, too. Occasionally, and not too often, he was a good critic, but as a young man he never handled ideas adequately. He could never separate them from the creative halo.

What touched him went into the melting pot and became part of that general mess of nerves and temperament. I doubt if he could ever, at twenty-five, have made a good critical summary of the world of his time.

Which makes me think, if I could exclude from my thinking things like Keats's *Letters* and some prose of Shelley's, that sound criticism is no part of the young poet's armoury. It may be a drawback, it may create a censor too early, put spies in the obscure factory, and rationalise the complex. Every writer knows his vocation from his schooldays and his attitude towards the world is born in him. It is the spirit-skeleton within the skeleton, and all his urge is to get this plain to himself. I do not think that one arrives at it through thought but through experience, and the young poet's way to experience would seem to be the way of a son with a father; that is, he imitates some older poet, sees things through his eyes, adopts his ways and rhythms of speech, and at the same time, even while the process of identification continues, the personality inside him is building up towards a revulsion. When that comes, he strips a skin like a snake and is more himself. One's philosophy of life, indeed, consists of a long series of revulsions, each revulsion being a broken marriage of some kind or other. We skin-strip till we find the skeleton, so it is doubtful if a keen critical faculty is essential to the poetic make-up. That will arrive soon enough.

I am not surprised then to find in some cases that the intuitive critical sense of those young men is somewhat ahead of their experience, ahead too of their practical achievement. That is natural.

Examples.

Well, take Anthony Cronin first, he is the most vocal of our young men and a man who critically faces up well to his world, a young man who allows nothing to scare him from saying his say. But his note on Scott Fitzgerald in the May issue of this magazine made me wonder a little. This was a good summary enough of a fairly usual kind of American talent, but he brought in as a 'great' example of first-person narrative Evelyn Waugh's *Brideshead Revisited*. Now, I have the greatest respect for technical excellence and I find Waugh an amusing talent enough but as a great example of anything except salesmanship he just does not fit in. He is Anatole France at secondhand, his stuff just salted enough for benefit of the Bourgeois.

What no young man realises is that it is always disheartening for an older man to come down on a lively youngster. The role is not sympathetic enough. The old bull stamping the ground, the schoolmaster lifting the ferule, the bawl from the rostrum, they are all present in the mind and create a sense of guilt. As a critic, I say I am criticising a poem. But as a poet I know I criticise a person, a person and poet become one in the poem. There is no blotting it out, this sense of guilt, of hurting one's never-forgotten younger self. And it is only an evasion to do the job in an uncly, heart-to-heart way. That way is the way of superiority.

On the other hand, when a poet prints a poem, it is offered for criticism. And there is the public for the poem to be considered, a public that is one's own public too. This, basically, is a selfish attitude. It boils down to this, that most poets consider their own stuff the best there is, and that all their criticism is consciously or unconsciously a propaganda for their own kind of poetry. A grand example of this type of criticism is Patrick Kavanagh, who moves through the fair wagging a shibboleth like a shillelagh, drunk with masterpieces still to come. If we accept a critic's job at all, we have to allow for personal bias and for one's own indecent motives. We must at least approximate a reasonable fairness.

So if I say that the four poems printed in the last issue by Anthony Cronin do not do that young man justice, I am putting the thing as fairly as I can. I allow for his integrity. I know he is making a serious study of the ways of the psyche and I know that nothing is as difficult to fix in a personal idiom as the wayward motives and intentions and remorses that make up a single action, but it is just no good to say it in another poet's language or the language of any particular clique. Auden has been first in that world and his idiom is so personal to him and to his imitators that even a hint of his presence kills the effect of a poem. Wasn't it Pound said 'Make it new'?

And this is not new:

> The clocks have different tones
> And the night is heavy with rain
> As they lie awake in the dark
> And go over it all again
> The fearful who cannot work out
> The equation of loss and gain
> Something went wrong they say
> Something along the line.

My point here is not to pull down a promising young man, nor even to pull him up, for he is certain to find his own way in his own time—there is a kind of initiation by imitation, as I said before—but to save other young men from a wasteful model. The thirties are dead. Bury the decade, then. Not even young Englishmen use the ghost nowadays. But in Ireland, it seems, we are as usual twenty years behind.

The only other contributor to the symposium whose work I know is Valentin Iremonger. A book published by him last year made me regret a hasty diatribe I did on him some years ago, before I had seen his work in bulk. I can apologise now. Iremonger came under the influence of the thirties, as every Irish poet of his generation did, and it wasn't his fault but the fault of a time. The failure was in the generations between Yeats and himself in Ireland when no urban poetry was written, stuff that could give the growing population of literate city-folk something that would take the spark. At the time the Audens and the Day-Lewises were striking young rebels against everything that hoary tradition stood for, how was he to guess that they would end tamely as professors of poetry, traditionalists themselves? Iremonger has a delicate sense of fluid rhythm and he seems to have read well in modern American poetry, with some advantage. There is no reason, indeed, as far as I can see, why his next book should not be the young man's book we have been waiting for.

In all this talk I have dwelt on the influences of the old on the young. But there is always the psychological interchange. No poet is ever a settled man; daily he builds his psyche anew, his everyday world, and it is a truism that one poet stimulates another to the building. It was with something like excitement, then, that I came on a critical remark of young Montague's. He said the Edward Garnett school of writers 'of close natural description and poetic undertones' has attained 'a certain fixity as the Irish school of writing'. Is this true? Certainly, of the short stories of Liam O'Flaherty and Frank O'Connor and in the earlier O'Faolain short story. But Montague doesn't enlarge enough on what could be a new approach and when he discards the easy give-and-take of country life as an approach that has lost its meaning, he seems to forget that most writers in prose are country-born, MacManus, Kiely, *et cetera*. And there is no future in Kafka, since we can't all live on the borders of insanity. What then? American brutality, the tough he-man with the bleeding heart, Hemingway à la mud? And *Tarry Flynn* is no different from the Garnett school, except that the near-poetic moments are given more than usual prominence.

And certainly not Graham Greene. Or Waugh. Or the infinitely boring Sartre.

The English 'Catholic' writer gives me a pain in my neck. He wears his Catholicity like a mark of caste distinction.

The main problem would seem to be the unconscious censorship the writer exercises on himself in face of the community, and this is the writer's problem everywhere except in the anonymous cities of larger countries. But if Mauriac could evade it at no great cost, why not the Irish writer? The answer is that O'Faolain ridiculously had a good novel listed by the prudes and it is a long time now since we had a novel from him. Why? No novelist is short of material in a practically untouched country like Ireland, yet here is a man who had a good deal to say almost silenced before middleage, at a time, indeed, when he should be doing his best stuff.

Why not another symposium, Mr Editor, this time by established writers?

Not that it would help. For the work that we are all looking for is the wonder-work that never happens. It is the dream that lures every writer, that drives the young man to the garret and the old man to drink; it has never been written and it never will be. If a good work does happen, it will not have its origins in any symposium, and not even in any individual, it will come out of some stir in the age and be entirely unexpected when it arrives. And some of us, I suppose, will not rate it at its values, as I cannot rate Kafka at his value. But I doubt if it will be an art in the Realist mode, since that went out with *Ulysses*, nor in the American mode of Penn Warren which is a cross between thriller and Garnett, and still I cannot see that any non-representational work of imagination—in prose—will ever have enough communication to be of representative and permanent value. Melville's whale, for instance, is important, even as a symbol, because the beast catches up the world of ships and seamen and taps a neurosis as large as the seven oceans. There is a daily logic somehow in the visual things the day presents, and if we kill the eye we see ourselves no better for being blind. Even in verse, if we do not bring things to the visual point, if we do not stamp words with the prints of things, we lose in direct strength and challenge.

The visual, however, is neither the real nor the realistic, but a help to communication, a lighting along the pathway that leads into the image. All good poetry must end in the image, and the image is a complex made visible, the end and the all. The Imagist school in some respects had the right idea but it made a miniature art out of a major issue, it confined its energies to the poetic subject. And there is no poetic subject. Each poem is different from any other and demands its own kind of language and approach, demands and enforces it, indeed, and a poem fails only when the poet does not follow the poem faithfully in the kind of language it wants from him. To do that he must kill the idea of style, of one personal style, which was about the only serious limitation that Yeats had since it confined him to subjects that lent themselves to lordly utterance. If I think, for instance, of an acquaintance I knew on and off for many years, who died some time ago, somebody—say—who left no deep impression on me, I do not inflate my feeling for him with prayerbook words. He belonged to the pubs and his history was the history of the drunk. So the thought comes alive in the most casual way and the history becomes the elegy. Let us call it R.I.P

Remember him
In the saddle lifting some well-bred brute
Over the timber,
So right from the tall topper to the polished boot.
He died, they say,
From too much lifting of the elbow,
With a great fall of pride
A half-crown touch. But he always shaved, poor Joe.

To a relative or a close friend, this poem would give umbrage. Quite wrongly. For a string of acquaintances are saying the same thing in different pubs, though they donned respectable black to bury him and murmured the usual words of convention in the ears of whoever was bereaved—which was quite right, too, of course.

But if I pin a history of the man to my board, it is with the affectionate truth of the artist. I am not lettering a stone but seeing home a nice old chap who has had a little too much. Had he been respectable and staid, he would never have delayed long enough in my mind to gather a poem about himself, but those who give all to a passion touch the poet on his softest side. We bow before something greater than man.

Perhaps that is our business.

—*The Bell,* January 11th, 1952

Editor's note: *The Bell* had recently carried statements by a number of younger Irish writers about their work, their aims and their attitude towards their elders. The novelist Francis MacManus was deputed to write a reply—which he managed huffily and badly. The banned novel by O'Faolain was *Bird Alone* (1936).

A Poet's Journal V

S OMEBODY took me to task last month for saying that a
poet remakes himself every day anew, as if with the
morning he fingered the clays and topped the psyche
with a fresh profile. Well, what about it? A man definitely is a
part of time and, to give the phrase a new turn, he is never the
man he was. Each day, indeed, makes some change in him,
even though the process of change only becomes visible over a
period.

And in a poet's work? I think he alters with every poem.
I went further once, and said a poet died in every poem, and if
I analyse what I meant exactly by that it must bring me up
against something that every poet believes in his heart, i.e.,
that he is in a state of possession when he makes a poem, not
every poem, but some poem now and again, and not all the
time throughout a poem. I do not say the poem is the better
for that, I do not say that one leaves the critical faculty aside,
but I believe that no poem of any use is ever made without
some degree of possession, and when a poet is in that state he
is something else than himself.

What he contacts then is beyond me. Perhaps an elder
psychology that the primitives knew, perhaps that all-seeing
person within that one guesses at in such a work as Dunne's
Experiment with Time, to whom past and future are as one.
Whatever it is, it is dependent on the poet for its temporary
expression, for its time-body, and the poet is dependent also
upon it, for the words that well up from line to line, for the

integrated passion of the utterance. I am tired of people who look on writing as a mere craft, but not as weary of them as of those who regard the writer's voice as the voice of God. I go back to Yeats, indeed, when I wish for an explanation that will give my reason and my unreason something they can hold in common. Yeats believed in the Daemon, the bodiless reality who made a body out of our reality, who could only feel and live through us, who is our other self, one who enlarges himself on our passions and leads us on to the kind of life he desires by all sorts of lures, even though it is well against all of our practical interests.

A Pre-Raphaelite doctrine, maybe. Emotion is everything. Still, Pater and Wilde do not exemplify it. One was not daring enough to believe in it; the other believed in it too much, mistaking sensation for passion. The best example could be Dante, who made poetry out of his ruin, or Baudelaire, who lived ruin in order to feel it, de Nerval who went mad that he might know emotion from the other side of things, all the eccentrics of life who were forced to dramatise an attitude so that they could feel, so that they could feed that abstract person within with the passions of life.

And poor Pound, escaping from it all his life, to be caught up by it at last in a cage-camp in Italy.

Je suis au bout de mes forces.

That from the gates of death,
That from the gates of death: Whitman or Lovelace
Found on the jo-house seat at that
in a cheap edition! (and thanks to Professor Speare)
hast 'ou swum in a sea of air-strip
through an aeon of nothingness,
when the raft broke and the waters went over me,
Immaculata, Introibo
For those who drink of the bitterness
Perpetua, Agatha, Anastasia
Saeculorum

Repos donnez à ciel
Senza termine funge. Immaculata Regina

Les larmes que j'ai crées m'inondent,
Tard, très tard, je t'ai connue, la Tristesse,
I have been hard as youth sixty years.

So my feeling is that a man is a projection in time of a personality outside time, a dual thing that could work each way, and while I needn't believe in this with the absoluteness of a doctrine, I can use it as most poets use any doctrine, as a working hypothesis, as fuel in the stove, as the negative and positive currents that come together in the bulb and throw some light into the room. Even Euripides, who scanted the Gods, was aware of other worlds.

The Gods ask feeling from us, and if we can't supply it they will invent ways in which we will.

We haven't very much of it. We react conventionally and make the usual gestures. And afterwards there is the examination of conscience, and we wonder how much was drama and how much emotion, how much lay in our own insistence on making ourselves fell.

And how much of feeling is suggestion? When I ask myself this, the void around me gapes. I question my own authenticity. I am confronted, like Baudelaire, with the horror of emptiness.

And that in itself is an emotion. Baudelaire's answer was to pick up whatever emotive fragments of himself he found lying about every morning and make himself anew into a person. 'An impure man of faith,' somebody called him. It fits most of us.

It is this up-against-it feeling that does make us creators, make us turn on special aspects of living so that the heart beats again.

> *Alors, o ma beauté, dites à la vermine*
> *Qui vous mangera de baisers*
> *Que j'ai gardé la forme et l'essence divine*
> *De mes amours décomposés.*

And as I grow older, it seems to me, too, that this abstract entity inside us needs a vision of the current world, of the world as we see it now, this instant, this truly present thing in which we live. Only a constantly renewing art is capable of this, an art that changes almost daily, that is eternally struggling to keep pace with time, an art that can present the new thing that is happening in a new way. What way that is, is for each poet to make out for himself. But I think the days of elaborate art are for the time being over, or should I say the apparently elaborate, for the essence of art still, as we learned at school, is to conceal art, but the elaborate stanza, as Valentin Iremonger remarked last week in a critique in this paper, stands out now as too much artifice; and the evident artifice gets between the listener and the thing said. It will come back, of course, as antithetical prose will come back, for the essence of change is the return of the departed, but just now our ears are all for the new tune, for haphazard rhyme and the line that completes a mission on its own, forgetting all about its feet while it makes its own running. The skills of versemaking are once again personal to the poet and not to the metricist, and a poem can make its own rules of rhythm and pattern.

The thing about form is that there comes a time when it becomes formal. Then it controls thought rather than releases it, and pens the poet in a convention.

Form, of course, is always necessary. Some subjects, indeed, will demand a rigid scheme or there will be a stumbling and a halting and a churning all over the place, and a consequent loss in rhythmic value.

And the rhythm is the thing, the undercurrent and undertow that counterpoise the onward rush. But the learned stanza carrying its rhymes like airs and graces has ceased, I think, to be part of our time and makes me think of something I read somewhere in Proust's occasional writings. He said that initially the great inventors of art in the nineteenth century were all regarded as vulgar by the public, no matter how the critics stressed their contacts with the artists who went before them. They had to lower the expression to compete with the changing psyche.

The poet's obscure vision of reality, indeed, is never apparent to himself until he is getting it into words. Then the battle is joined. And in the queerest way he must yield up the greater part of his brilliant equipment, discard his facility and his dictionary, throttle his eloquence, and kill a thousand metaphors, if he is to find that something new that makes his hair stand up with triumph. If he takes the easy way of his facility, he will substitute something else for his actual vision— as Auden does—nine times out of ten.

Indeed, it is of Auden I think as I make this remark on facility, and his book *For The Time Being*, which I have been re-reading lately and comparing with earlier stuff. In the earlier stuff the art compasses the vision satisfactorily—to be on the safe side, let me confine this to the selection in the Michael Roberts anthology; but in this book, where his subjects are Shakespeare's *Tempest* and some major incidents in the New Testament, there is a shocking misinterpretation of material, and what intervenes between the poet and the vision is, I suggest, the poet's own fluency and facility. He does not size up to his vision, he debouches, he takes his stand on platforms he has used before, and the same crackers come automatically out of the same pockets of language. The reflexes are fixed. I do not deny many brilliancies of image and fancy and stanza-building, but the cleverness seems shoddy in its juxtaposition to his subject. I do not look for dignity, now, or poetry with the quality of prayer or piety, I look for the VISION. He is a lightweight dancing round a monstrously large ring, and the floodlights dwarf him.

Strangely enough—but let me quote it first, lest I make my point with a sledgehammer. This is a poem spoken by an 'abstraction' called Sensation.

> My senses are still coarse
> From late engrossment in a fair. Old tunes
> Reiterated, lights with repeated winks
> Were fascinating like a tie and brought
> Whole populations running to a plain,
> Making its rich alluvial meadows
> One boisterous preposter. By the river
> A whistling crowd had waited many hours
> To see a naked woman swim upstream;
> Honours and reckless medicines were served
> In booths where interest was lost
> As easily as money ...

Surprising as it may seem, I think Mr Auden has read Mr Austin Clarke. The poem 'The Fair at Wind Gap'. Indeed, I remember Clarke telling me they were together as judges in the Oxford Festival of Poetry back in '38, and that Auden, meeting Clarke for the first time was to be found that afternoon with the *Collected Poems* under his oxter. If Clarke didn't autograph it, at least he made his mark.

The only thing really derogatory about rhythmic reminiscence like this is that it indicates a too-ready acceptance on the poet's part for what is offered to him in the making of a poem. No modern writer has a more definite and personal rhythm than Auden, no one *plays* more with rhythms than he; still, in the poem above, there is the ghost of a young Austin Clarke, and in that fine poem, 'September 1939', there is the ghost of the elder Yeats. Why? I suggest that the reasons lies in his own brilliant facility. He has not enough defence in depth from the temptation of his natural fertility.

And on that account one feels that the conscious mind is responsible for too much of his work. I don't think his Daemon can be too happy about things.

—*The Bell,* February 11th, 1952

A Poet's Journal VI

*I*F A POET must always revolt against his time, then Lucifer was the first poet. And why the rebellion? Why this urge to explode oneself into different images, to take shapes other than the natural body we have inherited through time and flesh? Does the scientist revolt? Or the priest? Or that Socratic man, the politician, who thinks a timely logic will solve the illogical problem of events?

Optimists all, except the poet. The scientist moving step by step into some atomic explosion, doing good optimistically, yet increasing all the skills of death. He sees where things are heading all right, but the responsibilities he shuffles on to the shoulders of that great abstract monstrosity, man. Conscience is a democracy. A sin is a mob. But a world is a wave of feeling that carries us all along willy-nilly, the moron and the intellectual doing their equal parts.

History derives from no cause nor from any man. When I see Sean O'Faolain and Hubert Butler assigning a current political situation to this group of thinkers or that clique of actors, I think that they assign to the universe the simplicity of the crossword puzzle. There is no science in history but that of the unaccountable spectacle. A time happens like a gross god and determines itself in furies and lethargies, in fears and nightmares, as if inside the world there was a primeval genius, active and suffering. Why else the constantly recurring Promethean myth, the tortured saviour of mankind, the speaker of his horror, the first poet?

For horror it is. The cry can escape into poetry and it can be assuaged in a religion through symbol and acceptance.

> *Le prêtre est immense parce qu'il fait croire à une foule de choses étonnantes.*
> *Que l'Église veuille tout faire et tout être, c'est une loi de l'esprit humain.*
> *Les prêtres son les serviteurs et les sectaries de l'imagination.*

There are poets of that Apollonian type, men that can hymn things without expressing the chaos in which as men they stand, men who have the technique of belief such as the priest has, men like Robert Farren in Ireland, who can give themselves up unquestioningly to the miracle, but they are not in the archetype. They have solved the poet's problem religiously and what is left is technical, a residue that goes into the art of versification. Farren has not had his due from the new Irish schools for this reason. His talent is a throwback into the epical, the gathering of myths into a glory. The Columcille poem displays him to the full, clear, striking, cool, with the calmness of an ancient sun-age, fabulous with the faith that God was just on the other side of the ditch. With that he could invent new skills in verse-craft and make a science out of the rougher assonantal patterns of Austin Clarke and F.R. Higgins which in their turn derived from that friend of Rossetti's, Allingham, who came from Donegal: and to him from the Gaelic.

But for most of us it is the suffering of matter that makes us speak, an ancient consciousness that we have as our first mission to transmit the cry of things beyond ourselves. Man is mythic not logical, Aeschylean and not Socratic, and when Plato burned his poems and founded his optimistic god on syllogisms of sophistries he gave us the university of the atom bomb.

And out of my youthful reading, where Plato figured as some enigmatic talking machine, so clear in demolishing problems that stood erect again a moment after, comes that vision of the Condemned Socrates in his cell, who, having fought all his life against the music in things, against music as an expression of things, turned at last at the bidding of his god or his subconscious to the writing of poetry. A volte-face, even if it were only the turning of Aesop's fables into a new rhyme, for did he not empty the republic of poets, because he proved *logically* that poets were the imitators of an imitation.

All men, indeed, aspire naturally to the condition of art, for the problem of the duality of the world is solved, not by a logic, but by an aesthetic. There is neither good nor evil in the poetic cry, there is only a singleness, an acceptance of the haphazard will that inhabits the universe, the cry of chorus in the 'Trachinie':

> Do not come out, Iole, unhappy virgin,
> You have already seen enough of woes.
> And yet fresh sorrows wait you; but remember,
> All is decreed and all is the work of Jove.

Sophocles claimed that he did consciously what Aeschylus did unconsciously, clothed the sorrow of man in a piety of rebellion and brought man upon the superhuman stage, but with the fall back to the Rational, which might be called the fall of man, the poet has no superhuman stage in common with the world. We deal in concepts where the early Greeks dealt in feelings, because that is a current coinage. And so our speech is inhibited, our stage a three-walled drawing-room, our heroes the man who came to dinner. Eliot's psychoanalyst. Yet the significances of myth are always with the poet, always in the poet. And whatever redactions of primeval feelings were in the gods are still active and move through us in metaphor and image. It is our job to give those currency, and in a Socratic world make them available to feeling again. Wonder, sorrow, dread, we are surrounded by them as no age was ever so surrounded, and we cannot give them a common voice.

> *Profondeur immense de pensée dans les locutions vulgaires,*
> *trous*
> *creusés par des générations de fourmis.*

In a Socratic society, indeed, the poet has only the importance of an individual, analogous to the rural parson in England who is still a figure but no longer a force. Whom do I write for, asks the poet; to whom do I speak, asks the parson of his empty church? And the people, having lost the language, have also lost the God, and keep to their day's work, busily accumulating their deaths inside them.

I have never spoken in a language I trusted. I have always necessarily upholstered myself with the properties of communication, as if I were an American footballer taking the field. All modern art is a compromise, and the poet wears a fleece so that he may walk with the flock.

Pound bowed to necessity, and Auden loved it. Both are profoundly moved by the myth, Pound historically as if he annotated an ancient calfskin, Auden jubilantly as if he were commentating on a game of football and great Jove himself were hooking for his side. Both have done their best—as one might say according to their facilities, both sought to communicate through the symbol more plainly than Eliot, who thought the symbol of itself to be sufficient without the explanatory lead. No poet at this stage should need a tail of private philosophers to make him public. The essence of an art is to the whole.

And that is the trouble. The wholeness eludes us. We are the poets of fragments, our apparatus always out of order.

Il y a dans l'acte de l'amour une grande resemblance avec la torture ou avec une opération chirurgicale.

Those eternal mirrors of the modern man, this broken sensibility that sees itself by contraries. We constantly find ourselves in the arms of our opposites. We find our faith only by denial of it, as if the denial itself were a declaration of faith. And yet this is the kind of art we have to use if we are to get at the truth in ourselves and leave it free to affect others, a kind of truth by self-deception. There is no plain speech, there is only a large reading between the lines.

That is why I do not come back easily to the poetry of Yeats. He did not wring the neck of eloquence, he only gave it a twist, his particular twist. He had all the equipment except the art of self-abnegation. He denied all the right things in the wrong way. He would have his vision exclusive to a coterie, his church a church of one man, and yet he published himself like a drama and his speech has none of the hesitancies of the God-smitten. Still his power outweighed the faults, and man is declaimed poetically through a gorgeous instrument.

His highest handling of the myth began, of course, with the *Four Plays For Dancers*; and the later plays that followed that mode, though in prose with an inset of short lyrics, prolonged the theme. For me this is his greatest work, though not his greatest verse, and it is an added comment on the time to say that not even his own theatre will stage the stuff, instead of playing up the convention and training players specially to the art. It could form a magnificent groundwork for future poets, and call on them indeed for whatever they had. And they have something. And it is something important for us and our time, a thing not to be vended in the commercial theatre, where values are so bastard they have ceased to matter, but where the state stands a subsidy the poet has a right to sound a trumpet, not a commercial manager with a commercial gift of being ordinary.

To this art of Yeats a company should be trained, verse speakers, rhapsodists if you like, and a number of performances given during the season. If the state pays for all the courting in the kitchen stuff that now adorns the Queen's, it can surely dig out enough to finance what might even attract the intelligent tourist. Then there are the Greek plays with all their god-qualities. Those are what one might call the world's national heritage and as Irish to us as anything we have of our own. Why, one week in four could make a marvellous difference in a season's work; with a producer like Ria Mooney and actresses of the calibre of Eithne Dunne and Siobhan McKenna and some of the present Abbey group, who knows what kind of a movement could happen.

And what a relief it would be from the debased thing that now passes for Abbey Drama, with its Christmas finale of grotesque abandonment, the Gaelic pantomime. The man who thought of this should be offered an outhouse in Spiddal to house his activities and not the theatre of W.B. Yeats, for not alone does it signal the end of a movement but it has turned things right around to where the Abbey began and inverted all the values for which it stood.

If the Government wishes to spend money on the Irish

language, and I am one of those who stand by that policy, why not endow each country school with a 16 mm projecting apparatus, set up a little film colony, and produce homely fables that will serve as lessons at school? In that way, we should have Irish speakers almost as native as the native in a few years and make the learning a pleasure. The Abbey is an English-speaking theatre because we are English-speaking, and it is a farce worthy of the mind who thought out the Christmas farce to project a Gaelic revival through it.

In the meantime, there is no place for the poet with a play if he doesn't, like Austin Clarke, produce it himself.

—*The Bell*, March 1952

Editor's note: The 'Queen's' is The Queen's Theatre in Dublin, to which the Abbey Theatre moved after the 1951 fire.

A Poet's Journal VII

P OETRY should renew itself in every decade by refining itself from those impurities of time and place which give it a kind of temporary body in current taste. Taste changes, of necessity we react against the new which after a while turns into its own cliché; so we seek the different form, the way of saying the same thing, and once again look for the permanent to speak through the impermanent. There is no such thing as pure poetry. There is a soul and a body in all things, the ideal form and its earth equivalent; but the earth-form must alter in time and space and it is through this earth-form that the ideal must speak to us. That is the current language of art; and like any other language it is always in the course of amending its meanings.

While Mallarmé has saved us a lot of trouble in his fantastic pursuit of the pure and unabridged word that had no commercial connotation, his failure can be too much of a success for us who follow after him in time. Our time has gone to the opposite extreme. And in admitting everything to our verse, we lessen the formal value of the statement. We forget we speak of the permanent and *for* the permanent. We intrude ourselves, that current Selfhood which most of the poets of the past distinguished from the identity, from the *moi profonde,* from the timeless soul. This soul is the poet's concern. And the revelation of it must be his art.

There is no definition of this poetic identity more profound than that of the young Keats. It is rough, it has the approximateness of the young man approaching a truth for the first time for which he has to find a new idiom, but it has the mental resonance that creates waves of sound within the mind, and we go on, and almost without thinking, find it has become part of one's thought.

As to the poetical Character itself (I mean that sort of which, if I am anything, I am a Member; that sort distinguished from the Wordsworthian or egotistical sublime; which is a thing per se, and stands alone) it is not itself—it has no self—it is everything and nothing—it has no character—it enjoys light and shade; it lives in gusto, be it foul or fair, high or low, rich or poor, mean or elevated. It has as much delight in conceiving an Iago as an Imogen. What shocks the virtuous philosopher, delights the chameleon poet. It does no harm from its relish of the dark side of things any more than from its taste for the bright one; because they both end in speculation. A poet is the most unpoetical of anything in existence; because he has no identity—he is continually in for and filling some other body—the sun, the moon, the sea and men and women who are creatures of impulse are poetical and have about them an unchangeable attribute—the poet has none; no identity—he is certainly the most unpoetical of God's creatures. If then he has no self, and if I am a poet, where is the wonder that I should say that I would write no more? Might I not at that very instant have been cogitating on the Characters of Saturn and Ops? It is a wretched thing to confess; but it is a very fact that not one word I ever can utter can be taken for granted as an opinion growing out of my own identical nature—how can it when I have no nature? When I am in a room with people if I ever am free from speculations on creations of my own brain, then not myself goes home to myself; but the identity of everyone in the room begins to press upon me that I am in a very little time annihilated.

It is this 'openness' in Keats that made him a poet so young; things struck him as sensations, 'sensation' in his meaning being the entire complex of thought and feeling slapped on his nervous system like a sudden hand. He lamented his own openness because he was a manly little fire-eater whose body wanted to use him for life as well as for art, but as a poet he was lucky beyond the dreams of most poets in so far as this lack of selfhood let him plunge straight to the heart of things. He had no desiring self to use art as a vehicle of sensual reconciliation—as Swinburne used it, and Wilde, Yeats sometimes, and most poets often enough, too often for them to become major poets. One of my private definitions of great poetry, indeed, I derive through this personal factor and its intrusion of the poet's body-desires into his art. It is something on a par with the little alcove in the library, a use of literature for other than literary purposes, it is the major sin. It is also, in other variations, the way of Realism.

'*C'est horriblement ressemblant*,' said Cezanne of Rosa Bonheur's *Laboureur Nivernais*, meaning that the art-object had not ascended and come down again from the Mount of Transfiguration, having passed though the rhythmic changes into the pattern which is art. Nothing can exist in art as it exists in life. The artist connects one to the other. He is the meeting point at which they contemplate one another, two imponderables making mystic marriage, a poet making a poem. But because a poet must use a language which is abstracted from a current vocabulary and which must keep all the hints of its original if it is *to satisfy a man who speaks for his own time*, most poems cease to be poetry after a couple of generations of use. They 'fade on the page', as Robert Graves says: only the permanent continues its life, that thing in which the extraneous elements were least and the poet's time-body the least emphatic. The history of poetry is a history of lost causes and spent emotions, high indignations and high horses equally dust. What carries a poem is its language; the meaning that oozes through words like so much many-coloured oil is a matter of sound and syllables and nothing commonsensical that may be determined by any prose-précis.

So, a poem cannot afford any other object outside of poetry. Leave the ideologies to the ideologists. The current political or the current social question must solve itself in the prose world. Poetry has no public life. And no poet should listen to the lure of the utilitarian. He may have a smash hit with the journalists or the very young, like the Auden clique of the thirties, if he links himself to their external thinking. But a decade will show his corpse stinking to the high heavens with the sins of the temporal. He passes with to-day; and passes out, not on.

What surprises a young poet, indeed, is that his emotions

make such bad poetry. He has been taught by all the professors that poetry is emotion, that poetry is a simple retelling of the body's story, that it recollects in tranquillity its little teacup storms, and taps it down in its tacks of rhyme and hammerheads of rhythm. The sheerest bunk. A poem will find a poet ('A little thing that was presented to me,' said Rilke) and it can start out of nothing or anything except out of an emotion. And it usually starts with a word or with two words, words that come out at any time wearing strange aurae which excite; the rest is an adventure and a guess is as good as God. But to start a poem with an object which is outside of the scope of poetry is to beget an illegitimate on a newspaper-column.

I am not limiting the use of the conscious, now, when I pontificate on the role of the subconscious in the initiatory step that starts a poem moving. I think specially of Milton's *Paradise Lost*. Words here, for all the detailed mastery of sound and image, are not used poetically. They are the vehicle of a scenario, they are the carriers of a story, they marshal a long argument in an open forum, they do not exist for their own sakes but for the sake of a legal plea. They make a great rhetoric of propaganda. But the poet is speaking not as a poet but as a politician. And even if his object is to convince God of something or other, the work is no nearer to poetry than if it were written in prose. And prose, as Shelley knew, is the effective vehicle for all that is not *poetic in origin*.

Saeva indignatio is never enough, indeed, for the purposes of poetry, and I do not accept Mr Plunkett's assessment of Mr Kavanagh's poem, *The Great Hunger* (*The Bell*) as being at all final. No one will question its authority as a picture of a certain kind of living in a certain place at a certain time—and God knows I can look around me from where I write and see similar tragedies still unfolding themselves in LIFE—nor its virile presentation, not its vividness, not its adaptable rhythms, but the inspiration of the whole cannot be differentiated from that of prose. Words are used purely for communication purposes, not for themselves, not for the suggestive aura which words mix with words when they come together magically as in any good lyric. The poem is grand scenario-work, it is the work of a radio commentator of genius, but it is not poetry. Poetry, indeed, is not any selection of detail, such as the details chosen as examples by Mr Plunkett; those, while they are pictorial necessities to the scheme of a story, do not assist the lyrical meaning. They are a utilitarian asset or prop, they are part of the equipment of any good short-story man.

The lure of detail, indeed, is one of the temptations in the path of the young poet. Our descriptive apparatus is always aching to be used. 'C'est horriblement ressemblant,' said Cezanne, who understood the temptation. We are always ready to give ourselves to the fiction that buttresses itself on detail, anxious to get out of our own lives into the other fellow's. That is desire, the wish to intrude on experience, a kind of will to live as we see it in the messenger-boy who delivers the groceries with a 'Buffalo Bill' in one hand and a pot of jam in the other. Good description, with the actual detail that cannot be invented, with that visual feeling about it of actual experience, is one of the delights of secondary art. I have as much interest in big-game hunting as in chasing the housefly, but I listened to a man talk for two hours not long ago because of his way of describing the approach of a tiger to where he stood with a gun waiting. He caught three flying glimpses of the beast only as it leaped the higher brush towards him, to disappear in between the low brushwood, and I got the picture because he said that in the first glimpse the tiger's face was no larger than a housecat's, and the second appearance was tiger-size, and the third, when it was no more than a leap away, so gigantic that it was an outsize in terror. But to admit the visual is to use words as drudges, to carry the non-lyrical load of story or platform.

Words, indeed, are stimulants and the poet dishes them out so that others can share his drunkenness. Art has nothing to do with any kind of imitation of the visual, though the poet must use words that are visual almost in their impact. One of Rilke's secrets, for instance, is that he brings forward the abstract noun into the foreground so that the foreground is thinned to a gauze, the poem, then, becoming a series of perspectives that run away back into some infinity, 'l'éternité qui gronde à l'horizon, la destine ou la fatalité qu'on apperçoit *intérieurement sans que l'on puisse dire à quelles signes on la reconnait!'* Realism has the pictorial appeal, but as Yeats said long ago, leave it to the painter.

A young poet seeks a philosophy but finds an aesthetic if he is lucky. It is a critic's job to insist on the difference. And we have no critics in Ireland of any aesthetic size. Our 'possibles' leave us early and acclimatise themselves to other cultures. A critic like Enid Starkie is a loss, but how else is she to practise her *mêtier* if we have no Baudelaire or Rimbaud to offer her to study? We have left Yeats to American college-men, the definitive Yeats with all the *et ceterae*. And if there were an Irish equivalent to the God-drunken Rimbaud, who would there be to give him his place? Not Padraic Colum who pities poor Cathleen for her lack of singing-birds. Singing-birds! Are we caged canaries? Or the simple thrush who stirs with the sun? This kind of simplification is one of the annoyances one doesn't expect from a practising poet. We do not think simply any more. We are too involved with our souls. And our writing is a complexity that mirrors what we have found in contemplation. When Colum sang, there were some remnants of folk-belief in which he could be absorbed and in which he was part of the country-plan of the time. That time is now time past. And with all respect to him we cannot, even if we wanted it, have it back again. What we do need is a few trained souls who will take what we have to offer, a difficult in-looking poetry that will not rely on dead attitudes for buttress—poetry with no message that is apparent, that is no guidebook to Ireland, is no national monument, that is nothing, indeed, but poetry. '*J'ai tendu des cordes de clocher a clocher; des guirlandes de fenêtre a fenêtre.*'—any poetry, even a poetry of praise.

Which makes me think of that sonnet of Rimbaud's of which I was tempted to make an equivalent, a work of rage let me say because of the number of rotten translations that passed for it in English, and in despair, too, because of the wild and jubilant delicacy of the original. I quote it for what it's worth from the *Dublin Magazine*. It was one of the magics of my youth.

MA BOHÈME

So I tramped the roads, my hands through my torn pockets,
my old coat just a ghost about to vanish;
I was your tramp, Muse, but rich, with worlds to lavish:
La, la, the marvels we dream of, we mad poets.

I walked with my buttocks falling out like moons
Through holes in my trousers, rhyming, my head in the air;
I took a room each night in the Great Bear;
Stars over my distant hair had the soft swish of gowns.

And I listened, excited with dew as with strong wine,
At my ease in a ditch, a mood, a creature of starshine
In the good September twilights, a man apart.

—*The Bell*, April 1952

Editor's note: The translation of Rimbaud's 'Ma Bohème' appeared in the *Dublin Magazine* of April–June 1948. Fallon omits the final three lines.

A Poet's Journal VIII

I MADE a note to get hold of Eliot's last essay, that on poetry in the theatre, and every day I forget to send for it. Why? It is something I should do since Eliot is one of the first-class critics. Perhaps it is *The Cocktail Party* put me off. It is such a bad play as a play, and even Eliot himself has ceased to call it verse, I believe.

I did hear Henry Reed's eulogy of it on the Third Programme, I heard one talk anyway in which he made my own point about the poetry of situation, which is that while lyric poetry is a verbal art, and purely verbal without any extraneous elements, the poetry of the theatre demands another kind of language, a language that will have a functional use first in demonstrating a situation. A play is a situation and its rhythm is that of the scene and not of the word, so words must be used to carry the scene and not for their lyrical value. Where poets like Austin Clarke slip up is in making a play as if it were a lyric, thus mixing the genres, loosening the lyric meaning and losing the drama, making a hybrid art out of a lack of understanding of the differences between the two media.

For the primary consideration of the theatre is drama and drama is a visual kind of poetry. The action, indeed, is almost independent of words, as the old silent screen proved to us, and I have seen several good plays in which the language was scarcely adequate put over by the strength of the situation and by good acting. The cult of Realism, indeed, almost demands inadequate language since people, for the most part, have come to speak in clichés; but I think we will accept any language on the stage provided there is good acting and the inner meaning is well mimed. How much is lost we never know and how much more dramatic good language can be than bad we do not even try to guess, except when we have the play before us in manuscript. And then how tawdry and trite even the good situation seems, when the language dramatically does not live up to it. It is the theatre carries it off, the spectacle, the mime, the poetry that only the theatre can give.

The Cocktail Party makes dull reading. It is also tired, like a canvas that has been repainted many times—before its death. I have heard this dullness commended as 'letting the situation speak for itself'; and I have heard the character-group commended likewise as being a satire on the usual West End play. But the satire is so obscure that the play has been accepted in the West End merely for its play-properties and not for its satire. And, also, I expect for its preachiness. People, the large middlebrow audience, seem to go to Eliot now for their religion, which is not indeed his fault but is something merely which indicates that the more ancient symbolism is losing motive power.

What is important about the play is that it is prose; it is limned in verse form, but it is plain, deadpan prose. In other words, it is an admission by a poet who is also a playwright that he has found verse inadequate to the needs of the stage.

Which brings me back to Yeats who, in the later plays, used prose too. And the later Shakespeare also, who without rhyme or reason dropped from his pentameters into the more casual rhythms. Why?

There are some speeches in *Hamlet* that seem to cry out for versification as *speech*, as in that scene in the Third Act between Hamlet, Rosencrantz and Guildenstern, and yet the action quite properly demanded the quick-changing rhythms of prose speech, and the playwright quite properly obeyed. All stilts were off and the play is immeasurably the better for it. After the Elizabethan flowering, indeed, the stage settled down comfortably to the everyday speech-rhythms, just as the fourth century in Greece sought an equivalent in the theatre for the language of the ordinary man, the man of the time. That verse did come again was a mere fashion of the Court of the second Charles and has nothing to do with popular demand.

So, in one way, Eliot can be said to be on the right track. If one is to deal with people one meets in the streets everyday, they must have their semblances of everyday reality. Their speech must seem to be the natural speech they would use in certain circumstances. At least, it must deceive us into believing it is.

Any good playwright, however, can lure us into a suspension of disbelief. Shaw got away with murder, and used the stage as a soapbox. And Christopher Fry can orate by the folio and keep us a-tiptoe. But—

There is, as Eliot is aware, a difference, a difference of spirit one can call high spirits. Fry puts things over in a dance of fun and his questions are cloaked in wit. Verse is the natural vehicle of wit, as witness the limericks that are trotted out eternally in the local, but if a theme asks for its full and horrible impact, it will not allow any obvious artifice in words to come between stage and audience, not nowadays when we have lost the verse convention. I think we can only truly feel something that is of our time, something that wears the dress of our time, and we do not go to *The Lady Is Not For Burning* to feel but to enjoy, we do not go to explore ourselves and our capacity for feeling but to enjoy a spectacle of wit and blistering comment that is only half-apparent because it is removed from the world we know and given a literary, not a realistic value. If I put something back in time, I remove a dimension and work on a flat surface, I engage myself automatically to a literary background. I can make comedy out of that, but never tragedy. For tragedy belongs to one's own problems, and those are contemporary, they are housed in my own feelings and if I am to make them felt as art, they must wear the everyday clothes of my own time since that was the way I encountered them.

One only learns that this is a fact through one's own work. And one can waste a long time in discovering something for oneself. I am not drawn very much to our modern stage because it has, in Dublin at any rate, frozen itself into a three-walled convention where there can be only a theatrical poetry of situation and no metrical poetry, no verbal enlightenment such as a chorus can give. A poet needs to break down those three walls somehow and let another world through, so that, indeed, some of the characters bring a comet-tail of something larger that the human along with them. And still, because the convention is so set nowadays, we cannot depart from it at any great extent. The convention has been a part of our education and it forbids me, at least, to be interested in any vital way in modes like Impressionism or Expressionism. They have failed. They gave us a silhouette and not man in his proper dimensions.

The functionalism of Jean Cocteau—the Cocteau of *The Infernal Machine*—is perhaps one way to manage the missing dimension, if one is ingenious enough. This is to make the very scenery an active participant in the action. I remember, for instance, how the stone of an old ruin became in that play the pedestal of the sphinx simply because a girl stood behind it with shoulders and head showing. What a poet is really after, indeed, is that extra dimension, the God, and the trouble is that the lyric genius and the mechanical so seldom come together. It is a great ease, indeed, to work for the radio, where all the world's your stage and each eye is turned inward to create its own 'correlative' scenery, but it is only a shelving of a pressing technical problem. One just wants to share one's vision in common with a number of others, and have immediate response.

So, almost against my will, I have hammered out a technical scheme which may bring off one play at least, and pushed back those cramping three walls so that two kinds of play seem to go on at the same time, one intruding as comment or chorus on the other, the main action prose since prose is the speech of our time; the comment coming through as if the general subconscious had found a voice. There are occasions in a play when there are natural silences, silences which actors cover up by inventing a bit of business, and I have used those for verse. But if it comes off—that is, if it ever reaches the stage—what then? Another search through the technical for the metaphysical, another weary time jamming pieces of puzzle together.

Still, the metrical fellow inside me is not happy. He has

looked around and seen that no verse play of a tragic nature had found a place in the public consciousness—that is, no verse play that had its situation from our own time; and yet he thinks the thing could be managed without surrendering to the prose convention. After all, if bad prose can carry a situation, why not good verse?

But Yeats answered in the negative, Shakespeare was moving that way at the end—and indeed, he came to prose when he touched the scenery of his own time—and there is Eliot and *The Cocktail Party* deliberately—or is it deliberately—dimming words till they have the cast-off feelings of pieces of orange-peel. A tragic theme, indeed, asks for the theatre to speak and not the man, not the lyricist who needs only one ear into which he can whisper.

So, it seems to be always a question of theme; inside the theatre it is the theme that matters, the broad plastic gesture where a feeling is loosed in something other than in language, the mime of an inner spectacle, so that a good play—if we follow the argument—should have almost enough common appeal to make it at least a minor commercial success. A pleasing thought for a poet with a play—practically a prose play—in his pocket, success monetary being always a part of our dreaming.

But how successful, actually, was this William Shakespeare? It is generally accepted, or has been accepted up to lately, that he made for his time a considerable fortune from the plays. Yet some recent research shows that only some few of the plays were acted often enough to prove they were successful. And every other playwright of his time who depended on playwrighting for an income, died in penury, even the bold Ben. Some, certainly, were only written for court—or near-court—performance, for a court-clique, and couldn't have paid well, so it seems he must have made his pile in another way. An interesting question for the researchers, a point for those who believe in the psychology rather than the large-domed front. So, reading *The Cocktail Party* makes me want again to get that new essay of Eliot's. To-morrow, certainly.

—*The Bell,* May 1952

Editor's note: Henry Reed was an English poet whose poem 'Naming Of Parts' still figures in verse anthologies. He also wrote dramatic scripts for the BBC. The Eliot essay in question was *Poetry and Drama*. The verse plays of Christopher Fry (1907–96) had a huge vogue in the post-war years but have dropped out of the repertory. Some of the theatrical innovations Fallon mentions were incorporated into his own stage play *The Seventh Step*. However, he later suppressed this work.

A Poet's Journal IX

WELL, I turned up T.S. Eliot's essay, *Poetry and Drama*, a pamphlet of 28 pages or printed matter, price 7s. 6d. I also found a readable copy of the plays of Euripides, in a somewhat Victorian translation, of course, for which I paid a like sum. I make no comment. But I think to myself that the cost of living is going up.

But 7s. 6d. is a small price to pay for an experience and for any contact with a shrewd American mind. Eliot, as a critic of technical things, has much to be said for him. He makes a kind of business analysis of art. He comes right down to the necessity of capturing his audience; that is to say, of being himself a success.

Nothing wrong with that, provide the audience is the right kind of audience for an artist. But then, what is the right kind of audience?

The stage, in the *Noh* plays of Yeats, asks for a very small audience of sympathetic poetry readers who must be artists themselves, insofar as they are required to give themselves to difficult poetic concepts and lend their ears to verse which is too lyrical for the ordinary and untrained hearing. This kind of art is not much different from any poetry reading, and I am surprised that Austin Clarke doesn't make his weekly radio readings out of such stuff instead of throwing us all that minor English muck that waters every Edwardian anthology. It would be interesting to compare the poetry royalties paid by Radio Éireann to those paper-poets of Georgian England with the royalties paid to Irish poets, taking them person by person—excluding, of course, that last diversion into native talent in which every living poetaster was pulled up squirming from his little piece of Irish earth and given his glorious quarter of an hour of dowdy life. Selection, after all, is a criticism of life.

But the stage, as I said before, is the one art which employs a material which all people share in common, the ordinary stuff of everyday life. This is a truism which we keep on forgetting. People, vitally, are only interested in making themselves feel and every good play is a melodrama in which the ordinary person expands his feelings. For a couple of hours he lives at an intensity that is rarely required of him in his everyday life. And this is his release. It is also his justification.

If we bring things down to ground level, if we examine ourselves carefully day by day, it is a surprise to discover how little we do feel and how much we can make ourselves feel if we put each straying incident of our day into its place in the imagination. For the imagination has gathered emotions into types, and when the type is touched, the juices flow.

So the type is the ground-work of the theatre. And in the type all people are at home, the groundling and the god, the pit and the box. These are the playwright's people. And for those he makes his spectacle.

And it must be dramatic. It must invent ways in which people will walk to the very top of themselves, aye, and out through the top, since to go outside is to contemplate. The drama, indeed, is the supreme vehicle of self-contemplation. And even bad plays have a portion of this large quality of self-extension, for on the stage, less than in any other art, the quality of the craftsmanship can be bad provided the theme is strong enough to provide its own approach to the emotions. It is, indeed, a case of giving the stage a theme and allowing it to do the work itself.

The poet does not readily understand that the stage is a place of action and not words. An entirely different metier. I have even read a diatribe on the theatre by a prominent present-day Irish poet in which he damned the theatre for being theatrical, for being an art out of all touch with some imaginary everyday, non-dramatic realism. Yet most people think in actions and live always at some pitch because of the inner spectacle with which they present themselves. If nothing happens to them of any worth, they will invent something for themselves; life, indeed, is lived more in a reverie of its dramatic possibilities than in its actualities, and even the poet, whose father is the word, has a reverie which only astonishes by its particularisation of events and people. We are all in a way our own private theatres, and it is this theatre we transport along with us when we visit one that is public. Those of us who make a trade of our mental scenery, who are what one might call the professionals of the reverie, will be harder to please than those who have not developed their pictorial qualities, their capacity for making their own dramas; but the others, the untrained and the unlettered, will substitute for the bad play and the bad craftsmanship, all that feeling they give to their own half-formed reveries; they are accustomed to the half-said thing and when it becomes visible in any kind of recognisable shape, they are so overwhelmed with gratitude and so complete in their identification of themselves with the spectacle that they have nothing left over with which to become critical. Give them a situation they know, and they will do the rest.

The theatre, then, is a theatre at only one remove from one's private reverie. But that remove is the difference between art and life. And astonishing, as art should astonish. If I see the *Hamlet* of Anew McMaster or Mícheál Mac Liammóir, I can reflect on it, even when the art of the acting is of the major kind, because it is a play I know almost by heart; but if I see a play I have not seen before, I must allow it to arrange my emotions as it wills. I am no longer in control of myself. Afterwards I will criticise, and even be niggardly of my praise when the critical faculty has time to become dominant again, but in the moment of the action I am removed out of myself by some power of spectatorship which kills the active critic. That is the power of the theatre. And that is the art of it. An art that even the worst of plays can share provided the theme touches one's private world.

Look, for instance, on the note in the 'London Diary' of *The Irish Times* (May 15th) concerning a play by Priestly and

Jacquetta Hawkes, in which four characters sit together on the stage before microphones and talk to each other in three acts, gradually exposing their identities in a situation that should have as much drama as an afternoon in a cocktail bar. Yet, because they were typical people, and the typical dreams were uncloaked, the play seems to have come over to the crowd. It probably has as much permanence as any other West End success, but it must have had that immediate psychological repercussion which is necessarily one of the most important qualities of any play. Every good play, indeed, must have that quality, and let the highbrows bawl as they will.

Not that they bawl too much, or even enough. For it is when a play has resettled in us and its ferment of feeling has died into our elements, into our personal reverie, that there comes a moment in which it must be judged. And this judgement is not conscious, and not a process of our consciousness, but is arrived at and speaks almost before we are aware of it. It is our whole private feeling or reverie passing judgement on some intruder who has enlivened or disturbed it, who has drained it of feeling proper to itself, or enriched it by a future of different imagery. We are the worse for every bad play that is produced. We lose each way. Feeling has been filched from us under false pretences, and a gate closed, perhaps, on a way of feeling that could have enlarged us if it had found a more plausible imagery.

So if I put theatre first and craftsmanship second, as their relative places in theatrical art, I must admit, of course, that they are both essentials to any literate audience. And I must admit, too, that a good craftsman can put over a non-dramatic theme. But very few poets are good craftsmen of the theatre. It is a carpenter's job—

> My curse on plays
> That have to be set up in fifty different ways.

But a theme can carry a poet if he allows the stage to invest for him and if he puts a sock into every character's mouth, and if he revises and revises and revises till he says in ten words what he first said in ten score. We are so used to words that we forget our actors and the natural silences of speech, in which a look can be as large as a paragraph and a simple bit of stage business more significant than the most voluble of explanations. What we have to do is not to write down to people, but to shut up and let them do their own underwriting. Collaboration is the word.

And I still want to write a play which will be a play in verse. And I still think *The Cocktail Party* is not a verse play. Eliot, while he writes now to a theory that prose and verse should not be used together in one play, believes also that 'prose should be used very sparingly indeed; that we should aim at a form of verse in which everything can be said that has to be said; and that when we find some situation that is intractable in verse, it is merely that our form of verse is inelastic. And if there proves to be scenes that we cannot put in verse, we must either drop develop our verse, or avoid having to introduce such scenes. For we have to accustom our audiences to verse to the point at which they will cease to be conscious of it; and to introduce prose dialogue would only be to distract their attention from the play itself to the medium of its expression. But if our verse is to have so wide a range that it can say anything that has to be said, it follows that it will not be poetry all the time. It will only be poetry when the dramatic situation has reached such a point of intensity that poetry becomes the natural utterance, because then it is the only language in which the emotions can be expressed at all.'

Well, there's the gospel according to Saint Tom. But to me, with *The Cocktail Party* in front of me, the word poetry does not seem more operative than the word prose. And on the stage, I understand—I have not seen the play myself—that there is no discernible difference at all. What, then, is this verse he speaks of? Metrically, each line with a caesura and three beats to it. But verse is never the measure of poetry and the emphasis of drama cannot stomach regularity for long periods. Different tensions require different schemes of versification, different line-lengths, different metres; and it seems to me that if one keeps the same scheme, one cannot alter the levels of feeling as quickly as in prose. Eliot's line, indeed, is not nearly as flexible as the iambic of the later Shakespeare, the Shakespeare of *Cymbeline* where the dramatic properties are sustained by a counterpoint of sense AGAINST rhythm, that is, Shakespeare begins a new line in the middle of his pentameter.

> All of her that is out of door most rich.
> If she be furnished with a mind so rare
> She is alone the Arabian bird; and I
> Have lost the wager. Boldness be my friend;
> Arm me, audacity, from head to foot,
> Or like the Parthian, I shall flying fight,
> Rather, directly fly.

I quote at random, and not much to the grain, but I am convinced that poetry differs only from prose in the degree of its tensions and that those tensions are emphasised by verse forms. But if those verse forms are used to contain a prose speech, the tension leaves them, and one might as well make the play in prose where one's rhythms will be that of everyday speech. This can be an advantage in so far as it is not rhythm that counts in the theatre but word-content, a sense of meaning that does not owe all to sound, as in a lyric where sound can be a meaning in itself, but words used in their everyday stresses in the way in which one talks to a friend.

—*The Bell*, July 1952

Editor's note: Seven shillings and sixpence equals about forty cents in euro currency. Austin Clarke had a weekly poetry programme on Radio Éireann for many years.

A Poet's Journal X

W HEN someone remarked that the inauguration of the President of Ireland was marked by the non-attendance of the poets, I made enquiry and found that Austin Clarke, at least, was there, representing either himself or the Academy of Letters. I don't know whether this Academy is recognised as an official body, like the French Academy, but it seems to me that there should be some official method of recognition for the writer outside of the measure of his creative capacity, which is at any rate something not to be measured by any official mind. If the members of every little commercial body in the country are to be recognised at certain times by the State, it is only right that there be a literary body in existence, too, to obtain similar recognition on behalf of the writer. Personalities aside, it seems to me that such a body should be chosen on a sort of services-rendered basis, the older men being pushed up to where the sun shines brightest, the young being honoured only by proxy, no matter how good their promise or even their achievement, for official recognition is somehow the kiss of death. It means that one's work has been absorbed so well that the digestive process is completed, and the public is ready to be shocked again by new food.

Coupled with another thought, this reflection brought me to the position of the poet in Irish society to-day, and by society I do not mean the top-drawer stuff, but the country as a whole and the lower middle class and the farming class in particular. And it seemed to me that somehow as poets we are not pulling our weight in the community. Take ballad-making, for instance.

A ballad is not hard to make. Any competent man of metre can make one in a couple of hours at most. It is so easy, indeed, it does not demand enough of a poet. So, he leaves it to others, following the tradition of isolation that began with Baudelaire. I follow that tradition myself, believing always in the fascination of what's difficult, and am excited only by the thing that comes as a symbol and brings more than one plane of living along with it, but I am prepared to agree with anybody who tells me there should be a simpler art on an everyday level for those who have not my own preoccupations. A poet need not be on top-gear all the time, and he never is anyway, and there may be a case for a more popular art, and for a popular artist like Thomas Moore. I confess to a prejudice against Moore, begotten, I fancy, in those early days when I read the *Autobiographies* of W. B. Yeats, but having occasion to write some things to a melody in the last couple of weeks, I learned that there is a technique in song-making as in everything else. I am one of those people who need to have a tune beaten into them with a sounding-fork, or whatever you call it, but who are unreasonably stirred by any old folk-air with its half-notes, and off-notes, and notes that appear to be born from a different scale than the one I was brought up to. The Greek mode, you will tell me, and indeed you may tell me anything about music and I will believe it, but whatever mode they are made to, those native melodies strike so many chords in me that I lead a life of luxury while I listen.

A melody, indeed, is quite capable of working its miracle without the addition of words, and I dislike opera of all things because of this top-heavy structure of fat tenors and bulging sopranos, trite plots and tame passions, but a folk-song seems only built to be spoken to unheard instruments, and a man on an island or a woman in a pub, without even a jew's harp, can cope with it in an exact and just way without seeming to need an accompaniment. The voice, there, is the thing. And the voice is a major accompaniment to the thing said as it goes up and down the scales. Every word is heard and every word is a note of music. Between them, a poem becomes a song. And it was as song that poetry began.

I am not quite certain if the best poetry can be written to a melody. It is too difficult, perhaps, for the immediate comprehension that song demands. And song, too, makes its own special demands. It limits rhythmical innovation, it calls out for vowels, and it is very choosy about your consonants. In one word, it explains the melodiousness of Elizabethan and Jacobean verse, and it explains, too, why such a poet as Donne shows up so harshly against the background of the age. Indeed, I am inclined to think that he made his poems against that background, as if he counterpointed against a music that was not heard but taken for granted. Which is just the thing that most poets do with the poetry of those who are immediately ahead of them in time.

A song, I find, goes against one's grain in many ways. First, there is a definite and unescapable scheme of rhythm, an annoyingly definite beat to anyone who has made his art wayward in order that his own rhythmical feeling may be apparent to him. This is like going to school again and joining a common chorus. But when I took into the piano a song I had built from the Irish, using my own rhythms, Norah O'Leary would look up at me in comical despair and say—I am afraid. And that was that. I would change words here and there hopefully, and Norah would squeeze them into their musical formations, but the result was always the same; if I wanted music to my verse, I would have to have a new melody specially arranged for them, and since that was not the thing I wanted, my verse would have to go into the wastepaper basket and work begin anew. Finally, of course, I found some permutation that almost pleased me—but didn't please the melody enough—but I am forced to conclude after a lot of trial and error that if one wishes to put words to any established folksong, one has to work in line with all other song-makers and think of the song and not the poem.

The result of all this is that I keep the Irish words and music before me during a trial shot and that I work to a discipline that would put any modern poet in a red rage. Emphatic words must fall where tradition has already inserted them, vowels must open where the mouth must open, and one must choose one's consonants so that they can travel daintily around the precincts of the Albert Hall—if required. It may be good for me. But I have no feeling of virtue. I only feel I am defeated by all other poets who have been assigning their vocabulary to music since time began.

No tricks seem to work. I have tried all the standard ones, just to get away from the look of convention that I see on the page I have typed out, but when the singer begins, the song is arrested here and there like a tiny stream into which a branch or a log has fallen, and I know tradition has beaten me again. And a glance at the Irish convinces me.

And when I read the Irish words, I have no excuse to offer at all for intruding an English song in their stead. Successions of singers have fined and filed away all obtrusive voice-difficulties in those traditional things, and a man has only to open his mouth and exhale himself in song. But I was fiddling about in an effort to come to terms with all those people who would sing if they had songs, people who have no Irish and who dislike the rotten translations usually dished out. The Irish too, while as near perfection as anything can be in sound, is in nearly every case as imperfect in meaning. One can feel one song overlaid by another and another, and all the alterations and adjustments that take place when words are taken on a journey from one side of the country to another, with singer after singer amending it as it was added to the local repertoire. Literal translation, indeed, while it is an admirable thing, is not I think a necessity; so I never bother much outside of the scheme, and I use this as I like. The Irish remains after all for those who want it that way.

And this brings me back again to the chore that a poet might do for his community, putting real words to those old airs. I think I myself have failed completely in so far as I wrote out of an Ireland that died thirty years ago. I kept a Galway folk-feeling in my words and wrote in the usual themes. 'Casadh an t-Súgáin', for instance, suggested a middle-aged man drinking his substance in a public house, bemoaning his hard fate. 'Ar Éirinn ní 'neosainn cí hí', a man remembering a young girl who married another man before he himself was of an age to be deemed marriageable. In 'Pé i n-Eirinn í', I tried a modern subject but drifted into the eighteenth-century fashion of naming Helen of Troy and Deirdre. In this song, too, I muted the vowel rhymes a little by substituting other vowel sounds—

> If she had a tail of bright fishscale
> And a comb for her hair in its yellow coils ...

I must confess, however, that the ear is not altogether pleased by the variation when the words are sung. One's resources, indeed, are limited to what the ear expects and I think, now, that one must leave to the music and the singer all rhythmic wandering that lures the poet to find his own effects. Those have to be put aside very sternly.

But it is a question whether one can put a modern poem to such melodies. They have such an atmosphere of their own, they are all eighteenth century Ireland, period pieces; and having explored that side of myself I think that any stuff like it that I would do again must be necessarily pastiche. In other words, a chore. But those songs were alive and being sung in my neighbourhood when I was a child, and it was rarely that some big-friezed farmer from Turloughmore or Carnane, on a fairday when prices were good, wouldn't break into one of them in Glynn's public house in Athenry. That was the respectable period of Victorianism, however, when no woman would put a foot in a public house or be seen swallowing a jorum, otherwise, I am sure, I'd have heard a lot more of them. As it is, I have vivid memories of women sitting patiently on a high-creeled cart in the rain and mud of a fairday evening while Pater Familias gave his special rendering of 'Caisléan Ui neíll' or 'Máire ní Gríobhta' inside the stacked tobacco-smoke of that little packed pub. I was not particularly impressed at that time, perhaps I was ashamed of my reactions to a muse that only belonged then to the back parishes; and in the years that followed, indeed, I ran away from such stuff, only to complete the circle years later and find the ground under my feet moved when someone or any one started up one of the airs I knew.

F.R. Higgins, writing of those songs, insisted always on calling them aristocratic. He is quite right, of course, if lineage means anything. But to me they are the expression of country

Ireland, of a folk-Ireland that has now dwindled into a society of folklorists, something that irritates because it is too earnest, because it is a kind of religion of the museum. That kind of atmosphere drives our young men to do other things, for they sense a businessman in the archivist and a fake façade in all things Gaelic. But I have contacted a teacher or two in the country who are battling to give their pupils something to put against the tin-pan invasion from America, and I know there is a liveliness of feeling in existence still on which any Irish poet can draw, if he would forget that literary Dublin is not the whole of Ireland.

And that is the point. Poems like Patrick Kavanagh's *The Great Hunger* may please the man who likes a material that has sociological implications, but one has only to see a horse fair at Carrickmacross, as I did a month ago, to discern at once that if there is an economic tie between life and virility, it applies more or less to the odd-man-out. Economics, indeed, make virility a necessity, and any picture of life that does not take *élan-vital* and the male upsurge into account is biased. There is no single truth in any spectacle, there are as many truths as there are participators, and if one takes the dull, hodden grey of one man's picture of the countryside as truth, it is a truth that must be qualified by the pictures of others. This country is alive in ways no cityman or expatriate countryman can know, and it surprises me every day the amount of traditional literary intelligence that is to be found in it.

So if I think we should rely more on our own people for a literary response to the things we do, I think we should also seek ways to come closer to them. Irish literary movements have never gotten under the skin of the country people, and I doubt if 99 per cent of them will understand a difficult poem; but all our poems are not difficult, and if we approach the simpler ones with a regard to local ways of speech, or even use a common theme in which to be difficult, we may find there are those who listen to us in the depths of the country, or even in the streets of Dublin.

I doubt, however, if making new songs to old airs can help. But for some, perhaps, it may be a way out of themselves, and a way, maybe, into the heart of their own country.

And that, strangely, has some compensations. It must be like having a home somewhere where one may go now and then on holiday.

—*The Bell*, November 1952

Editor's note: At one period in his career, Padraic Fallon became closely involved with ballad-writing, mostly for traditional Irish airs. Some of these appeared in print, while others were written for radio. A number have entered the ballad-singer's repertory.

II
Memories and Essays

The Unique Genius

Cyril Tourneur is one of the major biographical puzzles left us by the Elizabethan dramatists. A couple of sentences would accommodate all that we know of his life. He was engaged in composition between the years 1600 and 1613. The former year saw the appearance of *The Transformed Metamorphosis*; and in the latter year there is mention of him in a letter from Robert Daborne, the playwright, to Philip Henslowe, the manager, from which we gather that he was a professional writer. Of his life, otherwise, there is no certain fact; his face is blacked out in the brilliant mosaic we have of his age, and though we have had some brilliant guesswork from Mr Allardyce Nicoll—whose book from the Fanfrolico Press contains a complete collection of all the works attributed to Tourneur, with suitable and admirable theme-decoration from Mr Frederick Carter—that Tourneur was one of a family in the service of the Cecil family, there is nothing really to connect him to our lives except 'the unquenchable and burning fire, the bitter ardour and angry beauty of his verse'. It is a great pity, for to read his plays is to be involved for a long time in a maze of speculation about the man behind them.

Certainly none of his contemporaries, his equals or near-equals, give rise to such curiosity. Tourneur belonged critically to the earlier portion of the Shakespearean tail. In some ways he imitates his master, as, in other ways, he uses Marston or Middleton. Yet he was, uniquely, a person and, in *The Revenger's Tragedy* at least, sublimated his sources and fashioned himself a manner that, for innovation and individuality, is second only to Shakespeare and Webster and, perhaps at his best, Marlowe. There is nothing that I know of so entirely strange as the personality that gestures so urgently in that play and still he matched it from his resources of vocabulary and invention, found a phrase or devised a situation to meet every turn of his terrible theme, and in the result achieved a self of such power as to place him, if not among the very great, at least a long step above the 'minors'. Unlike Shakespeare or Webster or Marlowe, whose whole personalities no one play could contain, *The Revenger's Tragedy* seems to express all that there was of Tourneur. We feel, after reading it, that we know all about him and are tempted, on the instant, to make it the hinge of our speculation on the man himself, on his private life and his background—above all, on his great obsession, his devasting hatred towards life.

Tourneur, indeed, must have been a living death-motive if he stood in such relation to life as *The Revenger's Tragedy* stands to literature, and if he were inspired as the play seems inspired. In the play, his hatred and loathing and disgust are such as would have been unutterable had his genius not come made to measure. In *Hamlet* Shakespeare realised the same motive and, in a lesser way, in *Lear*, and made it seem an important phase of life experience, credible because subordinated to humanity and expressed through characters who must be recognised as human. Tourneur, in *The Revenger's Tragedy*, realised it—with a difference. He projected it in characters which are but personifications of all the vices, and have no reality outside of adolescent nightmare. There is no reality, as we accept the word, in it or in *The Atheist's Tragedy*; and it is, in part, because of this lack that I am prepared to differ with Churton Collins and assert that Tourneur's genius was not of the kind that finds and develops itself gradually but, on the contrary, a precocious and sudden flowering in adolescence and, furthermore, to assert that his genius was of the kind that isolates itself in one masterpiece in which there is complete, if temporary, union of the man with his neurosis—a sort of bridal night—and, thereafter, disintegration.

It is futile, I know, to drag a theory by the hair from the

two plays of Tourneur's that have come down to us; and his verse gives one no help, for it is, with the exception of *The Transformed Metamorphosis*, of the type that is made to order. If there were even undisputed external evidence to add to the entries in the Stationers' books that *The Revenger's Tragedy* was written before *The Atheist's Tragedy*, as I am convinced it was, the ground would be less liquid but still treacherous enough. Satisfactory proof would require at least another half-dozen plays indisputably Tourneur's and the dates of their printing; and there was but one that we know of, *The Nobleman*, and it was lost in transit. As something is needed, however, to explain why *The Revenger's Tragedy*, printed four years before *The Atheist's Tragedy*, is so much the better play of the two, is so much tighter in texture, so much more urgent and powerful an expression of the same view of life, and to explain why the author of such work—and a professional writer at that, who must have been thrust, of necessity, and quite often, into the society of his fellow writers—should seem to have passed practically unnoticed through his own time, I think we cannot do better than seek the reason in the writer's own character as deduced from the plays and from *The Transformed Metamorphosis*. The only excuse I can offer for such barren speculation is the worst possible excuse—that to appreciate a writer's work is to speculate about the writer. ('What porridge had John Keats?')

Little but a middling talent shows in Tourneur's first acknowledged publication, *The Transformed Metamorphosis*, a long riddle of a poem which is so obscure that the author did well to inform his public that it was a satire. At this time of the day one would never guess it. That he was very young then, in 1600, there can be little doubt, for what there is of style in the poem—and it is certainly curious—is derivative of the fashionable school headed by Hall and Marston, whose mannered innovations none but the very young would be likely to imitate. The only thing to be deduced from this production is that the author was young, and a would-be satirist.

The next thing attributed to him, and not by any means unanimously, is a prose allegory, *Laugh and Lie Down, or The World's Folly*. This has very little of the Tourneur quality; and if I mention it at all it is to emphasise his preoccupation with the 'sins' of the world, and his pose as satirist which was, in reality, a way of living at second-hand. (Apropos of this, there is Churton Collins' remark: '... he loves to satirise that he may secure for himself the luxury of prurient description'.)

Two years afterwards, on the 7th October, 1607, to be exact, was printed *The Revenger's Tragedy*.

It is nowhere definitely stated that the play was Tourneur's. His achievements, before this date, give no promise of such craftmanship in construction metric, or of a vision so intense that in spite of wild distortion and grotesquerie we, even in this sophisticated day, must give it room in the sum of our experience. The consensus of scholarship, however, assigns it to him; and there can be no doubt, I think, that the mind behind it and the mind behind *The Atheist's Tragedy* are one and the same.

I have to state now the difficulty that exists for some commentators in the fact that *The Atheist's Tragedy*, the lesser of the two in all ways, was undoubtedly the later play. The fact that it is in no way comparable in power or in unity of character to *The Revenger's Tragedy* is the holdfast of the few who do not consent to Tourneur's authorship of the latter. It is also the stumbling block of those others who, wishing to see Tourneur as a complete and mature personality, would read into him the natural development and growth of normal men, and have *The Atheist's Tragedy* as Tourneur's first play in time. It is quite possible, of course, that it was, and that it was apprentice-work laid aside for one reason or other and tricked out at a later date when it had made something of a name and had a greater stage experience. The objection to this, and it is strong enough, I think, to rout it, is that if Tourneur's mastery of his craft was increasing in the usual normal way with age and experience, and if *The Atheist's Tragedy* was rewritten after *The Revenger's Tragedy*, why does the former show greater crudities of form and manner and graver lapses in taste, and deterioration everywhere, when all could be remedied simply by the application of a master's rule of thumb? There can be but the one answer, I consider, to my question. The play was composed by a Tourneur who was himself deteriorating and who, if he were aware—which I beg leave to doubt—of his lapse from his own high standard, was unable to remedy it.

At any rate, I see no reason to doubt the evidence of the Stationer's Hall where *The Atheist's Tragedy* was entered in 1611. Both plays are young and both marked, in different ways, by immaturity of experience. But *The Revenger's Tragedy* has the heat, the sudden energies, and the violent nausea of a young man at his first rebound from life. The versification, too, is younger, and more varied in temper than in art, and is of the kind that orders itself internally to a vividly apprehended vision rather than the kind that can be arranged by a craftsman out of his knowledge and experience of what is fitting; in trying to describe it, one single, so-often-misused adjective springs up in the mind: 'dynamic'; and as integral a part of the action of the play as limbs are to movement. I am not particularly widely read, so I pay it no great tribute when I state that, outside of the mature Shakespeare, I know of no dramatic verse as inspired from play's beginning to play's end; and it is on this (to me), very vivid feeling of the play's inspiration—that, in fact, it ran away with Tourneur—that I base my intuition that his genius was the brief kind that flowers suddenly in neurosis, and, having expressed the man in terms of his neurosis and the neurosis in terms of the man—a psychic unity—wholly and completely and for the first time, thereafter dwindled down to its real size and became mere talent, a talent that luckily outleaped itself.

It is at this point that speculation about the man Tourneur begins, and finds itself faced by a void. Naturally, having my private image of him, I look for anything that will help me mirror it. Nobody, I tell myself, could have been born with such a loathing for life as Tourneur's two plays show him to contain; no man possibly could entertain it and live; certainly, no man bearing it could attain maturity. It can be pointed out against this that Swift's hatred of humanity was as great as Tourneur's, and that there can be no doubt of Swift's maturity. There is, however, no real analogy, for Swift was mature before the virus took its violent way with him. We can account, too, shrewdly enough, for Swift and for his man-of-the-world cynicism, for we know so much about him that, for all practical purposes, his body corporeal might be sitting still in his study at St Patrick's or pacing along New Street. Whereas Tourneur, if there were not so much of the body in his plays, might, for what we know to the contrary, never have been in the body at all. To allow Mr Nicoll's supposition that he was one of a family of Tourneurs in the service of the Cecil family would furnish us, indeed, with something in the nature of the background we require. The prime psychological factor in loathing towards life is, if we except physical disease, more likely to be founded in a feeling of social inferiority than in anything else; and to imagine Tourneur as the son, or close relative, of a high-graded servant—a clerk or steward—and with, possibly, the run of the great house in his youth and the favour of the family, which would allow him to be tutored along with its own members and, while he was still in the child stage, to mingle quite freely in its more homely social doings, would be to account in some degree for such a factor. One can suppose the awakening of a proud boy to his dependency and to the slights—perhaps, kindly enough—attendant on his anomalous status. It has been the theme of many romantic novels. There would be a withdrawal into the self and a counterbalancing quickening of the fancy; and, for the plays show all the extraordinarily sensuality of the introvert, an escape into the fleshly imagination. There would be solitude, certainly, for he would be given no menial position in life—perhaps, an extra secretaryship, something confidential—and an unique upstairs-downstairs angle of vision which is, indeed, the very angle of the plays as I read them. To deduce anything of his background, however, from the play, is to go more by guess than by God, for if he was of that type of subjectivity to which I consider he belonged, he would not heed very much the form of the exchanges that went on around him in life, but would be concerned, rather, with their spirit. His stage situations, in their logical fantasy, show him to be no realist in our sense of 'realism', but they have the kind of reality that only a solitary, in his brooding, can give to the interchanges that go on around him and from which he is precluded, interchanges simple and normal enough when comprehended in relation to life as a whole, but of dark significance to a rich, limited adolescent. It would be absurd to look for the Cecil household in the plays ...

> Secured ease and state; the stirring meates
> Ready to move out of the dishes, that e'n now quicken
>   when they're eaten,
> Banquets abroad by torchlight, musicks, sports,
> Bare-headed vassailes that had ne'er the fortune
> To keep on their own hats, but let horns wear 'em.

He took, I think, just as much of his imagery from life as his fancy could befool to his liking, but in the way he returns again and again to those mighty banquetings and revels and their imaginary consequence in sexual luxury, there is something less suggestive of the poet in his garret than of the accounts-clerk penned at some middle distance between revellers and servers, and constrained by youthful pride and position from mingling with either.

It is all, however, in the air and, if it be gathered that I am trying to prove that Tourneur's genius was, in reality, a talent that outleaped itself in order to express fully the man in terms of his neurosis, it must not be understood that I consider it necessary to account in any way for the neurosis or for the making of *The Revenger's Tragedy*, which, of its isolation and very nature, must almost be adjudged a divine accident. In regard to the isling of his genius, I would be on safer ground, as I said before, if *The Revenger's Tragedy* could be said with certainty to be his sole masterpiece; we would be assured, then, of what Churton Collins styles 'the narrowness of his range of vision'— a summary phrase which is, in my opinion, exact and just. As matters stand, Tourneur seems to have expressed himself fully in this play, and there is not in it the signs of any future possible growth, of any deep inner concern with humanity, of any further ranging over life. His eyes are not trained on life at all, but shut upon his vision of it, and we have no doubt that he will never see anything but this vision. Webster, who 'was much possessed by death', has left us a demonology not less violent, but in no single play, late or early, do we feel the limitation there is in Tourneur; the impression he leaves is that his protagonists have in some way objectified his great pity. 'He must go on,' we think, 'it is necessary for him to go on making occasion for his pity.' It is not so with Tourneur.

Narrowness of range or vision is, in itself, no criterion of youth or of slender experience. But when it is enshrined in such a rich vocabulary and in such breadth of expression as Tourneur's in this tragedy, one feels that there is nothing else within him to be expressed and that his art has turned out all his pockets and stripped him naked. We can behold him in this period of *Vindice* more clearly, I think, than we can ever hope to see him later; for after this, if he is to live at all, he must invent for himself a less terrible vision of the world. This trimming of the candle is undoubtedly a later phase of experience of which *The Revenger's Tragedy*, with its great firing of both ends, shows not the least trace. Now there can be no doubt that Tourneur did fashion himself some sort of a niche in the world, there is evidence that he spent some considerable portion of his later life in The Netherlands, with which the Cecil family had political connection, for he was in receipt of a pension of £60 a year for services rendered there, and it is unquestionable that in 1625 'it pleased the Lord Viscount Wimbledon, when he was made General for the Cadiz Action, to make Choyce of him to goe as Secretary to The Councell of Warr ...' and that, at about the same time, he acted as Secretary to Sir Edward Cecil: all this leads one to believe that he did adjust himself to life, a feat, in his case, which was possible only by the sacrifice of his authentic first vision of life to his 'will to live'. In other words, he had to divide himself in order to live.

The author of a single masterpiece always intrigues by reason of an accidental-seeming element in his achievement. The achievement seems, in fact, bigger than the man in the way that fire is bigger than the fuel out of which it is wrought, and it suggests a sudden unity for which he himself is not quite responsible. Greater men, on the contrary, are of a size with what they create, they are quite the equals of their inspiration as well as its origin, and seem to touch no element that is outside of themselves. In this respect, it is to hammer a driven nail to bring up Shakespeare-*Hamlet*, Shakespeare-*Othello*, Shakespeare-*Lear*, which we recognise as moods of the one man, and less than him because he ousted one to make room for another. In

Tourneur, the mood is static; it remains with him, and there is never any question of him ousting it. It is greater than he is, and he is forced to search out through all his deformities of self in order to express it, and then to invent more. Now, it seems to me that there is more of a self in *The Revenger's Tragedy* than in *The Atheist's Tragedy*, because what invention there is in *The Revenger's Tragedy* is in strict accord with the theme; his obsession seems to obtain from him a complete surrender and to have kept his art, sternly, within its limitations. There is a full, straight, narrow current from beginning to end, and no dwelling on the external scenery of lust, and no unnecessaries of humour—for his grotesque humour was an 'invention' and not at all of his element. It is the man in his entirety, complete without subplots; and the whole man and his vision—or mood—are expressed more strictly and accurately than they can be expressed again. It is apparent, so strong is his obsession, that he must return again and again to express it, but he will come with more of an 'invented' self; his energies, acclimatising themselves as best they can to life, will have branched from the first integral stem, and he must loosen his art to make room for them, and allow it to dwell on the parts rather than on the whole—suffer disintegration.

This, as I see it, is what makes *The Atheist's Tragedy* a lesser play in all ways, except in variation of metric. The obsession is the same, the characters might be duplicates, one of another, but there is a wholesale relaxing of tension. The Tourneur in it is dispersed, he has spread himself into backwaters of humour and the conventional happy-ending romance; it is an older Tourneur attempting to save himself, heavily and with dreadful, painful effort, from his authoritative first vision, a laborious, pitiful attempt to accommodate himself near the imaginary norm—to see the world as others see it. There is fine talent shown in individual scenes, long dallying escapes into lust, and much sweet verse, lingering and artificial, but extremely competent. But the inspiration there is in it seems to be a left-over from *The Revenger's Tragedy*, and the play, altogether, an attempt to give form by craft to what in the earlier play created its own form, to the force of the latter, its hatred and despair, while at the same time seeking to accommodate the new elements of self-heavy humour, conventional honour, heroics that his adjustments to living have forced him to invent. The difference between the two plays is, indeed, exactly what it should be if my reading of the man is correct. *The Atheist's Tragedy* attempts the wider range, but in so doing it emphasises the narrowness of its author's real range. In spreading himself, he lost his drive.

That neurosis was the big factor in his brief genius is an emotional assumption which not everybody will admit. But, while not seeking to erect anything over him in the nature of a brazen monument, I submit that it offers a solution of some points at issue without any juggling with the facts available to us. It would explain, first of all, why a play printed in 1607 should state better, with greater power, intensity of feeling, and far greater unity of self, a certain singular state of mind than a play printed four years later. It would account, too, for the isolation of all his genius to one play, and account for the manner in that play, for its suddenness, and the startling feeling one has about it from the beginning—as if something damned had burst all sluices, with Tourneur riding it headlong in a brief urgent freedom to the final weir. Finally it would account for Tourneur's lack of objective humanity and the nightmare atmosphere of the two plays in which there are no people, as we know people, but abstractions of the terrible birds that feed on him inwardly, stilts and sticks tricked out that he may fit his cap on them. Not one, three-dimensional, honest-to-god human being among them all.

If I am right, then, and *The Revenger's Tragedy* was the first and the fuller expression of Tourneur's attitude towards life and if I am right in saying that this attitude was dictated by neurosis, it would follow that any other work coming from his hand—while, naturally, being concerned in chief with his peculiar obsession—would show more and more the invented self in which he endeavours to accommodate himself to living. *The Atheist's Tragedy* is near enough in time to *The Revenger's Tragedy*, and still it is a disintegration of genius, because there is enough of this invented self in it to enable him to escape from the insupportable terror of his real self. The more he accommodates himself to conventional life, the more he will stress those elements in his art which are foreign to him—humour, heroics, and the like, which have no part at all in his integral vision. His work will be more lashed and driven, clumsier and less unified with each succeeding effort. His inspiration will be out of the mood of *The Revenger's Tragedy* always, but his craft, coming out of what he imagines to be conventional and normal, will be continually growing away from it. In the end, his real self will be a side-issue to his invented self, or perhaps lifted up as an Aunt Sally to be stoned; and I suggest that any other play coming after *The Atheist's Tragedy* would stand in relation to it as *The Atheist's Tragedy* stands, in art, to *The Revenger's Tragedy*, and would be a further disintegration of Tourneur's real vision. There is some evidence that this was so, for the lost play, *The Nobleman*, which was printed in the year after *The Atheist's Tragedy*, is styled a 'Trage Comedye'. And what had Tourneur's vision to do with the comic?

If *The Atheist's Tragedy* were lost along with *The Nobleman*, we would have a great quarrel with Time, but would have, still, the essential Tourneur. In his occasional verses he is as minor as any other minor Elizabethan, and he left us no lyrics. But in *The Revenger's Tragedy*, there is the most important dramatic verse outside of Shakespeare and, at their best, Webster and Marlowe. He had remarkable stage sense and was cunning to create melodramatic situations, but this quality—even backed up by the close texture in which his patterned characters are woven, and the unity he confers on them by his passionate horror—would not have availed to bring his name down to us were it not for his living, dynamic verse-speech. It brings within our range of experience, and makes human, a phase of life that is so uncommon as to be almost incredible; it never gives one time to pause and mutter with Hippolito, 'Nay, brother, you reach out a' th' Verge now.' And it preserves, in no mummy-form, one of the oddest, most to be pitied figures of a great time.

''Tis well he died: he was a witch.'

—*Dublin Magazine*, July–September 1937

Editor's note: Since Fallon wrote this essay, modern scholarship seems no nearer to clearing away the obscurity surrounding the life of Cyril Tourneur (?1575–1626). *The Revenger's Tragedy* was printed anonymously and not until 1656—long after Tourneur's death—was it attributed to him. The attribution has been strongly contested, however, and over the past century and a half many scholars have favoured Richard Middleton as the play's real author.

The Native Roots

DÁIN DO EIMHER AGUS DÁIN EILE
by Somhairle Mac Ghill Eathain

AUNTRAN BALLADS
by Douglas Young (foreword by Hugh MacDiarmid)

POETRY SCOTLAND, NO. I
edited by Maurice Lindsay

(all from the publishing house of William Maclellan, Glasgow)

T O T O U C H on the new back-to-the-native-tongue movement which is beginning to make literature in Scotland is willy-nilly to make contact with a major Irish controversy, the Irish Language. There are many arguments, pro and con, for a Gaelic-speaking state, they have been columned and platformed for more than half a century, and have so saturated us that we are almost unable any longer to see the issue clearly and without passion. You grow purple if you are of the Empire breed, and prate of global economics, the gigantic axle at Westminster, and our place by proxy in the sun that never sets. Or, if you are of the native stock by blood or inclination, you grow wild and almost wordless thinking of a broken culture, and are all for the new State glasshouse and revival. There seems to be no middle way except that of indifference, for the values involved, like those of religion, are outside of reason. You are born with a silver con in your mouth, or you sharpen a pro as your grandfather sharpened a pike. Reasons, either way, you will have in plenty; reasons as ready-made and formal as those stylised statues which the sculptors of the Decadence took out of stock as a ready fit for the head of any patron. And like all reasons, no doubt, a mere masquerade for very different and maybe selfish motives.

To an issue which was never clearly a racial issue, time has brought the usual addenda of complications. The hard nucleus of the opposition, however, is still what used to be called the Protestant Ascendancy Party, people who, whatever Ireland may mean to them, look naturally to England as their motherland and have no reasons to desire any other culture. To many of those, Gaelic as a museum language would be palatable enough, but they claim that a Gaelic-speaking state would cut them off from England and from the wide horizons and large monetary movements of the Empire where, with their school and university contacts, they have moved always as freely as any born Englishman. To them Ireland is a suburb of the great city of England.

And they reason that it can never be anything else, now that transport is a matter of moments and that sound-waves have made nonsense of the sea-waves as a frontier. Race movements, in fine, political and cultural, in this spaceless but spacious world should no longer be selfish and separatist, wilful in their meanderings, but grand currents towards an eventual single identity where all would merge into ... what?

This, as political theory, seems sound enough, but it is cultural nonsense, for the essence of civilisation is not the similarities of its parts, its common sameness, but lies in differences that challenge each other, fight mentally, merge and sunder, take and give, always fluid as thought is fluid, a never-ending change. It is suspect, too, because it requires that Irish Ireland should be the first to yield up her national identity to something that seems very likely to be nothing but the old dominant-race theory in a new form.

Now the most unlikely thing in the world is that Ireland will surrender the English tongue as a means of communication. It is too valuable for cultural and economic reasons. Why then are the loudspeakers of the minority so active? It cannot be Gaelic alone that they fear, for a countrywide common use of Gaelic, with English always present as a second tongue, would erect no barrier between Ireland and England. What is it then? Is it mere race antipathy? Or just the natural reaction

of a deposed autocracy who have seen all their work as con-
querors and all their hereditary privileges go wallop in a couple of decades? Or is it that there is something in the shape of
the Gaelic state that they, as inheritors of the freely-questing
mind of the eighteenth century, mislike and distrust?

Perhaps there is.

There is, for one thing, a literary censorship, a rabid exhibition of provincial obscurantism which makes an open mockery of all intellectual freedom. They are entitled to take this as
an indication of what could happen if the country, by the use
of Irish, shut out the world and all those liberal standards
which the free minds of Europe have struggled for centuries to
erect and maintain, often against bloody persecution and
nearly always against the grain of general opinion. They can
make a lot out of this and, quite rightly, they do. They are the
only people, except the writers themselves, who are outspoken
about it, for being in so small a minority they have no need to
play the electorate as other parties do. So Ministers of State,
thinking in terms of parish wiseacres, are goaded into senatorial dicta which bring ridicule on themselves and their offices.
This, we think, is government by the forge and the crossroads,
by the ingrown spinster and the inhibited puritan, by the self-
appointed vigilante who would excise life's major temptation,
Life itself, by act of Parliament. Can such an atmosphere breed
a Goethe, or even a Shelley? And what would we do with a
Baudelaire? Or a Villon? Or any country poet with the hardi-
hood to write another *Midnight Court*? Liberty, certainly
would become eventually something disreputable, something
which wise men left to that queer fellow, the censored writer.

And one almost forgets that in another Irish capital, the
Minister of Literary Censorship has something like a counter-
part, with bigotries and electorates to balance ours, and that
no party has a monopoly either of folly or wisdom. Same man,
different clothes.

The truth however, despite any cynical political use of it,
is clear enough. Whatever about the Irish State, the Irish language, handicapped from the start by the dead hand rather
than the Red Hand, has a gelded, not a gilded, future. No
writer whose job is human nature will use it, for a writer needs

an audience, not a social pillory. Writing in English he can find kindred spirits in two hemispheres, writing in Irish he will find his name in *Iris Oifiguil* or in whatever periodical the Censor publishes his list of the damned, without even the comfort of a nice cheque for royalties. It makes a difference, all the difference in the world.

Yet those, really, are red herrings drawn across the real issue, whether Ireland is or is not to be a Gaelic-speaking state. The majority, through the state machinery, have given a definite affirmative, but in practice have qualified it by not taking it on themselves to learn and use the tongue. This mental laziness, indeed, rather than any set opposition, is the chief problem of the revivalists, and the minority have made the most of it, playing to the lowest common denominator on the one hand (pleading a kind of law in culture by which the good is ousted by the bad) while with the other they beckon to the intelligent by sponsoring the uncensored mind.

And that, for the moment, is how the battle stands.

Two intelligent minorities fighting for a vast area of inertia which may come alive one way then another, as all democracies do eventually. That the revivalists must go on *à rebours* until they complete the job is, I think, essential, for the Gaelic-speaking state, even more than any economic reason, was largely the inspirer of the separatist politics that have brought us where we are to-day. For that reason alone, it should have its chance. Language must mean something, must have another use than that of plain communication. Matthew Arnold and others separated what they identified as a Celtic element from English literature in general. And surely this element should express itself better in its own tongue, a tongue that developed out of the psychic structure that was natural to it, and which has indeed, in the words of Valéry, that '*purété*' which is '*le résultat d'opérations infinies*'. Gaelic is rich in music as few languages are, with words active as images, a gift from God for any poet who would have the luck to speak it from his birth. To let it die now would be, if not race-suicide, something at least for which the future would never forgive us, something a great deal more obscurantist than a literary censorship, which the next election or the election after that, or the election after the next election after that, may by some happy chance cancel and annul.

This long dissertation leads me almost in pity to the men in Scotland who have begun to write their poetry in Gaelic. If after fifty years of elaborate and enthusiastic revival there is in Ireland no audience for a Gaelic poet—and an audience creates a poet as an age or period does somehow create its own way of psychic satisfaction—what must be the position in Scotland where the language has been carefully elbowed even out of the back-hills and the bleak seaboard? Ireland at least had a political movement powerful enough to carry its cultural house on its back. Has Scotland, where education has not the home bias we have in Ireland?

That the rebuilding of it has begun, there can be no doubt. I have a book of Gaelic verse before me as I write, by a young man, Sorley MacLean, which is as promising as a young man's verse can be. MacLean, who was badly wounded at El Alamein fighting the Germans, does not work in the patterned verse which Mary MacLeod of Harris invented for the Gaelic-speaking world around the end of the sixteenth century, breaking up the old tight models into verse of free vowel metres. That Gaelic lends itself to this involved and deliberate vowel-play is now a matter of history, for by the middle of the eighteenth century the ancient consonantal modes and measures had almost entirely given way to it. There arose then in Ireland the hedge-school poets, who might be called the first Irish Realists on account of their use of everyday themes and the near-propaganda uses to which they put their verse. They used speech as plainly as any modern poet, yet they kept to the 'sounding' words that Dryden insisted on and to the strict patterns they had taken over from Mary MacLeod and made verse memorable enough to be quoted in study and farmhouse two hundred years later. Sorley MacLean, except for an odd poem here and there, disdains the pattern and makes verse after the fashion of English, using assonance, however, where English would use rhyme. There is no reason why one should expect more pattern from a Gaelic poet than from a poet who writes English, especially at this time of day when the fashion is to strip and strip until the thought walks naked, but patterns that would seem stilted in English seem to be the very texture of the Gaelic, they shape the language and only, incidentally, ornament it. I am thinking, now, not of Egan O Rahilly's 'Gile na Gile', where the art with its classical delicacy is almost too obvious, but of poems like Blind William Heffernan's 'Caitlin ní hUalacháin' of which Yeats made an approximate rhythmic version in his famous song of that name, or, say, Seaghan O Tuama's 'Bean na Cleithe Caoile', the first stanza of which is:

Níor thagair liom ceart, beart na briathar aoibhnis
Leabhar na ceacht, na rann a dheilb díreach:
Níor cataigh me ar fad go teacht am sheirbhíseach
'S am reachtaire cearc ag Bean na cleithe caoile!

A rough finish is part of the art-technique of the Romantics and was adopted to give an appearance of immediate inspiration to expression. But now that thought, rather than any representation of emotion, is the major theme of our time, the technique must alter too, and pattern with all its intricacies be admitted again. Sometimes, almost in spite of himself one thinks, Sorley MacLean drops into an assonantal arrangement not unlike that of any poet of the Maigue.

An tugadh d' fhonn no t' ailleacd ghlórmhor
bhuam-sa grainealachd mharb nan doigh so
a' bhruid 'am meirleach air ceann na h-Eorpa
's do bheul-sa, uaill-dearg, 's an t-sean oran?

In many more poems, however, he adopts the more usual folk versification:

Tha barr a' chiuil
air dún a' mhullaich:
tha 'n ró-chrann ur
fo dhriuch'd gun tuireadh.

The important thing about this young Gaelic poet is that he can see to-day in terms of yesterday and to-morrow and not isolate himself in the romanticism of the past or lose his prophetic soul to the political economy of the future. He is logically nationalist, and equally logically a Communist, but he is a poet first, standing in the midstream of today, and the current is visible through his verse. There are many fine poems in his book; 'The Heron' for instance is a cunning piece of work, introspective, but definite, while 'The Highland Woman' has a very effective rhetoric, and might have been written by Wordsworth had he passion enough to follow his own social logic outside the bounds of Bumbledom.

> *Is thriall a tim mar shnighe dubh*
> *a' drudhadh tughaidh fardaich bochd;*
> *mheal ise an dubh chosnadh cruaidh;*
> *is glas a cadal suain an nochd.*

This stanza, in the Scots of Douglas Young, another young Scottish poet, reads as follows:

> Her time gaed by like black sleek
> throu an auld thaikit hous-rig seepan;
> she bruikit aye sair black wark,
> and gray the nicht id her lang sleepan.

Young is not so apparently a poet as Sorley MacLean, and would seem indeed to belong to the poet-type of our own Padraic Pearse and Thomas MacDonagh, poets who find a good deal of their self-expression in separatist politics. To read his book, *Auntran Ballads*, one needs besides English and Scots, a knowledge of Greek, Gaelic, French, Latin and German. It is, however, mostly in Scots and good humour, and goes well as a companion book to Sorley MacLean's, of whom he has made many translations. Young, indeed, seems to be a driving force among the young men of the new movement, and if he doesn't make a poet, is certain to be of consequence otherwise.

There is another sign of the Scottish awakening before me as I write, a magazine called *Poetry Scotland*. This, however, does not back up the native movement to any large degree. Five out of the seventeen Scottish poets represented write in Scots, with Sorley MacLean the only Gaelic representative. The magazine has four sections, Scotland, England, Wales and Ireland, the English, Welsh and Irish poets being included because the editor, quite rightly, does not believe in a 'strictly national outlook in art'.

It is a pity, however, since there are so many thriving English poetry magazines in existence where all the young English poets of importance may be read, that the section was not devoted to some other country whose verse is more difficult of access, Russia, Spain, or Spanish America, any horizon indeed that will help push the English background into perspective.

Whatever may come of this movement—and what a fine publisher it has secured in William Maclellan of Glasgow, a book-producer of lovely quality—it is there anyway, slender perhaps, but active, with no large figure yet if we exclude the widely aspiring Hugh MacDiarmid who seems to be writing more plain English nowadays than Scots, but indicating, in MacLean especially, a promising in-seeking trend that may connect Scotland to its own root once more. We must wish it *Sláinte 'gus saoghail.*

—*Dublin Magazine*, July–September 1944

The Poet in the New Ireland

O F LATE years Irish Letters have been represented mainly by writers of prose, by novelists, by short-story men and playwrights, good talents working out of realistic backgrounds who fit without any sense of intrusion into the lists of their London publishers. This is so normal nowadays that one is likely to forget that for many years no year seemed complete that did not bring forth a book from some Irish poet, Yeats or another, and that it was on this book that our stock rose or fell abroad. Poetry, indeed, seemed of late to have fallen on evil days, and this in its way could be a theme for social or political speculation. Why, since the death of Yeats, has the bottom fallen out of things? And why should a great creative epoch seem to end with the death of one man?

Analysis, of course, will only bring out those kinds of generalisations which serve as springboards in discussion. Yeats, for instance, was a summary of the Empire Irishman, meaning an Irishman who lived his early years in an Ireland dominated by England; and for all his Irishry his two feet were very firmly planted in the dominant country, in literary England where his taste was formed, and though he lived to witness the climactic changes of the new Irish State he was by then a fully fashioned world figure who had no inner need of the native community. When he did write for home consumption he made a mess of it, for he wrote for a people who overnight had changed, for an Ireland with a new set of values, a naked country that had started to shiver in its skin.

Poets who followed inherited a psychic mess and rang their bells for a non-existent congregation. The new Ireland had more immediate interests. It required a new front, a new Establishment, and that had to be thrown up quickly, with father-figures in Senate and Dáil to insure the homely virtues of field and fair. Indeed, as a fragment broken off an established empire, we had all the insecurities of the unwanted child, and if we bolstered ourselves with anti-divorce laws and the censorship of letters it was, I suppose, only to be expected. What could not be anticipated was the dearth of new poets, or indeed of any kind of real writer in the new State who could compare—even on handicap terms—with Yeats or Joyce, or even with Moore and Shaw, men who could shake and startle a time because they belonged naturally to the larger community of letters and had honed their talents on the European stone.

The problem for poets living in Ireland was to make poetry out of entirely new conditions. Most poems are made AGAINST the grain of a time but they are still of their time and place, and necessarily so. The community in which they are made participates in them whether it likes to or not. There is a country in every statue, a civilisation in every poem or any other work of art; and eventually, though it rejects it for the moment, it will belong to the community where it was born. But for thirty years we had been living politically and at high tension; and from the Treaty onwards inhabiting a sort of hangover, living on the outskirts of ourselves in eighteenth-century ruins, not Lever's people anymore, no more the Playboys of the Western World, but a people now confined by facts and economics who must explore willy-nilly all the new mysteries of Statehood. There were only two poets then of any quality whose development was synchronous with the revolution, Austin Clarke and F.R. Higgins. They were alike in some ways, but what strikes one now at this remove of time was their difference. Their approach to the new world had nothing in common.

The difficulty with verse, of course, is that it never rises out of immediacy. It must take its own time and use its own plasm. Its rule is to have no rules but order, a static concept that will translate itself to no definite current situation except by analogy and its various corollaries. The great myths, for instance, are poetic vessels. They live because time past is—poetically speaking—still alive in the present. And that is how Clarke faced modern Ireland when he returned here to live in 1935. What he saw here, by analogy, was primitive Christian times, saints and hermits and a lot of very active demon tempters leapfrogging round the pious landscape. And out of this, serious and cold, and with all the implications of tragedy and irony, he developed his vision of the Catholic conscience, seeing this as the poetic task of the moment but leaguing himself with times and attitudes that were long past. With Higgins it was another story. He borrowed his poetic shape from J.M. Synge.

Synge, of course, was never an original. And the *Playboy* came out of a thousand ballads. The extravagance is that of 'An Mangaire Súgach' or Owen Ruadh O'Sullivan, and it is not at all as daring as Merriman's broad conception of the clerical militia or the Church Triumphant. But the attitude was similar, the swagger that exists in any place or state of revolution or in any community that must escape from its own boredom. Higgins was a romantic. He wanted to dissolve himself into the Western blues of Paul Henry. Indeed, for one short year he transferred himself there bodily, only to return to the pavements and his dreams. To pull a currach on one square scone a day is not a poet's work after all, but what is remarkable is that the visit to Hy Brazil, or Lough Gill, left him with an unchanged vision. He still believed that a lyric lived in every bawneen and pinched lavishly from Mrs Costello's collection of songs from Muighe-Sheola. The point I am making is that, unlike Clarke, Higgins lived in the shadow of Synge. He prolonged the oration.

Both had one thing in common. They wanted their work to seem Irish. And in this, oddly enough, they kept in step with the new State. Each felt the need for new patterns to express their Irish identities, their will to be different from English poets. They wanted a native literature in English. And if either happened to be a native Irish speaker, I think their verse would have gone into Gaelic—at the time anyway. Later on perhaps, like Dante Gabriel Rossetti, they might have rescued their books from the corpse of Kathleen, for the dead is not an audience suitable to a poet who must live and ply his trade among his peers. He must do that—even if it is only to live on credit.

Most poets after them left the Irish thing to take care of itself, the argument being that it is poetry, not race, that has art-importance, and that any value race has must come through anyway as part and parcel of the experience that made the poem. With this, of course, it is not possible to disagree at this time of day. It makes my work no more Irish if I use the stylistic devices of Gaelic verse. It is still a device in any language. And English, after all, has its own genius that mints its worth in its own way. It seems to me anyway that every theme invents its own technique, and rhythmically-born begets its own chronography as it moves along. It's only when a poem fails that we see the person of the poet—as we see the bad actor in the part he has not allowed to possess him and use him, preferring to stamp on it his own personal image.

Synge's importance, if he has any real importance, is not in his verse but in the vitality of the link he forged between the swaggering eighteenth-century figures of the Merry Pedlar or Owen Ruadh O'Sullivan and the dying folklore of a more modern day, Lever's Squireen translated into homespun.

Editor's note: This untitled essay was found folded away in a volume of Synge after Fallon's death. It bears no date but probably dates from the mid-sixties. 'An Mangaire Súgach' ('The Jolly Pedlar') was the eighteenth-century poet Aindrias Mac Craith.

Raftery: Poet of the People

FIRST there's Callanan's picture of the (rival) poet. I take this as gospel somehow, perhaps because it fits into my own image of the man, as it certainly does arrange itself into the time and the place, a Connacht still populated to the limits, with full fairs and markets, crowded courts of law, tensions everywhere, hunger next door but one, famine in the offing, fun everywhere there was a public event. Lever and Lover are never too far off as regards the public face of things, the 'boys' around the kennels, the crammed kitchens of the big house where barefoot girls were honoured to serve for nothing, the big house itself which must never be left out of the picture since it was the local pinnacle eternally visible.

Says Callanan, the Craughwell poet, of the poet born away in the County Mayo, in Killeadan, about 1784, two centuries ago;

> Pitiful the fellow who came here on top of us;
> His hat rented from the dunghill,
> Yellow as snuff that blithe article
> With its tow cord keeping it in one piece.
>
> The wrapper round him had its uses
> And showed them, for it housed many a dab of butter;
> His trousers trailed to the ground,
> Filthy too with holes uncountable;
>
> And O and O the sacred rag of his vest

That scarcely covered his middle pelt
Where the belt showed a bright buckle when the belly
    was empty,
And opened when he was full.

For all that he is the poet of the people, the ideal of a time
when a poet shares the general psyche and writes out of it,
when he is no different from the next man in texture or feeling, when the herd feeling is his too and he can sit down and
make his poems by any fireside knowing the man on the sug-
awn opposite him knows exactly what he's getting at, since the
terms of reference are held in common. The difference between
him and Callanan, however, was that of the settled man and
the man who must make his way in the world. Callanan was
a snug farmer near Craughwell, where his people still live; his
verse was made for the delectation of his friends. I doubt if he
were particularly interested in stirring up a mob, or siding in
the continual tug-of-war that went on between big house and
cabin, this not always obvious until something disturbed the
usual status quo, such as a big trial or an election, or even a
charge levelled against a priest of getting a local girl in the
family way.

    It's a magical world for a poet if he can speak the thought
and will and wishes of all. For a youth gone blind, utterly
handicapped in a world where the struggle yields even the
slightest of rewards to the strong, it was a tool that had of
necessity to become his way of life. Callanan was to say of
him, by way of denigration, that—

    There is nowhere from Galway to Doorus, and on
    Down to the seashore below
    Where this scold couldn't be found orating,
    Talk he must on everything, sport or authors.

Callanan, of course, could sit back and thatch his house at his
leisure. Raftery had to build his and then keep it out of what
came out of his head. In a hard time he was a hard man, I have
no doubt about that. He would have learned early that people
only prized what they paid for, only gave the places of dignity
to those who claimed them and stood by their claims. With his

beggar's bag he tramped the country around Athenry, Craughwell, Gort, Clarinbridge, all those bare roads towards Oranmore and Carnmore up to Loughrea, Cappataggle, Attymon, Kiltulla. There was Gaelic spoken in those places when I was a child, not by the young, but by the old, and Raftery formed part of many a session at the fireside where old men would gather after dark. This, I can remark, is my own experience. Here was a native poet alive-alive-o. Which means he was still contributing.

What did he contribute?

I have thanked God many a time for Hyde's book, myself a fool by profession not taking advantage of the opportunities I had to get a good knowledge of the language. This book, of course, and my own experiences almost make up for it. And I did get many a well-known stanza off by heart unconsciously, the ones that sing.

> *Ach míle glóir do Dhia, níor caill me leat mo chiall,*
> *Cid gur maith a cuaid mé as, a cúilín fáinneac,*
> *'S nár rugad aon fear riamh do chuirfead a lámh aniar*
> *Thar Nansaigh Walsh nac dtiuradh grádh dí.*

English it, Pádraicín Ó Fallamhain.

> To God all the glories that I didn't lose my senses for you
> But how did I come through, O heart's delight,
> Where every stunned man's head is still turned back
> Who watched you pass the road.

Let me go on, now the humour is on me. In English only for the reader. (I can still lather out the words native to my long-stalled tongue, grandmother's language):

> A sight of her on the road
> And that was a star in the mist of a winter's day,
> Gold head, and the hair tumbling to her shoes,
> A gale of it that blinded the eye;
> And the virgin nipples might as well be bare
> No cloth could ban the beam, light
> Strewed the roadway after her, she swam
> Her own white shadow like the swan.

This was a blind man, but then Homer too saw the eternal image of the goddess in a young girl's flesh and bone. I do admit that the terms were conventional, God knows what fellow burning like a candle felt those words first. Not that I put much faith in any passionate and swearing human male. It's much more likely to be the cold man in search of a passion who will sing it to life. Extravagant praise never makes the skywoman come to earth in any man's arms. It's beyond the beyonds, as they say. But it does sound all the echoes somehow that hover above and beyond ordinary living. In making those woman-poems Raftery was following a convention a lot older than the language he composed them in.

It's in the turmoil of the times a man like Raftery would find himself in full. O'Connell, Emancipation, the eternal discourses round the million fires, the potheen glow in the hedge tavern, the wars against the Tithes, warring nations; here the poet was both newscarrier and publicist, his column a word-of-mouth affair, his fee a night on the settlebed by the ashed-down turf fire, or if a bit unlucky a mere shakedown in the barn. Raftery, as a matter of fact, died in an outhouse. The Catholic Rent is a sort of peasant Catholic mythology, like the King Billy affair to the North.

Listen to a stanza. It was made after some gathering in Loughrea in favour of O'Connell.

> I hear stories going the rounds;
> On the 19th day a hundred persons shall gather
> To confute the perjured people who believe not in Mary
> On whose lap sat the King of Graces.
> At the Last Judgement each person shall be called
> And punishment meted for the people with the
>   broken seals,
> James and Charles who turned their coats,
> The harlot Elizabeth shall feel the hand above,
> With Cromwell on the ground and O'Neill over him,
> And if Billy gets away on his white horse
> It's only to meet up with Sarsfield.

This, of course, was preaching to the converted. It's the secret language of the downtrodden, the burden that lifts them for a moment, the burden of song. Raftery had no known schooling, he was on the one level at all times with his hearers. It was his business to speak out their inmost thoughts because they were his own also.

So for the condemned Whiteboy, one Anthony Daly. Daly was tried for shooting at a man, and his only defence in court was to say, 'If I were to fire a gun at you, don't think I would not hit you, even though I have only one eye.' He was hanged on Seefin, a hill in the country near Craughwell which the people say still bears the marks of the gallows. I think myself that it was used for the ancient mysteries, considering there's a cave on the summit also. And the procession that followed Daly to the gallows might be representing many a similar ceremony in the very distant past at such key points in the calendar as Solstice and Equinox. The poem Raftery made is extraordinarily active metrically.

> *Tráthnóna Aoine an Chéasta*
> *Bhí na Gaedil faoi miorsa aig na Gaill,*
> *Comhtrom an lae caedhna,*
> *Do bhí Aon-mhac Mhuire in san gcrann.*
> *Tá súil le Mac Dé 'gam*
> *'Sé mo léan, a's gan mait ar bith dó ann,*
> *'S gur b'é Cullen 's a chéile*
> *Chroc Daly, a's go dtugaid díol ann.*

I think what mostly attracts me to Raftery is the feeling of the world around him. It's a peopled world. He can write a lovely modern poem to a carpenter who lived near Castle Taylor, detailing the actual steps of the work, the sash in a frame dovetailing, banisters and rails in the making, swingles, harrow and drag rake—

> He'll contrive cleverly car, cart, or coach
> And a coffin for a dead man,

—then praise him for his drinking capacity, 'if he were up nine nights who would see the signs of a drop on him ...' He'd have liked it in McDaids.

And what a mythic ploy he could stir up, bringing Samson into it with Solomon, David, and the fall of Troy, Priam agus Hector, Aongus as Alba, Cuchulainn and Hercules burned to the bone. Lovely. And all to save some cleric's reputation which was in hazard by reason of an accusation of seduction. Wakefield and Waters are the evil dealers in the case. The marvellous pulpit rhetoric of this roadfarer,

> *Umlaig a Bean, 's déan aitrige craibteach*
> *A's tá do gréasta le fágáil ón gcléir,*
> *Umlaig san maidin, agus síl an adhar,*
> *Oir atá Dia grasamhail 's ní déanann Sé bréag ...*

Which my meagre poeticising turns into ...

> Humble yourself, woman, repent, repent,
> Grace furnishes the most meagre priest,
> Bless your face in the morning, let your tears fall,
> God will receive you.
> Think of Judas and his pointing finger
> Repent for him who betrayed the King
> Who was born in a horse stall for us
> And died painfully on the tree.

Whisper though, I have a man's fancy that this poet is not always a mealymouth. 'The Wedding at Shlahaun Mor' is an account of a gigantic hooley,

> Tara was like it, where hosts
> Drank night into morning ...
> And many a girl fine and bright, skylike
> In form and fashion;
> It were a nice thing
> To be conversing with her on the side of a couch ...

There is a menu for as many fairy hotels as could be raised on any wizard's wand from here to Coney Island. What is applicable, however, to modern times is the way the beggars, the eighteenth-century hippy, collected to the fruitful place as if a bell clanged in their secret innards—

The devil a rake of a bacach who heard the news
But seized his equipments and his beggar's suit ...

A man of many parts, then. He had to be. To eat he had
to rhyme, to rhyme he had to take his world into his hands and
dish it out again at fireside and public house.

While I'm at it, I'd like to say that the credit of this book
must go to Douglas Hyde certainly, and to Lady Gregory who
put him on to the job, but other unknown and unsung people
were at it long before the great lady of Coole heard about it
at all. For instance a man of Galway University named Cawley who, of course, hailed from the Callanan country of
Craughwell.

Editor's note: This article/essay was originally commissioned for a
series in *The Irish Times* but never used. It is undated but was written about 1972. The Gaelic folk-poet Antony Raftery (Antoine
Raiftearai, 1779–1835) was a major presence to Fallon from childhood, since his poems and songs were still sung or declaimed then
among the Galway country people and anecdotes about him were
common currency. In particular, he was remembered in the area
around Craughwell, where Fallon had relatives, and Raftery is buried
in Killeenin hard by. Fallon made free translations of two of Raftery's
best-known poems, 'Mary Hynes' and 'Raftery's dispute with the
Whiskey'. He also made him the central character in his powerful
radio play, *The Bell for Mister Loss*.

Athenry: Childhood Memories

EDITOR'S NOTE: these recollections of the poet's birthplace in Co. Galway form the bulk of a long letter he wrote in the early 1970s to his second son, the editor of this book. They were intended as a guide to a projected article or broadcast by a leading Irish writer, which did not in fact materialize. Certain sections have been omitted that are either of a purely private nature, or might cause annoyance or resentment to the families of some people mentioned. The poet's own idiosyncratic system of punctuation and capitalizing has generally been retained.

Fallon lived in Athenry from his birth on January 3rd, 1905, until the age of eighteen when he joined the Customs and Excise in Dublin (excluding, that is, the periods spent away from home in boarding schools). Inevitably the town plays a major role in his poetry, especially the poems written in the last decade of his life. The street where he was born is now named after him. His father, John Fallon, was a successful cattle and sheep 'jobber' until deafness virtually ended his career, while his mother was largely reponsible for running a small hotel in the town and a butcher's shop.

Douglas Hyde's (bilingual) collection of poems by or attributed to the blind poet Raftery, with a commentary on his life and times, was published in 1907. Fallon possessed a well-thumbed copy of this work, entitled in English *Songs Ascribed to Raftery*. The Cawleys of Craughwell were related to his own family and one of them, the Paddy Cawley mentioned below, was elected to Dáil Éireann.

*I*N MY TIME it was shabby and downfallen, the street ends decaying forlornly into bog on one side but mostly into good limestone country whose inhabitants were mostly the Galway Ewe, the fourlegged one. Other inhabitants were frieze-dressed farmers who spoke Irish among themselves. They were dropping this almost traditional universal wear, but from the north of the town, Turloughmore *et cetera* they used to come even to the early twenties, mostly to Glynn's pub which is still there and run by a Glynn who is the very image of his old father. Glynn's is entirely unchanged since my time. The old kitchen is used as a snug nowadays, but I often bobbed in there with one of the Glynn boys. The kitchen full, Mrs Glynn cooking *et cetera*, almost like a country cottage kitchen. (Then both were 'off the land'.)

Farm life was all around. Many people had cows, including us. Many used to stable them in the backyards which would have no entrance but through the hallway, such as Finn's who lived near Sweeney's in our street. Finn's actually had three or four stallions and those, if not afield, would be stabled in the backyard and mares to be served would go through the hallway. When the men would all be out on the land—they had a few widely spaced-out farms—the girls would act as stud grooms. One of them said to me one time: 'I've lifted ones a damn sight bigger than yours.' The same lass—much older than my confrères, used to steal on us at the swimming place out in Curran's field. Believe it or not, I never saw anything awful in it, I was so young. I think that was all she ever did anyway, though an old naughty, clerk to my cousin an auctioneer, who used to fool about with the young ones was mooted as a TRIER. This was an old sex-mad, rosy, Pan-faced, limp-legged man who used to invade every kitchen in the town and have the ladies squealing with the pleasures of 'idle' pursuit. I doubt, looking back, if he were even potent.

The town was lively in a way no place is nowadays. The Volunteers were drilling, trouble of a kind in the air, eternally Athenry was involved in this kind of thing, the Land War was never as bitter as about Athenry. There were 'cattle drives' going on well into my own twenties. A man's cattle would be driven off land he'd leased or taken, or off a landlord's land, and driven wild through the country. Right or wrong, people always seemed to sympathise with this though there were, of course, real hardships. The Irish countryman is no angel, where his own concerns are touched he's a bastard of the first

water. The 'Fight for Freedom' was as much a war for bits of
land as anything else, basically it was against the Anglo-Irish,
not England.

Meetings and marches, drilling. I knew Liam Mellowes,
who stayed across the street from us at Morrissey's. He and
Larry Lardner and Stephen Jordan used to tell one another
dirty stories while waiting for Volunteers to turn up in Murphy's yard down Castle Lane. I KNOW that, I heard them.
Jordan was a TD for untold years and would have got anywhere on a marvellous speaking voice and sheer cheek, if he'd
had a day's schooling. He was a cobbler. He was involved with
the eldest daughter of the only other cobbler in the town and
wouldn't marry her. So the other old boy, a most lovable character, on the odd occasions he'd get drunk, would take up his
stance at Jordan's door and abuse him. It was another daughter of his who got out in front of the police barracks when the
military came to Athenry in 1918 and said 'Ye wouldn't look
at anyone, would ye? Well, go to hell now, there are men
enough for us all without ye.'

Looking back, the best fun was the occasional winter
play, usually St Stephen's night, usually one of Redcoats versus
Green, probably Boucicault. A very popular one was 'The
West's Awake' or 'The Dawn of Freedom'. (In Ballinasloe after
the truce, the Ballygar Players put it on with the protagonists
in modern uniforms, the English in khaki, the Irish in green
Free State uniforms.) I wanted Telefís Éireann in the anniver-
sary year to do a programme I had in mind when asked,
namely a child's Easter Week, showing the concerts and plays
leading up to it in Puppet form, old photographs *et cetera*, and
drawings. One of the best stage men I knew was Sonny Morrissey, of the family (of two, boy and girl Julia Mary) where
Mellowes stayed. Sonny was a great figure destroyed by the
time. He could come into a schoolroom, tell stories he'd illustrate on the blackboard in a flash, and literally have us falling
off our seats laughing; he had all sorts of sleight of hands
tricks too, but the bottle was his master. Actually he'd a habit
of getting a car to some country pub, having a time of it, and
ending up with a country girl. Sonny emigrated to South
Africa, got a job as a railway clerk, and died almost at once.

He was supposed to emigrate for his health, but …

The ball alley was one of the places one haunted, there was so little else to do. Hurling dropped out in the badly troubled years, though it came along big later, but those Sundays were highlights in the calendar. I only played once for Athenry, chiefly because there was no team, or I was away in college, and once also in handball at which, by Athenry standards, I was about fourth class. Athenry always had a class handballer—your grandfather was one, and your granduncle Ben, but both never took it seriously.

It's only lately I've had an objective look at the town. One always takes places for granted when young. About 70 per cent were unmarried. One might have a small job, railwayman or something, and the family would live off him, no work to be found except maybe labouring on the Department farm. In my time only a draper's sons, myself, and the son of a widow with money were able to go to boarding school. If you did go to school, it was automatically assumed you were going to be a priest.

The fairdays were big days, all held in the street. People guarded their glass by putting hurdles over windows (cattle fairs), but sheep and cattle were just held in rough pens against housewalls. To get out your own door, you had to push the sheep aside. There was a great welter all day, but the fairday being over, the streets were a foot in mud and manure and there was a horrible feeling of 'finish', of hangover, especially in winter nights; mud even got into the house on people's feet. There's a tradition that I was a very busy jobber as a fledgeling, went and bought sheep, marked them in the usual jobber's way with raddle, and the man came into my mother to be paid. I can't recollect it.

Only man alive now with a tongue in his head to tell of things, is a retired Garda sergeant called Peter O'Regan in Swangate, Athenry. We're the same age, went to the Christian Brothers in Galway by train each morning, 8.40, and home on the mail arriving 3.30, I think. At one time I mitched a bit, talked Petey with me, and was seen by my father running along the parapet of that bridge that spans Lough Atawla—he was in the train. I don't remember it. Petey told me last time I saw him—for a month he was terrified lest it get to his father's ears. The father was senior sergeant in the old RIC, and a very strict man.

Another relic was the funeral system, pipes of clay were filled and left with saucers of snuff on the kitchen table of the Wakehouse. I got very sick trying one out, aged *circa* six. Often wondered how a claypipe was smoked. It always stuck to my lips, even when blowing bubbles with one.

On eve of Mayday after Benediction, we used to carry out the Virgin's statue to the old rampart wall in front of the chapel (there's a bungalow there now) and gather beech branches in the rampart freshly leaved and plait them in a semicircle over her like a shrine. Nails were put into the wall and candles stuck on them and we'd gather wood and turf through the town for a big bonfire. This didn't last. I think I wasn't more than ten when it lapsed.

I had the advantage of TWO houses actually. The Ivy Hotel offered new faces every day or every week, travellers stopped there, there was a 'commercial' room (called the Coffee Room) for them specially. Often the lads, shopkeepers' sons, *et cetera*, would have a little hop there in winter, and we had on Sunday nights, for some winters, about twenty people who'd play pontoon at the big dining room table, bank clerks, railway clerks, teachers and elder pupils from the Agriculture College. Usually a bit of a concert after it. Surprisingly little folksong, I was starved for it when young. It was smart to know the latest music-hall hit. A nice girl wouldn't dream of singing a folksong.

The town was very lively after school hours, especially in marble season or bowley-rolling or tops. I remember the water scheme being put in, the streets being mostly rock under the surface, and the way the navvies—all locals, some of whom I never thought had left the country at all in the course of their lives—set into their jobs of drilling and blasting so professionally. There's a method in this that seems traditionally based. One squats and turns the big drilling chisel, the man using the sledge lifts it always to an unchanging rhythm drawing in his breath as he lifts his arms, expelling his breath in a grunt at the exact moment the sledge impacts on the drill. Having seen them at work, I know forever the ways of the MacAlpine Fusiliers and all the gangs who made America's railroads. Let me tell you they did work. At that time, it was a man's pride to do MORE than his share. Since he had to live in a place, it was necessary if he had to keep his head up.

Before the water was piped, we used to draw from a well on the Moor, a field of Finn's across the river from Leonard's Lawn. The Leonards, all spinsters, died without leaving any Leonards, and the lawn gate when I passed there a couple of years ago was locked. I meant to take that up in the *Connacht Tribune*, but forgot. One went through those big gates, kept left to stepping stones over the river, and the well was just a few yards away. Trees grew along the walls on the way, and I remember my uncle comfortably letting down his trousers to have a bog one lovely May morning, and another man joining him, both chatting away as pleasantly as in a public house. Why that morning sticks in my mind, however, is that there were lovely echoes, a voice sounded muffled and wonderful at a distance. Nearby is a watch tower. Many's the stone-throwing battle we had there, nobody hurt, and I don't know why. The little stream was full of trout. Come middle February and we'd be at them with a hare's ear or March Brown. I must have caught a few dozen fish in that reach at the lawn, but they were shrewd trout and the waters shallow, so a few in the bag was a triumph. My uncle fared better. My father thought it below his skill to bother with anything less than big rivers and salmon.

I think that will have to do. Maybe writing this will start me on something.

*

I FORGOT the Raftery connection, through Nicholas Moran our farmhand who used to quote him at length to me in the field where I used to help out at turnips, haymaking, especially with sheep. (I was an expert 'drover'.) Nicholas was from Coleswood, about four miles towards Clarinbridge from Athenry. That was Raftery's chief haunt. His cousins, the Shaughnessys, were bitten by the same bug. I heard a lot of tales about Raftery and Callanan—whose descendants are still

around Craughwell, they're called the HARE Callanans—
some of which I've made into stories, like the making of that
poem to the little hunchback girl as if she were Venus herself.
Raftery was nobody's pet spaniel, he was the vicious poet
aware of qualities in himself which his neighbours didn't have,
and there was only one way to assert them, by asserting himself. Behan was a jauntier version of him, Sidney Graham
another not so masculine, Kavanagh hadn't the 'cutting' or the
guts to face the physical thing in country or fairday pubs. So
Antony must have been a good bit of a man and a bloody
awful nuisance too, as you can guess from Hyde.

And by the way, Hyde got most of his stuff on him, and
ditto the Gregory lady, from that collected by one of the Cawleys of Craughwell, a doctor in Galway University. All of that
side of Athenry-Craughwell to Galway was a place of wild
men, terrific hurlers and masculine. It's the country of the Galway Blazers also. Paddy Cawley told me that Dr Cawley gave
his collection on loan to Hyde and never got it back. This was
on the occasion of rearing a new tombstone to him in Killeenin,
the village near Craughwell, it was there the Volunteers HQ
was set up in 1916. I came into it one day with your Mother
and it was autumn and the callows below seemed like a lake
and men were thatching ricks of hay all over the village, it was
like something out of a Jack Yeats illustration of J.M. Synge. I
love that kind of village life on autumn days, harvest over winter icomynge in. By the way, it was Cawley also who made the
collection and got the tombstone. And as an addendum, told
me very privately by Paddy Cawley, Raftery did not die in the
house where it's said he did, but in an outhouse. They like to
keep it a secret down there to save face. Raftery, to them, was
only a tramp who could make a nuisance of himself.

Nicholas thought Callanan the better poet, of course.
Reminding me of the scholastic quarrel of my earliest youth,
Tennyson versus Browning. Callanan being local and a
respected farmer and a bit of a wit, was first of course in his
own neighbourhood. (Nicholas thought he met Callanan
when he was a small boy, but that couldn't have happened, I
think he must have met his son, a big man with a long white
beard. Or seen a Wm Blake vision of Yahwah.)

III
Ireland's Poets and Playwrights

EDITOR'S NOTE: Yeats was, inevitably, a towering and rather awesome figure for a young poet of Fallon's generation, the Irish generation which came of age in the years between two world wars and in the infancy of the new Irish State. The following five review-essays—particularly the first—show how firmly and insistently he had grappled with Yeats' work and mentality, how much he meant to him as a whole and how largely the great man's presence loomed. In the thirties, after all, only a minority of readers had come to terms with the later poetry: for the bulk of the literary public Yeats was still the author of 'The Lake Isle of Innisfree' or 'The Fiddler of Dooney'—as a glimpse of many contemporary anthologies will show. Much of the middle-period and late work was still regarded as abstruse and hermetic. However Fallon, as a young writer not yet out of his twenties, realised fully the epochal importance of *The Tower* and *The Winding Stair*.

From the late forties Fallon swung predictably against his former master, as the review of the 1959 Jeffares biography indicates. This was not only a personal, subjective reaction, it was a common one at the time, reinforced by the stagey, consciously hieratic aspects of Yeats' personality which were still remembered well in Dublin. However in the last decade of his life he returned to something closer to his original reverence, and he tended to react strongly if anybody spoke slightingly of Yeats in his presence.

Five Aspects of Yeats

THE WINDING STAIR AND OTHER POEMS
by W.B. Yeats (Macmillan, London)

S O FEW poets complete the first exciting crescent of their promise, that it almost marks an epoch in poetic chronology when one comes to the full. Most of them, of course, achieved according to their genius; others—the little less-than-great—seem to have been prevented from complete development by some flaw, some split in the bright stone. Wordsworth, for instance, is an approach to a masterpiece; Tennyson, Morris, Swinburne, in the end were their own life-less conventions. Having made, early, from inspiration their particular casts of the Mystic Face, they seemed content to repeat it again and again, taking the easiest way out of that toil which, having creation as end, is rightly a never-ceasing labour to enlarge the boundaries of being, a continual effort at growth where each sap-filled inch is its own reward—a wider aspect, an increased illumination. 'Energy', Blake says, 'is the only life'; and certainly the spirit which bloweth where it lis-teth seems to linger longest where it finds a varying body, a shape-changing energy that casts up body after body for imag-ination to inhabit: there It can renew Itself in 'eternal delight'.

Mr Yeats, more than any I know of, has given ear to the harper in 'The Marriage of Hell and Heaven', casting skin after skin of opinion till now, at the age of sixty-eight, he emerges as nearly naked as a poet may, as bewilderingly fresh as the Old Woman of Beare might, youth in her veins again, an old skin already yellowing in the dew beside her. His is a logical, laborious growth; yet, long ago, who could have foretold that *The Wanderings of Ossian* would lead at length to *The Tower*, to this—*The Winding Stair*; that the enchanted sleeper under the summer hill would awaken in this midnight, the coldness of the moon about him, his mind, once a disc reflecting a land of sun, now a very moon-metal turning in dark and light. So it is; and yet no volte-face but a natural change; a progression—if one may change a figure—that, now reading backwards, seems to have tacked as erratically but as surely as the year to its seasonal ending, Spring and Summer melting into this Indian Autumn where all the passions and savours and colours of the year, refined to essences, to ghosts, are gathered in a brief, pale tumult, a sort of airy dance before the final fall into the Great Memory.

This period of *The Tower*, *The Winding Stair*, is important—more important, I have come to think in spite of myself than any of the earlier periods, drunken though they were with vision of the golden lands, because in it he has come to realise intellectually an attitude that was once romantically sensuous. Himself now, unclothed, is his theme. He projects it in no blue wandering among the islands but in an unflattering, hard light. If he uses symbol, it is not to turn the key in a golden casket but to silhouette an emotion in its archetype, so that, while bare and stark in itself, it seems still in some queer fashion to take on the dazzle of an auroraed thing whose life is here and in eternity. He loses in colour, of course; indeed, in this book, if we except one or two poems on which he uses some faint washes—'Byzantium', for instance, where the primary of the title suffuses the whole poem—there is no colour but light and darkness. He has gained, however, in intensity: there is no diffusion; the embodied things leave the darkness of the wings, pass across a lit, bare space, and are lost again in the darkness of the wings. It is a technique that may not be used lightly; it is too honest, as honest as if the poet put himself under X-ray; any commonness will show clearly as a broken bone. To his credit, it may be said at once that, apart from some epigrams that are distinguished enough if taken as lulls, as bookmaking, and two things or three that were as well expressed in the prose of *Discoveries*, he emerges with no diminishing of stature.

His art has always seemed to me to be an elaboration in emotion of one or two ideas—or convictions, call them as you will—which appear to have come into the world with him already formed and fleshed. The colour of the early phases, the drama of the later, come out of his attempt to cast life into this pre-conceived image. Unity of Being, and all it involves, a semi-divine state where body and soul, Time and Eternity, all antinomies would mingle in a musical notation, seems to have haunted him from the first. Out of it, in his youth, came that ideal art which had its setting in the magical countries of Bran and Maeldune: there, outside Time, he found his special unity by imagining it, an earthly paradise, impermanent because the human appetite sickens from an unalloyed sweetness, because even there the murmur of the world comes, resistless though its token may be only an apple branch drifting to the quiet of the shore, telling of the wildness, the tumult, the thundering glory of the storm that broke it. There is always the desire to pit force to force: 'all progression is by contraries': and so we have this later, bitter-sweet art, with its dyads Time, Eternity, Sense, Spirit, Self, Soul; a never-ending conflict, intellectualised at last, brought into consciousness and seemingly all the more bitter for that since the divided issues, with the corresponding division of desire, are come to be the more plain.

> The Soul. Seek out reality, leave things that seem.
> The Heart. What, be a singer born and lack a theme?
> The Soul. Isaiah's coal, what more can man desire?
> The Heart. Struck dumb in the simplicity of fire!
> The Soul. Look on that fire, salvation walks within.
> The Heart. What theme had Homer but original sin?

The choice is made clearly enough there; yet the poem is one of a set he has called 'Vacillation'. He returns again and again to the same theme as if in the pull of the two poles he must, of necessity, lay the sticks for his nest; as if there alone the solution of his special problem was to be found. The Heart, star-haunted, carrying soul like a cold bubble on its back may not be altogether happy among the market-carts, in the loudness of the Tabarde Inn; yet remembering the merry tumult, dark-and-bright love, the red of war, how may it be content with the pure space of Spirit? It is in a balance of contraries, inevitably, he comes to his rather warring unity if one may name unity this storm centre where opposites clash and mix in times of crisis, forcing him to continual statement of choice; inevitably too in each resolution of such crises, there is a rich realisation of the opposing elements, an intensification of each that is at the same time a dilation and an intermixing of boundaries. Thus in a vivid way, life and death intermingle, heighten each other by contrast, each taking a shadow of the other: Soul in life, critical of the Heart's experience, enforces some selection on it; Heart in death makes out of its memories of experience a superhuman, mirror-resembling dream; humanity is always the more human for the pale star on its forehead.

The compromise reached in *The Tower*, that violent, beautiful book, was a bitter and angry thing in comparison with the more harmonious arrangement I find here in *The Winding Stair*. There, one had the feeling that the poet, reacting too hastily to the brunt of age, had in a passion, against all his natural inclination, tethered Heart to Soul's chariot and stood back among the crowd to watch the bitter triumph. It was not final, of course. Indeed I suspect the poet as I would suspect an orthodox monk who sat in inquisition on himself, condemned himself to heresy—and to the torture: it would be too final, the unreasonable finality of—say—suicide. So it is no surprise now to find Heart dominant, unrepentant; spinning a darker, more passionate Maya: and the poet again drunkard of its heady juices. In a fine poem, 'Dialogue of Self and Soul' he makes the choice

> My Soul. I summon to the winding ancient stair;
> Set all your mind upon the steep ascent,
> Upon the broken, crumbling battlement,
> Upon the breathless starlit air,
> Upon the star that marks the hidden pole;
> Fix every wandering thought upon
> That quarter where all thought is done:
> Who can distinguish darkness from the soul?

But the Heart, brooding on

> Sato's ancient blade, still as it was
> Still, razor keen, still like a looking glass
> Unspotted by the centuries ...
> Wrapt in a bit of old embroidery, torn
> from some court-lady's dress ...

finds in those emblems of Love and War as in microcosm all the rich life, the passionate story of humanity—its own rich life, and refuses to ascend. It cries out

> A living man is blind and drinks his drop.
> What matter if the ditches are impure?
> What matter if I live it all once more?
> Endure that toil of growing up; ...

He does not desire to be delivered 'from the crime of birth and death':

> I am content to live it all again
> And yet again, if it be life to pitch
> Into the frogspawn of a blind man's ditch,
> A blind man's battering blind ...
> I am content to follow to its source
> Every event in action and in thought;
> Measure the lot; forgive myself the lot!
> When such as I cast out remorse
> So great a sweetness flows into the breast
> We must laugh and we must sing
> We are blest by everything,
> Everything we look upon is blest.

There, fully realised, I find the significance of this later phase; a phase that sets, as it were, a considered seal on his youthful intuition, on an attitude that seems to have come with him into the world, on Forgael's cry to Dectora as he gathered her hair about him;

> Beloved, having dragged the net about us,
> And knitted mesh to mesh, we grow immortal;
> And that old harp awakens of itself

> To cry aloud to the grey birds, and dreams,
> That have had dreams for father, live in us.

It is an attitude that seems to remember bursting trumpets and the descending brightness of the Will that took the dark tumult of the earth about it: that, if anything, is the permanent core in him, the life-shaper—almost in spite of the poet himself, who has always seemed to trample on his heart at the beginning of a labour only in the end to find it has spun its enchantment about him, stolen his golden thunder, and woven from the very stuff of his imagination its own image in the middle air:

> However they may take it,
> Before the thread began
> I made and may not break it
> When the last thread has run,
> A bargain with that hair
> And all the windings there.

It has usurped too, I think, that gigantic philosophical labour of his, 'A Vision', where the soul's eternal flitting from phase to phase of the Great Wheel seems to be but the defeat of Time, a defeat once realised in imagination, now realised in the philosophical intellect—an eternity of bodily life.

> All, all those gyres and cubes and midnight things
> Are but a new expression of her body
> Drunk with the bitter sweetness of her youth.

Out of it—illusion if you like—has sprung certainly a new beauty, cold, magical. Not a line in this book could have been written by a young man, it is so purged of sun colours, so luminous of itself: and yet in it there is the freshness, the singing quality of a new poet who is not yet a convention of himself; one, say, who has let youth go by without a song, holding its emotions, dreams, discoveries close to the heart all the time, brooding on them till they are essences, matches in the imagination; till the whole man at a touch is lit like the Moon, a tumbling wildness in the shadows of a skin. So some poems shine marvellously, like that one 'In Memory of Eva

Gore-Booth and Constance Markiewicz', when after a muted
reflection on their youth, the time he knew them

> Two girls in silk kimonos, both
> Beautiful, one a gazelle.

And on their age, 'withered, old and skeleton-gaunt,' the poem,
suddenly is found to be in a state of fire, the bird winging from
the burning nest:

> Dear shadows, now you know it all,
> All the folly of a fight
> With a common wrong or right.
> The innocent and the beautiful
> Have no enemy but time;
> Arise and bid me strike a match
> And strike another till time catch;
> Should the conflagration climb,
> Run till all the sages know.
> We the great Gazebo built,
> They convicted us of guilt;
> Bid me strike a match and blow.

In that cosmic image the human origins of the poem are forgotten; names, synonymous to most of us of minor poetry and
major politics, come to personify universal tragedy, humanity
wrecked on some bitter glory.

This mysterious quality of image is found all through the
book, notably in 'Parting', where in a sudden line the lover in
woman, the beckoner, light, elusive, assumes in one gigantic gesture the compelling shadow of the earth, as if a beam had suddenly discovered that dark outstretched body, the huge unappeasable breasts where desire would meet an equal infinity;

> He. Dear, I must be gone
> while night shuts the eyes
> Of the household spies;
> That song announces dawn.
>
> She. No, night's bird and love's
> Bids all true lovers rest,

> While his loud song reproves
> The murderous stealth of day.

> He.   Daylight already flies
> From mountain crest to crest.

> She.   That light is from the moon.

> He.   That bird ...

> She.   Let him sing on.
> I offer to love's play
> My dark declivities.

The same magical transformation is in 'Father and Child':

> She hears me strike the board and say
> That she is under ban
> Of all good men and women,
> Being mentioned with a man
> That has the worst of all bad names;
> And thereupon replies
> That his hair is beautiful,
> Cold as the March wind his eyes.

Who can explain why such plain words in a seemingly usual combination should set the mind in a whirl? The style is bare, devoid of ornament, yet somewhere in the swift, windy movement a face is mirrored, such a face as in our pondering we might imagine on the male East Wind, a creature elemental whose fires, nevertheless, because of their divine ancestry, have still an alchemical attraction.

*

READING and re-reading the book, my mind loses itself, I know not why, in the starlight of 'A Woman Young and Old'. This series of poems, left out of *The Tower* for some reason or other—the complementary 'A Man Young and Old' is in that book—is an imaginative interpretation in, for the most part, astrological symbolism, of the later philosophy. It is a breathless experience. It is as if one suddenly awakened in that dizzy shadow where the dead, even while dreaming back to the passionate body, feel at the same time the pull of that other brighter image—the body each had 'before the world was made':

> I long for truth, and yet
> I cannot stay from that
> My better self disowns,
> For a man's attention
> Brings such satisfaction
> To the craving in my bones.
>
> Brightness that I pull back
> From the Zodiac,
> Why those questioning eyes
> That are fixed upon me?
> What can they do but shun me
> If empty night replies?

It is strangely dramatic, an unending crisis out of which the poems rise with the ultimate violence of shot arrows, achieving a momentary liberation, a sort of wholeness of personality as though they had found for a moment their own half-remembered divinity, clinging to it

> on the track of the whirling Zodiac.

This series, more than anything in the book, is, I consider, the poet's reward for putting himself to school among unusual systems of thought. He might have come to maturity in some more conventional way but scarcely to such dark and dazzle, scarcely to this art where matter dark-as-night seems at times to attain to the condition of radium:

> Everything that is not God consumed in intellectual fire.

This series, I should say, and its next-of-kin 'Words for Music Perhaps' where the philosophy is a more local thing as if the passionate body rather than the ideal image engrossed those weird ghosts that sing their say there, Crazy Jane, Jack the journeyman, The Bishop

> ... Who has a skin, God knows
> Wrinkled like the foot of a goose.

Most of those poems are locked in a refrain, some effectively as 'Crazy Jane on the Day of Judgment':

> 'Love is all
> Unsatisfied
> That cannot take the whole
> Body and soul';
> *And that is what Jane said.*
>
> 'Take the sour
> If you take me,
> I can scoff and lour
> And scold her for an hour.'
> *'That's certainly the case,' said He.*
>
> 'Naked I lay,
> the grass my bed;
> Naked and hidden away,
> That black day';
> *And that is what Jane said.*
>
> 'What can be shown?
> What true love be?
> All could be known and shown
> If Time were but gone.'
> *'That's certainly the case,' said He.*

And 'Those Dancing Days are Gone' where the refrain seems to release from rags and wrinkled flesh a body airy and light as a summer's day:

> Come, let me sing into your ear;
> Those dancing days are gone,
> All that silk and satin gear;
> Crouch upon a stone,
> Wrapping that foul body up
> In as foul a rag:
> I carry the Sun in a Golden Bowl
> The Moon in a Silver Bag.

Whatever regret we may have for the Gaelic epics that died that the strange angry, laughing lyrics in this book should come to life, we cannot fail to admire the integrity of one who, finding the vision of evil as integral a part of his humanity as the mystic self whose kin is among the Gods, seeks to express equally the whole personality. What the Gaelic tradition loses, the Anglo-Irish tradition gains; for if he is in any line at all, it is that of Swift and Berkeley. Certainly he is not among those negative stoics, the internationalist poets who are flocked in Ezra's little Pound. When I was growing up I thought him to be the maker of his own tradition, the weaver of a new myth, the first of a line for whom

> ... Attis' image hangs between
> The staring fury and the blind lush leaf.

The makers of a new harmony between self and soul; necessarily an easier notation than Blake imagined, less ascetic than Dante's where Soul absorbed self—the saint's travail. Taking stock now, however, I remember that Blake's world and Dante's moulded themselves by their own weight naturally 'as drops of water', and that in contrast Mr Yeats' is a work of hammer and chisel and difficult balancing. So I find myself thinking of him as one of the last delicate lights of a sinking epoch, of a civilisation 'half dead at the top'—as a star trembling in the shadows with the horizon coming up.

> Pray I will, and sing I must
> and yet I weep—Oedipus' child
> Descends into the loveless dust.

> —*Dublin Magazine*, April–June 1934

W.B. Yeats: Man & Poet

by A. Norman Jeffares (Routledge & Keegan Paul, London)

YEATS IS in many ways the ideal subject for a biography; as in life he has all the qualities that count, the longevity that covers several interesting decades of change and fashion, the well-marked alterations in himself and his work that correspond with the changing times, his unusual interests such as magic and the milieu that surrounded it, his intervention in practical politics—or impractical politics if you like, for he was a member of the I.R.B. at a time when physical force seemed as far from sound policy as Mars from the Moon. Above all, this startling and picturesque figure who made all the world a stage had suffered from a famous and unsuccessful love affair with a political beauty who has become part of our Irish heritage: I may add, too, that not the least of his gifts to his biographers is that he himself was a voluminous autobiographer.

Yeats, indeed, had the faculty of enlarging his surroundings. He lived his myth from the first. In the Dublin Art School, before he could scan, he was the personification of what a young poet should be; and years afterwards when he was well into his sixties, and I met him for the first time, he was the personification of what an ageing, world-famous poet should be to a young man. And in between, what a life! But a life, all the same, that was not of the worldly importance he deemed it. Looking back on it, we can see now that he was the important figure, not Edwin Ellis who transferred to him Rossetti's interest in William Blake, nor Lionel Johnson who groomed the provincial out of him, nor Dowson nor Symons who were something of his wild oats, nor Lady Gregory, who looking around for an interest in which she could invest her surplus energy, chose him as she would another promising investment, not even the Abbey Theatre that no longer produces his verse plays. All of those people and societies, indeed, seem to have an existence only on the edge of what is important; but he, Yeats himself was and is so important that if he mythologised them itself until they had larger-than-life qualities, we have no desire to quarrel any longer with him about the matter. He took them and used them, and it is this use that makes them important.

Not that I think his importance is entirely assured. I offer this as a critical rather than an emotional opinion. We must remember that it is many years since his early verse appealed to the literary public. Dr Jeffares has not much use for it; and lately another Yeats biographer dismisses it very casually. And yet in its time this verse served a public as intelligent as the modern public. And the middle period also does not strike the sparks it did. Critics, indeed, concentrate on *The Tower* and *The Winding Stair* even though they must needs swallow in wry gulps the thought of the *Vision*, a kind of thought which is not hugely different from the early beliefs in faery which were at one time the stock-in-trade of the young man.

A lyric poet, of course, does not stand or fall by his beliefs or his philosophy. That is a modern heresy, a cult of impossible integrity. What a poet needs is thought that will enable him to create, to be fluent inside a personal pattern, but yet a thought that seems to be in touch with a greater authority than himself, for we have in spite of ourselves still something left of our primitive belief in priest or medicine-man. Whatever we think about plain speech, if we analyse it closely it is never enough; we want the sword upstairs or the secret altar, the stone mouth of the oracle opening like a strange flower. We want, indeed, what Yeats always sought to give, the feeling that the Gods have somehow got into the room. And any other kind of poetry is just conversation.

So to me, the most interesting side of Dr Jeffares' biography is not the incidents in Yeats' life, not even the man within the cloak, but the cloak itself and the man's continuous adjustments of it to his time. He stated somewhere himself that he was always aware of his audience, and this is important for it conditioned his manner. It made his speech a public utterance. You did not have to put your ear to the page to hear him.

And yet the most powerful portion of his later work has a meditative scheme; one would expect a pondering evasive rhythm, expect now and again a trembling of the air as if Pan piped; but what we get are axioms hammered out of bright metal, a clear and faultless clangour of speech that has no hesitation because for all its picturesque and Georgian in-setting of image, it only seems to put before us things we have already been pre-occupied about. Is this failure or achievement? And was Yeats just a figure that ends a phrase, who sums up in himself the best of the Edwardian, Georgian and fin-de-siècle eras—that is, experience we have touched through other writers? Is he the climax of an age rather than the forerunner? I may point out that one is not greater than the other, but poetically it is the forerunner who matters most to those who come after him.

And Yeats has given no hints as to how we may deal with our experience, he but sums up the methods of those who went before him. His personality, indeed, seems larger than his art, so much so that his last poems move along a much-too-travelled road, many of them looking like the work of a syndicate. I think, indeed, that while he sought for an altar all his life he ended on a rostrum, though I am quite sure he would have altered rostrum to Boiler as he always altered the penny-plain to the picturesquely coloured.

Dr Jeffares has written a good life and the Poet and Cloak are there in all their dimensions. He has done what Mr Hone, perhaps for motives of piety, did not touch; he has given us quite an appreciable contact with the actual life-material that went to the making of some of the poems. Sometimes this merely gives a name to an anonymous reference, but it is news to me that certain poems which seemed to come out of some wild fancy are actually related to living people. Some of the

'Fool' songs, indeed, are mere camouflage to cover real situations. And that is interesting.

But he could have enlarged on some things with advantage. For instance, a dissertation on magic as it existed in some circles in the nineties—in literary circles, I should say—would have clarified to some extent the poet's predilection for so obviously unpopular a theme for letters as it became later. And he could have emphasised the relationship with Ezra Pound, which altered his literary style and indeed gave him the play, *The Player Queen* in its present form as a comedy. And in his reference to the poem 'Leda and the Swan' I cannot find a mention of the shortlived periodical in which it first appeared, the Dublin creation *To-morrow* for which Yeats wrote an editorial that shocked the new middle-class, an impish act that seems to balance psychically all the senatorial avoirdupois he had accumulated in Merrion Square. Outside those little things this is a satisfactory book of reference.

—*Dublin Magazine*, January–March 1950

W.B. Yeats and Tradition

by F.A.C. Wilson (Gollancz, London)

*T*HE MAJOR questions of poetry are involved in any
study of W.B. Yeats, the basic attitudes at any rate, and
Professor Wilson comes to the point at once in pro-
nouncing *A Vision* as 'a product of acquired learning and of
the visionary faculty' which carries on the heterodox tradition
in mysticism. Most of Yeats' admirers regard this immense
skeleton as something that should have remained in the cup-
board, as some parade of mystery—mongering that should
have died with his separation from the Golden Dawn of
McGregor Mathers, but apart from the trimmings and the
Euclid, it is a book that reaches for the God's-eye view and
gives the man the dignities of his pallors and passions and the
image-making faculty that put the Gods in their various heavens. It combines, at any rate, all kinds of men into a worldly
scheme where they are at their highest moments, in full possession of all the faculties of Man, and at their lesser times,
rounding the wheel of reincarnation, partial-men, men in bits
and pieces, who live out a life in one part or other of their
being, but in touch with the Whole since they are part of the
Whole, with the Dance of Creation that is both within them
and beyond them, each in his way a God serving a kind of
apprenticeship to Man. Out of this Yeatsian view came the
great Yeats poetry. It has the benison of dignity.

It is not necessary, of course, to believe that Yeats accepted his own scheme or believed in it with no reservations. The tensions of belief work differently in life and poetry, and although Yeats thought deeply, he also sought the exciting synthesis of the world that gave him reasons for exultation and exaltation. The condition of man, the social animal stabled in the slums of the world who suffered wars and desolations of the flesh, he would not accept, as he would not accept the poetry of Wilfred Owen or any verse that dealt with such temporary states as wars, or even the naturalistic stage where everyday man was dolled up in his everyday problems; those were newspaper states of being, painful but not tragic in the highest sense, as the man run over in the street, who leaves ten squalling children after him is a newspaper item, a painful incident in the physical world but not a tragedy in the highest sense of Aristotle. A tear is an intellectual thing, indeed, and intellect is timeless, and concerned only with man as a passion of intellect. 'When the human soul can truly say and know "I am Brahma" or identify itself, in all its understood purity, with divinity, the way to mystical experience is open to it.'

He was, indeed, only open to the absolutes, to the prodigal sons who were saints or lovers, to the monopolising passion that drove man beyond the limits, so that the little self becomes identified with the greater and the spark in man enters the conflagration that is God. But because impermanent men are permanent man, with a history of God on his back and experience of God in the roots of his being, the modes of reaching God have long since left their patterns in the subconscious and are a part of the workings of our psychology, so all religions to Yeats had their validity. Their imagery remained and was enormously potent as emotional symbols, alive in the sense that they became inhabited when touched by word or reference, and for the poet a world permanent as tradition through which he touched others in making contact with himself, or with the total self he believed all men to possess. Seeking the material of his poetry, he made something less than a religion and more than a philosophy.

It is not extraordinary that the attitude is there in the poet before the material. Æ used to say that a man only comes into his own, that he is born with an intuition and knowledge which later he must acquire reasonably and with great labour. When the younger Yeats wrote about the Moods, he was anticipating himself. The Moods became the modes of reaching God:

> Time drops in decay
> Like a candle burnt out
> And the mountains and woods
> Have their day, have their day;
> What one in the rout
> Of the fireborn moods
> Has fallen away?

The largeness of vision, the God's-eye view, however, did not release him from the tensions required by his poetry. Professor Wilson makes a point of this in marking the contrast of his attitude to things with that of T.S. Eliot, a poet of an entirely opposite mode. Where Yeats exulted Eliot wept; where Yeats praised, Eliot denied. The one lifted the appetites into the cycles of the divine, into the human glory, the other wrote of 'Emptying the sensual with deprivation/cleansing affection from the temporal.' It is little wonder that Yeats saw so little in Eliot. His own vision came from his acceptance of Man as a temporary habitation of God, as some historical necessity of the Deity, while Eliot went skywise shaking out the ballast of the body, which in its humbler way must be always a partner in those higher excursions if creation is to count as following some predetermined and divine pattern.

Professor Wilson's study is devoted principally to the plays, the later plays, as dramatic expositions of the Yeats attitude. The *Noh* play, of course, could have been devised specially for him. His thought was as East as it was West, but both thought and play-mode are definitely against the stream of Western psychology, which experiments with space rather than with Time. As pieces for the stage they never come up to the reading. There is no engrossing bond between audience and actor, no psychic jolt in common. Verse that reads like revelation, as if oracles were on the move, becomes localised by accent and intonation, and God does not walk in the garden. What is terrifically interesting is Professor Wilson's analysis of

Yeats' sources, and his reasons for using certain symbols and imagery, following his own intellectual acceptance of the emotive value of a traditional body of law, old things shared in active participants in all art. I do not think Professor Wilson overdoes this exegesis. There are times when I fancy he overloads a simplicity, but I am quite willing to concede that many reasons for some word or phrase are turned into some overwhelming reason by a subconscious need. Yeats, however, was a thorough craftsman, the more conscious as he grew older, and—I may be wrong—I think he went for the sonorous and rhetorical jolt in the end, public expression, rather than the occulting reverie within. There is more purpose in the later poems than person. He had become acclimatised to a vision and it was no longer a voyage of discovery. He was pasting his posters on the Otherworld.

—Dublin Magazine, April–June 1958

Yeats the Playwright

by Peter Ure (Routledge & Keegan Paul, London)

WHEN A PLAY disappears into the study it emerges as being a bit beyond itself, the meanings of the parts having become greater than the whole, and the whole thing so bedizened and diaphanous with the veils of exegesis that the very centre of gravity itself seems to have lost aplomb. Mr Ure, however, is not out to disturb balance. He groups certain plays that seem to share a common theme, displays the plots and then proceeds to an analysis of both theme and technique. In no way is he creative at the author's expense, which means he has no theory, no abstraction of his own, on which to stretch the poet willy-nilly. What bothers me is that all this scholarship could be a vanity, for Yeats has been pushed off the stage into the study, and it is a truism nowadays that a play must be judged in the theatre.

There are sound reasons for this. A play is something that happens IN the audience. Interest, emotion, psychological awareness, are as much the protagonists as the actors who deliver the theme, and the resolution must come up out of the unconscious depths of the audience as if it had no author but itself. It is the impact that matters, the full and immediate impact in which all issues are solved at a stroke. There are no single strands of meaning, no side issues. A play is an experience, not a speculation, nor a poem to be read over and at

leisure digested. Its life consists merely in its theatrical existence. Either it lives in the theatre or it returns to the study as
a poem or a piece of literature, which is altogether another and
a different mode of existence.

Nobody knew this as well as Yeats himself. 'Because passion and not thought makes tragedy, what I made had neither
simplicity nor life,' he says in reference to his early attempts to
write *The Player Queen*. And there are many other such com-
ments on his own bias towards abstraction. He had no gift for
character, much wit but no humour except irony, and the liveliness of the streets was beyond his scope. He was basically a
literary man. And oddly enough, for the literary man, the theatre of the time did offer some kind of place, a foothold such
as the French Symbolist Theatre from which playwrights like
Maeterlinck derived, but while this engaged his interest for a
while he saw it for what it was, thin-blooded and without joy,
that high spiritual joyfulness like the famous silver trumpet. In
his own theatre he made many attempts to write for an audience. I don't know if he had ever a real success. The one inge-
niously contrived play—from an ordinary technical viewpoint—that I was certain would come off theatrically was *The
Player Queen*. It reads delightfully and I thought it was played
well. Yet on the stage it seemed diminished. With *On Baile's
Strand*, too, I had the same disenchantment. The bones of the
plot creaked. To me he was a dead loss.

Yet Yeats needed the drama, in the way he needed the
personal spectacle to valuate himself, but the spectacle he
wished to deliver was the only one in which a poet is really
interested, the lyric struggle between belief and abandonment,
the sort of life that is affirmed most naturally in the simple
undivided lyric, a narrow fountain-form in which one word
may mean the difference between beauty and disaster. This is
an impossible stage-form. It might come off if a writer was
preoccupied with people, but in that case it would be unnecessary, fine words making too many fine feathers, and Yeats
wanted his people all in plumes.

He was, indeed, completely in revolt against the Natural-
ist Theatre, decrying Ibsen, the greatest dramatic figure in the
last century, but perhaps this was natural, since Ibsen worked

out from a passion that penetrated his people, with an urge toward life, while Yeats on the contrary used the passion in reverse, in a returning sense as if life continually were accomplishing its own death. His was a static art because it contemplated eternity. It felt only the Neo-Platonic mystery. And the art of the Neo-Platonists was to use cloak and symbol and leave the final thing unsaid, to speak in riddles, in words 'published and not published', *editos esse et non editos*. Never was a personal religion less suited to the blandishments of the theatre.

This is not to say that the plays are impenetrable without exegesis. I do think a play must stand up on the stage, however, without footnotes, and that it cannot be a good play if it—during performance—keeps too much of its meaning to itself, or too large a residue of unresolved meaning when the performance is over. Until we have a real chance to see the plays, nobody can possibly say which is good, excellent, or merely mediocre. Perhaps this new Abbey will provide us with a Festival to the Founder? We read his plays, we read of them continually, they are referred to here and there and everywhere; but the number of people who have actually seen more than half-a-dozen must by now be infinitesimal. There is a real need here. And something else, a real debt to the poet who brought to the early Abbey his reputation and his genius, which should be repaid.

Mr Ure surveys the poet from his early beginnings, starting with *The Countess Cathleen* and working on to *The King's Threshold*—which play, by the way, had another ending in its earlier days, a happy one, probably taken from Edwin Ellis's 'Seancan the Bard', for this was a rare pinch by one poet from another, acknowledged in 1904 and then promptly dropped. Deirdre gets a chapter to herself, then the *Cuchulain* plays, grouped; and groups also in another chapter are *The Dreaming of the Bones*, *The Words Upon the Window Pane* and *Purgatory*. This chapter is called 'From Cradle to Grave', and is followed by another called 'For Reason, Miracle', comprising two plays, *Calvary* and *The Resurrection*. Grouped under a chapter-heading 'The Beasts', are three early plays, *Where There is Nothing*, *The Unicorn from the Stars* and *The Player Queen*, with—oddly enough—*The Herne's Egg*, an unplayable catastrophe much admired for its Neo-Platonic doctrine. As Mr Ure plays his hand, this works well enough. But why has no one ever remarked that four characters in *The Player Queen* have some sort of order of numbers, Septimus, Octema (the queen is an alter ego of a Saint Octema), Nona and Decima?

Transferring himself from form to form, Yeats finished without any form, leaving a nice naked stage to Samuel Beckett. The Japanese *Noh* play was a lyrical interlude, but it came out of a culture in which it was an indivisible energy and a traditional expression, and in which the climactic dance was understood in the very flesh of the spectators, a circumscribed and religious gesture with specific meanings. It could never mean anything like that on a Western stage. In selecting it as a new form that disencumbered the footlights, I think Yeats only succeeded in adding to the lumber.

But to be final about any play is impossible until the play is staged. I think the Abbey owes it to Yeats and to us all to give us that opportunity.

—*The Irish Times*, January 26th, 1963

Yeats' Vision and the Later Plays

by Helen Vendler (Oxford University Press)

THE MAJOR poets have all been concerned with major enigmas that have no answers in Time. And Yeats was no exception, being committed from the first, feeling that Man was a whole, a unity that structurally was part of the universe, with a memory beyond that of the body and a being of indefinite size that could never be contained in any hand-me-down suit of space and time or in any inherited set of religious dogma. His concern was not with the temporary but with the timeless, and his book, *A Vision* uses accordingly not the language of philosophy, but the metaphors of myth.

When Jung was at work on his theory of types, he had a dream in which he was asked some unintelligible questions by some learned assembly of a former age. He had the humility to conclude that the questions were unintelligible because they were couched in terms he did not understand and yet understood that they were related to his own studies. He found the answers in his studies of alchemy, or at least he learned the language, a language of symbol left over by the Neo-Platonists, pictorial and charged with meanings not easily comprehensible but invaluable in his studies of the occulted psyche. Yeats had studied this traditional *lingua franca* from his early days, working out of some direct necessity of his own, a drive in depth and height, and in a sort of illuminated confusion he set himself down at length, and at the end of his days, to bring it to order, in the way in which a man examines his conscience. He wanted to lay bare the physical skeleton of man, the boneless structure that is history, and all of this relevance he put into the only language possible to him and his subject, the language of myth. Jung would have understood him immediately. I don't think Mrs Vendler gets the gist at all.

She has set herself, of course, to make *A Vision* understandable, or at least acceptable as poetic logic, as a means to a better understanding of the plays. This, it seems to me, is a minor objective. Yeats has documented his own vision greatly. His verse is reflected in his prose. He prepares his readers, defines his world continually, throws them an up-to-date guidebook all the time, and indeed leaves them little to do at the end except to use their own sensibilities inside the special world he makes for them. So thoroughly has he done all this that he may have deceived many of us into accepting his world as the only world of poetry and himself as the only poet of consequence of his time. The point I make, however, is that Mrs Vendler uses the poet as her main source of enlightenment to his work, whereas she should have learned in the course of her study, as Jung did, the definite if effulgent meanings of the metaphorical language of myth. Instead, she has all the gush and certainty of a Freshman treading the tried and tired old academical trail of a doctorate thesis.

We can take it that Yeats illuminates himself. If anybody needs other illumination there are several commentators available. The poems, and their Neo-Platonic messages, are particularly well-served, and the plays have had a lot of attention in the course of which *A Vision* played its part as a correlative. What is important now is to get *A Vision* into proper perspective, not as Mrs Vendler does—in using Yeats alone with an occasional throw-in from Wallace Stevens, his almost contemporary, or using Blake, and Yeats' commentary on Blake, made when he was in early youth and under the influence of Edwin Ellis—but by putting it on the Swedenborg-Jakob Boehme line as another theory of everlastingness or by testing it against the Neo-Platonic remnants for those symbolic values which Jung discovered in the archetype.

Jung's theory of psychological types, for instance, would

have made a fruitful contrast with Yeats' tabulation of the moon-phases; and it is one of those curious historical coincidences that both happened to be working on the subject at the same time without any awareness of one another, working from different ends and with absolutely differing aims to arrive at conclusions that are not vastly different after all. Indeed, one seems to accommodate the other. Where Jung states that only here, in life on earth, can the general level of consciousness be raised, and that this is man's metaphysical task which he cannot accomplish without mythologising, since myth is the natural and intermediate stage between unconscious and conscious cognition, he might be speaking of the highest poetry. He does at least, out of a great mythic mind, give the poet the kind of specialised support that he could value, a credence of vision that only one fellow-traveller can give another. Yeats, at any rate, asked the big questions, as Jung did, asked them in a haphazard, fumbling, god-smitten poet's way, with a little knowledge and less scholarship but with a vast intuition that doubted itself to the last and with no awareness as to whether he was shaping his material or his material shaping him, or whether there was any final truth in his conclusions.

The main thing is that he did ask the question. His answers are mainly important to himself—and to persons with a cast of countenance like his, men of the same moon-phase, of the same psychological type. Mrs Vendler, in a way, makes a point of this, that the plays are expositions of the creative act, of the forces actually at work and taking symbolic form. Yeats dramatised this process and each play is a lyric statement of it, the statement becoming more emphatic as he cleared the stage of all props and minor characters. There is no play in the sense of the theatre, as we know the theatre; there is no problem, no solution, but stasis—and a description of stasis. I must grant that this theory seems to hold water. I must say too that it doesn't matter a damn. The conscious intention was never to demonstrate a theory but to wage with gigantic puppets the war out of which poetry comes.

Still, for what it's worth, I give her summary: 'The plays take up the primary questions posed by *A Vision*: how do we account for the perpetual vigour of the imagination? And how should we react in the presence of an obsolete poetic tradition? In *The Player Queen* we are asked to cast the old tradition aside, without regret, and accept whatever bizarre inspiration the new dispensation may provide. The *Dance* plays insist on the mutual subjugation of the Poet and the mixed nature ...' I'd better stop. I feel as if I'd stepped into some Leaving Cert. Examination by mistake.

—*The Irish Times*, August 24th, 1963

Æ, Poet and Visionary

THE HOUSE OF THE TITANS
by Æ (Macmillan, London)

INTO THE LIGHT AND OTHER POEMS
by Lyle Donaghy (The Cuala Press, Dublin)

*I*N THIS age when a culture seems to be seeding, no critic, probably, is all-round enough to respond equally and exactly to all the diverse forms of contemporary poetry. If he is to keep his integrity—and he must if his pronouncements are not to be void of the personal, the valuable factor—he must pronounce strictly in the order of his preferences, limiting his pronouncements to, or weaving his theory from, the measure of his own reaction. Response to poetry is always through its forms. Whatever can be said of an essence of poetry boils down to this—that it is like, say, the life essence, inseparable from its forms; it is whatever farm it inhabits. The difficulty facing a critic is how to divine the essence in forms for which his feeling is limited and when there is no infallible touchstone such as a tradition to guide him. A modern critic has only his own response to go on, and that is very fallible when there is no common mind. The modern mind is too various, too disparate, for any abstraction of the experience of one single mind to claim more than a limited, coterie value; by defining himself, a critic can expect at the most to represent only the thought of a particular school. Criticism, then, I imagine, should attempt in our time a particular, rather than a general evaluation; cultivating, out of the bewilderment of forms which the time offers, that particular form to which it can respond most fully, and confine itself there.

I do not feel in the least qualified to discuss Æ's thought. No discussion about his verse, however, can exclude at least some mention of it, for it permeates all that he writes. I need only say here that it has for me a fiery, visionary quality, an illumination as if it came knighted from the court of some planetary king. *The House of the Titans* is in the royal procession of his work. It is, in my opinion, greater than what has gone before because in it he has developed the epical element that one always surmised to be in his genius. The title poem is a fine effort of sustained imagination, of controlled music. The subject is a myth of Nuada of the Silver Hand. Of it, in *Song and Its Fountains*, he said:

A symbolic vision or dream was projected into the waking consciousness while I was engaged in meditation ... The dream pictures had a swift movement and as swift an interpretation. I knew as I looked on these images that Nuada was the heroic heaven-descended will, and he had come with other divine companions to earth to conquer it and bring wisdom to its dark inhabitants. But the brightness of the immortals had been obscured by a sorcery breathing out of earth ... the immortals only held sway over its dark inhabitants when out of the glory still within them they made lovely to the Fomorians their own bestial desires.

Then Lugh the Sungod came to Nuada out of the Land of Promise and showed him that he, Nuada, the power that was will, alone on earth was real; the other companions that had come with him were now but phantom images of themselves. By Lugh's power Nuada was lifted above himself and 'saw all about him the true immortals ...' They made promises to be truly with him at his labours until the great battle of Moytura to be fought at the end of time. The immortals then vanished and Nuada was left once more 'brooding in the great chamber' among the monstrous Fomorians. He has fitted the vision into a form as swift and subtle and various as the vision itself, scattering in the head-long movement a lovely stardust of imagery. It is eminently quotable if one knew where to begin ... and to stop:

> ... the builders reared
> Murias, Gorias, Findias, and Falias,

That were like living creatures, and towered and glowed
And changed with the imagination.

I have, as I said before, no qualifications to discourse on
the poet's thought, so I pass over the prophetic wisdom of the
latter part of the poem when Nuada sees in vision the Fomo-
rian heart caught into exultations and agonies which earth had
not known before the advent of the spirit and sees that heart,
having found in its depths 'the Magian mind that can grow
what it dreams on', pass away from itself and

> ... the high powers that only yield themselves
> To gentleness, awaiting its perfecting to give
> Sovereignty over all the elements.

It is a poem that quivers in the mind for a long time with more
than music.

Readers of the *Dublin Magazine* will be familiar with
many of the jewel-like lyrics in this book, 'Comfort', 'Incarnation' and others, all alight with the poet's peculiar quality.
Rather a breakaway for him is 'The Dark Lady', a longer
poem, which is a new interpretation of the relations between
Shakespeare and the Lady of the *Sonnets*. Whether one agrees
with Æ's theory or not—and some will doubt that the Mary
who has come down to us in rather contrary fragments of history could be so fine a creature—one must allow it as a distinct
possibility. The Dark Lady of the poem claims she was not
wanton with Shakespeare but made herself a hundred natures
for him, was wanton 'to his imagination'. She was so spiritually intimate with him that ... but hear her:

> I had not more easily as a small child
> Told my heart stories than I could to him
> Tell everything in thought, as if he were
> An ampler, wiser heart-nurse to myself.
> And though I was all love I shrank from that,
> The mating of lips and body, lest having all
> I should have less than love ....

And then Southampton came, 'a boy that stayed the breath ...
beauty that had no soul but itself,' and Shakespeare, 'the wise
soul'

Baffled in reading where there was not mind
Fell into dreaming and at last was stayed
On the body's miracle. And I grew sick
Seeing the dawn of an unnatural love.

She tried to save Shakespeare from that sin, giving herself to him, having no joy in the giving. But she was a dear friend to him, not a mystery, so he

Wandered away from me unto that one
Beautiful, baleful and uncharted star
Of boyhood.

She saved him by winning Southampton from him. She became Southampton's mistress. Shakespeare heard of it:

Never was there face
So ravaged … He threw at me a single word …
He never saw me again, yet I was victor
Slaying the unnatural with the natural love.

At a time when most other poets see life as chough, raven or hooded crow, Æ who finds it as more than a bird of paradise, is a very necessary antinomy.

*

THOUGH Lyle Donaghy sings as fluently and as urgently as a mating thrush, it is with a certain darker element. If one has any doubt of his poetry at all, it arises out of his very fluency. A spate is a good thing if controlled; uncontrolled, it is liable to spread among the shallows of emotion and become a mere mirror for a vegetable imagery. Mr Donaghy loves and is familiar with the outer aspects of nature; in verse, where an exact objectivity of an emotion is required, this love sometimes proves unruly and dissipates the emotion in a too-numerous, natural imagery. This, I would suggest hesitantly to the poet, is why some of his poems do not, for me, quite come off. I hasten to add that most of them do come off, come off in spite of a somewhat too poetic syntax. 'The Grave', for instance, with the ending:

And there's no earth
In sexton season's care, to hide the box,
Even now, from scratching ravens of the mind.

And that fine song 'We will go back'.

Somewhere about the great green raths our place is
Where the rich proud graceful orchids haunt
With cream-pink flowers like wounden torcs
Or Danaan horns that sound, insolvently,
    completed music.

The orchids host in the half-grazed grass of the rath
Like the music-sustained flesh of the beautiful dead
Never leaving the summit of the land-heap,
And no man knows their planting.

Often, too, a tight shoe fits him, such as 'A Thought of Suicide' and 'To a Critic'. There is a likeable folk inconsequence about 'Rose Adare'.

When I was courting Rose Adare,
I had no doubt what young girls were.
I talked, alluded to the showers,
Unpetticoated fifty flowers.
She always looked amazed at me,
And said she longed to climb a tree.
Now I will rise and follow her,
Knowing how precious young girls are.

—*Dublin Magazine*, April–June 1935

Editor's note: The poet, painter, crusading journalist, editor, agricultural reformer and social prophet who signed himself Æ (George William Russell, 1867–1935) was Fallon's literary godfather, as he was to many other young Irish writers—including prose-writers as well as poets. Russell was responsible for getting his earliest poems published and he remained an understanding patron, mentor and friend until his departure for England in 1933. As an altogether more humane, sympathetic, accessible personality than Yeats, who was generally cool and distant to younger Irish writers, Æ was a central figure in literary Dublin and kept more or less open house to all who sought him out.

Though Fallon's early admiration for Æ's poetry steeply declined with maturity—in fact, he once defined it to me as 'a vague blue landscape'—he continued to think highly of his spiritual stature, his fearless engagement with his milieu and its prejudices, his social conscience, and certain of his prose writings. The man himself he habitually spoke of with something approaching reverence. When complimented by some acquaintances on his laudatory review of Æ's *Collected Letters* (see below), he answered instantly: 'Well, I owed it to him.'

John Lyle Donaghy (1902–47) was considered a White Hope of Irish poetry during the 1930s, but today his loose, rhapsodic verse seems very much of its period. Born in Larne, Co. Antrim, he studied at TCD, did some acting for the Abbey Theatre, and later became a teacher. The breakdown of his marriage seems to have undermined him emotionally and his last years were clouded and unhappy. His final collection *Wilderness* was printed privately in 1942.

Letters from Æ

edited by Allan Denson (Abelard Schumann, London)

AN UNFINISHED poet, an occasional painter, a clair-voyant born and a natural contemplative, a religious without an altar, a believer without a God, a seer, a visionary, yet a man of affairs, an organiser of country cream-eries, an inspired journalist, a ferocious controversialist and the most gentle of men, here was a genius of a dozen vocations who mastered none of them, who was an amateur in every-thing, and yet emerges in my imagination as the one and only great man I have ever known.

Æ has died into his time, whereas Yeats, his 'oldest enemy and friend', has assumed its dimensions and a place in history. One cannot speak of one and not name the other. They call each other up like a simile. They belonged together from the first. They were the twin giants of our time, but while we made our verses out of one we carried them to the other. Yet nowadays few remember Æ and nobody has quoted him in twenty years. Indeed, the last essay of importance on his work is one of Sean O'Faolain's more youthful efforts, while around Yeats, on the contrary, the legends grow and the book trade prospers. He has become a business for ever.

Nobody, of course, will quarrel with this. A man may be many men, but an artist is the singular person from the first. Æ did not exist in his poetry or in his painting. He was the occasional guest, arriving with a week-end bag, a pencil and a paintbrush—and all the arbitrary values of the other six days of the week. He never realised that his were not the values of poetry, but those of the religious visionary to whom verse was the inspired shorthand of the Infinite, and if he laboured over it at all the labour was no more than that of the lily in the field that aches upwards towards some burst of bloom at the top. Most poets are aware that poems are 'given' to a poet. But they are aware too, and sadly, of the work involved in receiving the gift, and of the halts and hesitations it makes before it catches a rhythmic body out of a welter and pressure of irrelevancies. Verse to Æ was a one-sided experience. It was a direct nudge from the Gods. And while it was coming, he was bow-legged Buddha translating the cosmos into pastoral simplicities. He was profoundly certain of himself in those exaltations. They belonged to him, they were his right as a pure spirit, for he, as all other souls, had existed before time began and poetry was the speech of the Unfallen, and all beauty, indeed, only a recollection of this former and perfect state.

Poetry of that nature, single-headed and rapt, is not of this world. It is a hymn from the top rather than a cry from the midden-heap, from the mess of motives that is the actual personal life of the poet. It is no solution of the mess, since its basic premise is that there is no mess. We are perfect beings who chose of our own free will that famous marriage with matter which is the Fall. We chose it as a labour of love, to exalt it, to perfect it as another body fit for Deity, but in this titanic struggle we have forgotten our pristine will and purpose and it is only in certain states of trance or exaltation that we have glimpses of what we were—of what we really are. And those are the authentic poetic states and the only reasons for poetry.

Looking back now, one can see that this was one of the themes of the time: Madame Blavatsky and Number 3 Ely Place, Theosophy, the Buddha translated into some exciting Neo-Platonist mystery. It was religion minus the formal moral trappings. It freed the soul, released it from priestly control and allowed it its own ancient rights of personal divination and personal illumination. It was a body of belief into which Æ fitted quite naturally. He adopted the Eastern techniques for states of trance which made easier access to those actual visions that had beset his first youth. He really did have this other-world sort of experience, let psychologists explain it as they will. It lent him authority as a poet and a painter. It fulfilled the person but translated the poet. He got out of touch with his own body.

Among the letters collected in this book, the majority of them on mere trivia of a busy life, is one to George Moore which contains a terrifying assessment of Yeats as man and poet. It is almost forgotten nowadays that Yeats, like Æ, needed some other-world authority to sanction the authenticity of his poetry. And if he wasn't a seer he had to play necromancer and have at least a portion of the vasty deep at his disposal. It is doubtful if he ever had the immediate experiences of Æ, who never descended to tapping tables or listening to the babble of the earthbound, but he did assume the cloak of the Seer as if he hoped by some sort of sympathetic magic to assume the person also. And in a way it worked. The pose stuck and became a permanent attitude, and the attitude attracted its affinities and made verse, laboriously at first, but when he married and discovered his thought sieved into images through his new wife's psyche, he made most of the unforgettable poetry of his time, stuff that very likely would have remained unwritten if he had not undergone the labour of remaking himself. This Æ could not understand. To him the process of adjustment consisted in stripping himself of the world, in going around in a state of spontaneous combustion, in merging himself completely with the soul of things, in becoming his own naked self which for him always was larger than everyday life, a being like Plato's prototype. This was, according to him, the real state of nature, and only poetry made in this state was authentic. And yet about Yeats it is possible that he did hit on some half-truths that elicit the reasons for the successes of the poems and their failures.

He began about the time of *The Wind Among the Reeds* to do two things consciously, one to create a 'style', in literature, the second to create or rather to recreate W.B. Yeats in a style that would harmonise with the literary style. People call this posing. It is really putting on a mask ... The actor must talk to the emotion on the mask which is a fixed emotion. W.B.Y. began twenty years ago vigorously defending Wilde against the charge of being a poseur. He said it was merely living artistically, and it was the duty of everybody to have a conception of himself, and he intended to conceive of himself. The error in his psychology is that life creates the form, but he seems to think that the form creates life. He seems to have also thought, though he never said so, that if you make a picturesque or majestic personality of yourself in appearance, you will become as wonderful inside as outside ... He has created the mask and finds himself obliged to speak in harmony with the fixed expression on the mask, and that accounts for the lifelessness of his later talk and writing ... He bores me terribly now ... I want life and thought, and he talks solemn platitudes under the impression that this nonsense is arcane wisdom. Any bit of pedantry a couple of hundred years old seems to him to have a kind of divine authority. We go to hear him as we go to see the tomb of Shakespeare ... The only difference is that Yeats is his own coffin and memorial tablet ... Why can't he be natural? Such a delightful creature he was when young. And at rare moments when he forgets himself he is still interesting as ever almost.

What Æ did not see, of course, was that what he possessed quite naturally Yeats had to acquire by metamorphosis. He had no transports, so he had to invent them. The material of his early poems required a visionary background, just as the Faeryland of the Celtic Twilight required as a corollary some philosophic justification in its turn. But where Æ could speak authoritatively of this unseen piece of real estate, Yeats had to work on hearsay and the naïveties of the Kiltartan countryside.

At a Yeats Exhibition lately, I came across a long-suppressed poem which had as a punchline—repeated eight times in as many stanzas, and quite seriously—the refrain, 'You are wasting away, little Fairy.' And this was composed at a time when Æ had already discovered the serious burthen of his songs, and was already at home in his fabulous worlds—even if the poet himself was lost to them. And those worlds were as real to him as the Night was to St John. It is safe to assert that as a poet he was cursed by his capacity for vision, and that Yeats was saved for poetry by the lack of it. Mystical experience evades words, but the search for it can produce as a byline the states and tension out of which poetry can come. But then, poetry can come out of anything. Yeats went on from a poor start. The tortoise outran the hare. We have the two of them, so it doesn't matter, but it is extraordinary to think that a poet can be saved by his very limitations.

To the world generally only one of the twins is great, and certainly Yeats, the later Yeats, had most of the properties. His emanations have gone forth; they did not die into burly journalism or into creameries in the depths of the country, or on political byways before the guns arrived on affairs of state. But Yeats to the last carried some odd baggage from the Faery mound, and perhaps one of the gifts was glamour. He found the greater speech in the end.

These letters bring many forgotten things to my mind. Æ the impulsive squanderer of himself in matters mundane, social or political, an open letter to Rudyard Kipling which is not reprinted here, though the famous letter to the Dublin employers of 1913 is reprinted in full. How many know that it was he who drew an unwilling Yeats into the dramatic movement that became the Abbey Theatre, or wrote for the first little company of amateurs their first real play? Or that almost he succeeded in uniting Unionist and Nationalist in the common cause of an undivided Ireland, barging his way into the highest quarters, a bearded knight with a sword of peace? And for the editor of that tiny weekly which represented the views of the co-operative movement, he did make his office in Merrion Square the remarkable centre for another kind of life. He had a gift for people. And like the Ulsterman he was, he had a rebel sense of human rights. There was a McCracken heritage somewhere, spiritually if not in the true bloodline.

The last years were not too happy. He was a lonely man, and a sick man who had outlived his time. Where the long wave of events washed Yeats into the Senate, visitors at 17 Rathgar Avenue became fewer and fewer. The new statesmen took over and the *Irish Statesman* died. Time, never very generous, delivered its verdict, and a great Irishman packed up and went to London where another kind of verdict was given by his doctors.

Dear Seumus [to James Stephens],

... They allow me a year or thereabouts. Don't think I feel anything melancholy, I hold to the spiritual verities I have believed in all my life and would be glad and more cheerful if my time were shorter ...

Perhaps it was this quality that attracted me to Æ the man. He was a pilgrim in time, but at home in eternity. And even there, I am sure, for all the new starfire he is gathering, he will take a long time to shake the dust of Dublin off his wings.

—*The Irish Times*, December 14th, 1961

Austin Clarke:
Poet, Playwright, Prose Writer

EDITOR'S NOTE: The poet, verse playwright, novelist, critic and autobiographer Austin Clarke (1896–1974) played an important and fertilizing role in Fallon's life—as an early influence, as a close friend for many years, and as a model of dedicated literary professionalism. Their first meeting is described below, but later Clarke visited him several times in Wexford, and when Fallon visited Dublin in turn he usually 'looked him up'. With F.R. Higgins, they often formed a trio and are in fact shown together in the much-reproduced cartoon by Alan Reeves, which still hangs in the Palace Bar in Fleet Street, Dublin.

While Fallon generally preferred Clarke's early and middle-period poetry to his late, he always respected him and followed his output keenly. He was also instrumental in getting Clarke's verse plays printed. Though there was an age gap of nearly nine years between them, they seem to have regarded each other as virtual contemporaries and in the event, Fallon only survived the elder poet by a matter of months. The final piece printed in this sequence was actually one of a occasional series of articles which Fallon began to write for *The Irish Times* in the final year of his life; however, they were cut short by his death.

TWICE AROUND THE BLACK CHURCH
edited by Allan Denson (Abelard Schumann, London)

*E*SSAYS in autobiography are trials of strength with the past tense, from the pluperfect to the forbidden subjunctive, and the tensile strength of the person who emerges from the struggle seems in most cases to be diminished rather than augmented. We look for the extraordinary, for the ordination or the star above the manger, for the angels on the bedspread or the gipsy with the horoscope, and what survives the deep-sea dive proves to be the properties of everyman, nothing more or less than ordinary and common experience. One childhood seems no different from the other, the poet and the baker have eaten the same bread.

The real moments escape expression or isolation. When Austin Clarke refers us to a tiny boy poring over a small pool of rainwater in the background the mystery lodges in his heart or has passed into his life and work, it does not divulge itself to us. The picture is there, but the other dimensions refuse to come forward and coalesce. Yet there must be something vital in the poet's marriage with the rainpool, simply because it is an image that stays with him. The church steeple from down the street inverted itself till the bell tower and lightning conductor were lost in magical depths where a new, if circumscribed, world floated free, a seventh day in miniature over which a new creator rested. Significance is a word that has become maimed with use, but here I could tot up a lot of theory and reason it out that this was an experience that shadowed forth the poet's later attitudes towards the Church of his time. After all, another Irish poet was convinced that all afterknowledge, that all our intellectual pursuits only lead us to what we knew already in our dreams as children. So that our attitudes really are pre-natal and determined, and we choose to see as significant only the things that correspond to them. And didn't another poet say something about the world in a grain of sand?

So, roughly speaking, I am against autobiography. Like

Blake, I saw an angel when I was a child. I was reasoned out of my vision, of course, by a gruff aunt who thought quite rightly that visions were reserved for the pious as a reward for fasting and penance and bended knees, but I never blamed her very much for I was just old enough to doubt the veracity of my own eyesight, and really it could have been the middle moon painting her own face upon a cloud. Anyway it caused me neither consternation nor wonder, my hair did not stand up on end, and I felt no sense of dedication or delight. I noted merely that the face was the dear Italianate face of the Madonna in the local chapel—or one very like it. I mention it for one reason only, and that simply is to state that I still remember it plainly after almost three-quarters of a lifetime—and still without any feeling one way or another. So what significance—that word again—can a man draw from anything that happens in his unseasoned and wide-open childhood? Yet if the thing remains in memory, the bare bones of the affair, it must be working on some wonder of its own on planes of our being over which we have no control. We can never summarise, briefly or otherwise, what we are. That is where the poet steps in. In his indirect and illogical way he connects us to some reality we hadn't dreamed of. The experience, the real thing, seeks itself out in various mirrors at various levels, and when we see it at last we do not recognise it. It has turned itself into art.

I remember Clarke tugging me off a little road near Blessington to show me a field where once at twilight, he saw his first real bull, the bull that years later became the theme of Cuchulain, Maeve and Conor and inspired his best work. He is at pains to pin down the greater vision on the less and not Plato-wise, the lesser on the great. All the morning sunlight of the great epics that he trimmed to his quill he attributes, doubtless, to morning romps about the reservoir at Roundwood where he spent some early summers. Maybe he's right, maybe we do make a phoenix out of a duck egg, but if we do, then we are, I think, even stranger birds than I can credit. The genes must follow the genealogy.

Clarke's canvas, being a city boy's, is not as crowded with earthly wonders as if he had been born and reared in the country. Yet so intense was the country experience when it did come that it yielded for us, back there in the twenties, the best open-air verse of its time. The country, like the Gaelic revival, arrived in him with the fullness of a hereditary passion. It wasn't Georgian in any sense. If he mentions a thrush, it will be one that sang to Fionn or Patrick. If a landscape discloses itself there is a Patrician tongue somewhere banging a tongueless bell, and 'rain as quiet as the turning of books in the holy schools at dawn'. Clerics, rich and strange, haunt the countryside. Hermits battle with the devil in the thighs, but always along the Shannon-bed or the sedgy Boyne. It is a peopled Ireland—with not a tractor to be heard, but it is also the Catholic conscience simplified in landscape, with occasional ribald outbreaks and hearty humour. We are inclined to overlook the wild humorous streak in this poet, the reason being that the later poet has become so remote and glacial, casting his cold eye on life and death, and unfortunately these little essays will do little to amend the image of him we carry nowadays when the satirist is dominant. One small gem stands out untarnished. It is a Holy Thursday and the boy-poet with his sister is 'doing the seven churches', praying for the release of the souls in Purgatory. I like to imagine the throng of sinners he sent winging their ways to Peter's gate. Maybe, unlike the souls in Yeats' Don Juan, some will lie in waiting to offer their blessed mantles when his own time comes.

Belvedere, Mungret, the Jesuit's boy, Clarke knows his experiences challenge the vaster prose master, Joyce; so he gently spikes his own guns and glides over familiar ground. Instead, he gives us an unusual picture of the Dublin Maestro relaxing in Paris after doing his sentence a day. This has the humour of acid carefully applied. Two Belvedereans loose in the fabulous city, and they sit silently, or remember Mooney's. Maybe if they were two rugby players, they might have known how to enjoy themselves.

There is, indeed, such a curious, stilted innocence about those early days of the poet's career that I have a feeling he's pulling our legs. And yet, and yet—there's that visit to Shaw's flat, or rather to the Shavian gates of it, where our poet halted distressed before a large PRIVATE notice that sent him scurrying away. That's credible, if unadventurous; but I think it was not the notice that sent the young man on his way, but his own unacknowledged summary of the great man. There was a world dividing them, not a world of money or success, but of sensibility. There is a world of difference between a poem and a tract, and this Clarke saw for himself when he did meet Shaw—or, rather, when he sidestepped him one fine day at a railway station. This meeting, too, is set in brilliant acids, but, then, perhaps the subject was worth some vitriol.

Another large Irish—and more native—figure does not escape the loaded needle. I hesitate to mention this, because for once the portrait is not in scale, and the values those of the gamin towards schoolteacher. Nobody, after all, expected Abe Lincoln to speak with other than his native twang, and the accent of West Limerick to me only brings up memories of the great Gaelic that went into the speech of the poets of the Maigue. I doubt if Dublin adenoids are an improvement.

What makes a poet? Some tick but tell no time. Others are all face and moving hands, the works on view. We can see Yeats over the years synthesising his material, aggrandising it, even lauding it as if the material was the poetry, and then eventually we see it becoming the man and the poet. Clarke is much more modest, much more detached, more human if much less humane. At the beginning he had much more feeling for the myths than Yeats, but he saw them as plain story, as primeval West Limerick men having war and fun together, and the stuff has a life and richness far beyond Yeats' fumbling and tinkering. But in the end, Yeats brought all to symbol and moved the stuff all through the great mill again so that his life work seems a whole. Whereas Clarke has shifted his ground completely of late and gives the impression of two different men, two opposite kinds of poet. That both are good, that both are often far more than excellent, is not a satisfying answer; for the goodness of the one only undermines the validity of the other. If he were truly a good satiric poet it might be different, but often, quite often, he gets lost in the crimps of his own style. And so does the joke. We look for the point and see only the needle.

Where he alters scope, as in the plays, he is much more

his own man. There, problems of conscience, of sex and sanc-tuary give him the necessary passion and a violence of cohe-sion, and oddly enough it is on those plays that this little book throws light. A pietistic, dominant mother, a houseful of sisters attending convents, the overwhelming mystery of the flesh in a Catholic household; where an urbane Catholicity can cope with the growing pains of youth a Victorian matriarch could only show Venus retrograde in a Dublin side-street. The con-flict was there from the first, but there's no need for the poet to beggar it for it has served him well—as a poet. The shadows were all gathered up into the substance of the plays eventually, and perhaps it is there we are to seek the unity of the person, not in the squibs and the darts of his remote fencing with the religious orders around Templeogue.

This quarrel is louder than the poet, even if it is an old one and a European tradition; it is also a waste of time. After all, the poet himself must use some of the disciplines of the enclosed orders if the Muse is to have her rights in him and her observances. I suggest a new Order of the Black Church, the device to be a church steeple (sable) inverted, racking its bells on the depths of a tiny rainpool. I might join it one day myself.

—*The Irish Times*, January 22nd, 1962

COLLECTED PLAYS
(Dolmen Press, Dublin)

IN THE thirties or forties, according to local critics who were usually novelists or something, the condition of Irish poetry was parlous, yet small books big in content and of extraordi-nary high quality, were issuing from the Bridge Press, Tem-pleogue, unsubsidised; and there was an occasional Sunday night, unsubsidised, when the Abbey Theatre, through no effort of its own, filled up with an audience reminiscent of the days when it did mean something. Those, perhaps, were Austin Clarke's most creative days, but even allowing that, it still comes as a surprise to discover that his verse plays now number eleven and are so good that I for one look forward to the round dozen. And after that, another.

Each play is a lyric poem, an arch of plot, a density of personal ornament. The drama lies in the poet himself and not in the action or situation. And whether he wears a monkish habit, nun's wimple or goliardic feather, the theme swaggers on the skyline between two worlds, not that of Hell or Heaven, but the high wall of farce that divides the chaste from the unchaste. Here is a magnificently ribald tongue, here, too, the Altar Imp's view of Master Abbot, the politics of the lectern, the gossip of the refectory, the bright day of the soul and occasionally the dark night of the saint and its Celtic illumination, and all of this too robust for malice and much too witty to be wisdom. The poet is just the other side of the monkish coin. He rides with his trident over the same waters.

> Bend at this doorway, see the soul of Ireland—
> A poor old woman praying by the fire.

Made for a simple stage where the lighting is the scenery, some of those plays should go into every festival. *The Son of Learning*, for instance, was a success at the Gate when done there by the Gate Company. This is an exuberant piece based on the legend of Mac Conglinne, and could be used as a counterbalance to Beckett's men in barrels—where dead men do tell tales. It could be an innovation if both men were played on alternate nights served by the same company of actors directed, say, by Jim Fitzgerald. It is, after all, time we subsidised big talent, one that has been cramped too long in seeking its own ways and means, finding its own theatre, its own company of verse speakers, producers and props. Which is what Clarke had to do in the great glad days of the Lyric Theatre, founded by himself and Robert Farren. A poet's business is to write poetry not cheques, to manage rhymes not men, and it is our business to aid any native talent when we find it and push it into the front window we finance each year. The difference between a commercial talent and a poetic one is that between West End and week-end. There is no reason at all why we should subsidise the former. It will keep its end up anyway.

Economists have a term called invisible assets. And Clarke, poetically, comes under this. He spins no visible money, but like the guarded gold block in some American fort or other he creates the standard on which world credit is—or was—based. This book is such. The slender volumes tipped in blues, greens and greys, that used to slip out shyly to fervent subscribers here and there throughout the country, gathered into one, make up the best thing we have produced for a long time, and the Dolmen Press is to be congratulated on it. The book measures up to the poet and to the playwright, who is a poet.

—The Irish Times, July 13th, 1963

COLLECTED POEMS

(Dolmen Press, Dublin; Oxford University Press)

IN A WAY it is an impertinence to attempt to place any poet in the terms of time to come, but when a country cannot rise to any single striking figure, a worldwide structure, say, such as Yeats, or a seminal begetter like Ezra Pound, it needn't take the distrait libido too long to make the future plinth. Clarke comes after Yeats, and in certain ways ahead of him, picking up the vagrant output of the itinerant Colum on the way, dismissing Synge to his proper place on the boards.

Those are not large words, not too large I mean. I am aware of Clarke's limitations more than most because I was partly suckled on the song he made, he coming in time just that bit ahead of me to make the way into something native the easier for a younger man. It is the fashion now to rail at the native note, the Irish thing, and indeed nothing is so provincial as the professional Irishman, nobody as tastelessly vulgar. Clarke derived as much from Æ as from the Táin. He found a spirit transmitted from that great irregular that turned mythic the whole landscape of Ireland. This was the delicate thing that made landscape holy, that made it a living and historic being in its own right.

Think of Clarke now, and what comes first to mind is a place like Clonmacnoise, a riverland, green and slow, with the native stone mastering the flatlands in a single round tower, surrounded of course by the schoolmen and the craftsmen stone-chipping. Lauds going up and now and then the silver thud of the untongued bell.

He had translated Æ into almost Christian terms. I don't know if he ever arrived at any kind of personal image of Deity, but there was in him from the very first an almost frantic worship of landscape. He was always the city youngster escaping from the smoke, from the cabbies' corner, the too-populated slum street, not—and never—a boy just out for the day but a spirit returning to his birthright, into the natural growths like tree and herbage, into the waters that gave light to the air.

Once, confessing, he told me of the time in St Albans, in southern England, when he used, under the influence of Æ's *Candle of Vision*, wander the countryside seeking an actual illumination from things, aurae in trees and hedges, nymphs in the air above the streams. The world was alive to him in those times. And it was a life that never really died. I doubt if he would cut down a tree, even those that grew inward and left his study truly a green thought in a green shade.

*

SO IT WAS quite natural that his earliest verse should treat of mythic Ireland, and natural too that he should be the nearest thing to an epical poet we have produced this century, not that there is anything special about epic poets or any larger identification with the Muse.

The difference in Clarke's epic approach and that of his elders was that he was after the lyrical moment at the very heart of things. Something that his plays make plain, something a falling curtain at the end, all but snatches away because this active belief in him feared for its own sanity, for its own reality, I should say. He asserted nothing. When he built towards a luminous moment he set all the traps against himself, he lined up all the arguments against the supernatural to the very last one that broke the camel's back. This last crumbling when the world fell apart had always two interpretations; it was ambivalent as life itself, as two-faced as Gods are or oracles; the main thing was that it got SAID, got out of the void of the undeclared and the bodiless. Doubt or belief are no matter really when the visionary thing requires a medium, or needs a way out into consciousness, what matter is the unveiling of the image.

So much of his life belongs to this vital activity that it makes me unappreciative of his development as a satirist of modern idiosyncracy. God knows we need one in this sad scene. Yet his verse style is definitely against the obvious witticism. As Moore said of Yeats, the joke gets lost in the folds of his style. But don't let my opinion damn this wayward wandering of a Muse that grew bitter at the new Ireland growing up around him, swamping his native city, casting the great figures into the local sump, invading even his own very garden in Templeogue, where a Trinity man lived before him in most perfect seclusion, where I called when first he took it over, went around the garden to the murmur of a famous river, and sat many an hour among the books. It was important to him, this satiric comment, but in its anti-clerical simplification it was too easy to engage a talent as large as his. Satire is of another kind. It needs the belly-laugh.

It is very difficult to review his verse without an equal attention to the plays; they are two strands of a single whole. Up to the time the Lyric Theatre came into being his drama output wasn't very much, but there was a period then with stage available when he wrote several minor masterpieces, they in themselves being a sort of dramatic lyric in texture and point. I note now, and very surprised I am, that up to 1936 his verse fills only 177 pages of this collected volume, the remaining 388 pages separating themselves into collections for the following dates, *Night and Morning*, 1938, 11 pages; *Ancient Lights*, 1955, 11 pages; *Too Great a Vine*, 1957, 13 pages; *The Horse-Eaters*, 1960, 9 pages; *Flight to Africa*, 1963, 45 pages; *Flight to Africa II*, 16 pages; *Flight to Africa III*, 5 pages; *Mnemosyne Lay in Dust*, 1966, 28 pages; *Old-Fashioned Pil-*

grimage, 1967, 31 pages; *The Echo at Coole*, 1968, 61 pages; *A Sermon on Swift*, 1968, 26 pages; *Orphide*, 1970, 24 pages; *The Wooing of Becfola*, 1974, 24 pages.

*

I ENUMERATE this list just to show the sudden, almost unanticipated flowering of Clarke's middle and later years. The quality is something which must still be determined, the last verse is delightfully expert, and unashamedly enjoys itself in metrical devices of a kind not usually put into service by any craftsman, even one as jubilant as Clarke. In a note at the end of the book he describes a meeting with the American poet Frost, in which he is asked by the old maestro what sort of verse he writes and replied that he 'loaded himself with chains and tried to get out of them'. This act of ingenuity, I expect, gave him many unexpected lines and rhymes simply by the effort to put two and two together. It is likely also that the fact of search uncloaked more meanings and greater depths in some poems. His Pegasus was always under the cart anyway, and when the tensions of the 1938 volume *Night and Morning*, eased into more equable times, I fancy he unlocked himself by technical exercises and founded poems, some on sheer technique. Who would rhyme Pablo Neruda, bless him, with 'all in a doo-da'? And to the honourable name and fame of Ezra Pound he makes eight full or demi or semi-Poundian rhymes. Some he does not get away with, and the 'some' are more than the difference if one ponders more the spirit of the poem and not be dislodged by the play. The plain fact is that this was Clarke's way and method of work, and that he justifies it a thousandfold.

All the same, I have this hankering to surprise him in simpler moments, when the freshet was rising of its own sweet will and insisted on making its own way. His travel poems are almost as hieratic as the gilded altars of his Papal ministry.

> Gaiety of Religion chased us
> Away from Andalust,
> Shrines in a cathedral, enchased

Screenwork of silver, gold ...

This book, indeed, is not the matter for any quick simple review, taking in as it does the long life line of a magnificent talent. It will beget books, of course, be launched into the great American mills and taken, item by item, to the operation table. But nobody ever will find the thrill of a certain young man when he opened his first Austin Clarke, *The Cattledrive in Connaught*. For that alone I salute him now, and am greatly pleased that Liam Miller of the Dolmen Press should do him the kind of book that could most honour him. Here, if anywhere, is the monumentum of a poet, a book of fine design, model and layout, with a drawing, plural, but Bernard Childs' Salud.

—*The Irish Times*, 1974

Editor's note: Clarke's house in Templeogue has now vanished, making way for the rather ugly modern bridge named after him. Concrete housing estates crowd around the once semi-rural spot. The 'famous river' is of course The Dodder.

Elsewhere in Time

*M*Y ATTEMPTS to keep a daily journal of some kind
always end in empty diaries, empty that is except for
the first few pages, addresses, telephone numbers,
titles of books I want to get, and occasionally lines of verse,
the kind that jump into your mind out of nowhere.

Religiously I jot those down, and as religiously forget
them. A couple of years ago I came on a casual notebook I
kept for business purposes, lists of appointments and that kind
of stuff, results of enquiries and the devil knows what, and
found it full of quotations and some verse stuff that had
altered shape and value later on and gone into the making of
something. This is not like meeting up with an old friend. It is
to meet a complete stranger who has a nagging resemblance to
somebody you know.

What I'd like to do now is to rough into a few lines the
people I meet. I speak of first meetings, first impressions, both
of people and place; later, of course, to be compared with
closer acquaintance. At the moment, I think that one's first
impression of a person is fairly accurate. The camouflage has-
n't had time to get to work on you. You're not involved.
Mostly, however, those first feelings are entirely unprintable.
I'm speaking now of people.

Places are something else.

The death of Austin Clarke means for me an epoch
ended. A poet who is a generation ahead of you is a larger
influence than a poet two generations ahead, or three or four
as Yeats was. He had an epic sense that Yeats lacked. Read

Yeats, not the verse plays but the lyrics, poems with a mythological content, and then compare the lyrics, and the epic start
of the Cattledrive, in *The Cattledrive of Connaught*, *The Son
of Lir*, *The Frenzy of Suibhne*. I haven't looked at those for
years, yet when I turn them up they keep surprising me, with
their reality, their countryside, the archaic animism of figure-
and-landscape, but mostly their energy.

Beside him, Yeats is tapestry.

*

MY FIRST meeting with him was in '32, a few days before
Christmas. He'd come home from London and our session
was almost ending, 7.30 p.m., Palace Bar, when journalists
hurried into typewriters and poets looked into other places. It
was F.R. Higgins who introduced us (two poets, Smyllie said,
who never stopped fighting one another for disciples). He was,
somehow, exactly what I expected him to be, slender, light,
very quick to see a thing. And I was, it seems, brash enough to
lecture him—I can't remember about what—but he remembered it years later and brought it up, and I think it was only
after many more meetings, mostly in the company of our Elder
Seumas O'Sullivan, that the Clerical libido ran in my favour, a
confession which surprised me as I hadn't noticed the slightest
reserve in the man at all.

I think it was mistaken of Eavan Boland to hold a sort of
symposium on his work so soon after his death. If he sat there
in spirit it would be only to quote Synge, no—I take that back,
there were some very pleasant spirits at the 'wake', men I like,
but to tell the truth I feel myself that for all our drifting apart
in those last years that there were no people alive outside his
family who knew him as Mervyn Wall and myself knew him,
or, of course, the Campbells.

To grieve is a relative affair, I think the sense of personal
loss makes up the larger proportion of the feeling. Ewart
Milne, in a letter to *The Irish Times* some days ago, mentioned
the eternal man in the house at the foot of the Dublin hills, as
if he would live forever. And that was my feeling also. If I
wanted to call, he'd be there.

And now he's not.

I don't know if there's any truth in the rumour that some days before he died, he received an order to evacuate his house as it was required for a road-widening project. I suppose those sort of things happen all the time in bureaucracy, the good of the greater number etc., etc., but I fancy there's a great ironic face somewhere picking its moment and its weapon. But it should have happened hereafter, when he needed no more house room, no pines around his window, no birds, no river. And where was John Garvin, Keeper of the Joycean ghost, master of Dublin's fair city? Or has he, too, moved into private life?

*

MY FRIEND, Robert Farren, has pensioned himself off, I believe, his work well done, his civic work, though I would call it a national chore. For Farren was the man who cleared out the Augean stables of the Radio Éireann that was in the thirties. Nobody, no writer, took it seriously till he got in there and bulldozed most of us into giving a hand simply by raising the fees to newspaper levels, Leon O Broin overhead again, regarding the matter favourably as they say. Money, however, is not enough. He gave freedom of speech also. I got away with murder at a time you couldn't write even a small percentage of what is acceptable nowadays. And Clarke found himself with a weekly slot, a Monday night programme of verse-speaking that was to continue up to the last few years, a programme so unique that BBC personnel on visiting-firemen excursions always remarked on it as being the one thing that stood out.

This was the programme that enabled the Lyric Theatre to be born, giving Clarke fees enough to make it attractive to young would-be actors and to established actors who fancied themselves in rhyme and rhythm. Some are very big names nowadays, Liam Redmond, Cyril Cusack, Abbey and Rep people, Eithne Dunne, Gerry Healy, and my own Una Collins whom I only got to speak verse by writing it as prose. From this came the famous Sunday Nights in the Abbey, crowded houses if you please, for verse plays and verse-speaking, till Mr (duine uasal) Blythe put a stop to them on one excuse or another. (The sets had to be changed for the usual Abbey play on Monday nights, necessitating extra work on the stage staff. Fair enough, but then he charged enough too for the Sunday night.)

All in all, one could call the Lyric Theatre a Clarke-Farren venture, an amity made possible by Farren's understanding of his fellow-director. In more ways than one, he was the angel who trod delicately.

—*The Irish Times*, April 10th, 1974

Editor's note: The bilingual poet, playwright and critic, Robert Farren (Roibeárd Ó Faracháin, 1909–82) was a close friend and associate of Padraic Fallon during the 1940s and 1950s. During his long years in Radio Éireann—of which he became Controller of Programmes, 1953–74—he worked hard to enlist the talents of leading Irish writers, including Fallon, and fought internal battles to ensure that they were paid properly. Farren also served as a director of the Abbey Theatre from 1940 to 1973, and with Austin Clarke he founded the Dublin Verse-speaking Society which later became the influential Lyric Theatre. He seems to have been treated rather shabbily by officialdom in his later years, when Radio Éireann became merged with Radio Teilfís Éireann and moved from its old billet in Henry Street to suburban Montrose. The noted civil servant, biographer and historian Leon Ó Broin (1902–90) was for years the much-represented *eminence grise* of the Department of Posts and Telegraphs, in whose headquarters (the GPO) the Radio Éireann studios and offices were then housed.

F.R. Higgins:
The Poet as Folksinger

EDITOR'S NOTE: The poet Frederick Robert Higgins (1896–1941) was a strong influence on Fallon's early verse, along with his coeval Austin Clarke. Born in Foxford, Co. Mayo, the son of an RIC man, he was already quite well known as a poet before he was drawn into the inner circle around Yeats, through whose influence he was made a director of the Abbey Theatre. In his early years Higgins was a labour activist and also edited various magazines, while sharing with Clarke an enthusiasm for folklore and mediaeval Ireland. He was also deeply interested in popular balladry and drew Yeats into this interest via the Cuala Press Broadsheets.

Higgins's relatively early death devastated wartime Dublin and Fallon wrote a moving elegy in his memory. His best poetry is contained in the Cuala Press publications *Arable Holdings* (1933) and *The Gap of Brightness* (1940). However, his work went out of print for many years, until in 1992 Dardis Clarke courageously edited and published *F.R. Higgins: the 39 Lyrics* (Bridge Press, Dublin). Writers as disparate—and as fastidious—as Louis MacNeice and Austin Clarke paid tribute to the excellence of his verse technique and the quality of his metrical ear.

Somewhat overpraised in his lifetime, Higgins is correspondingly—and quite unfairly—underrated in our own. He is admittedly an uneven writer, but poems such as 'Auction' and 'Elegy for Padraic O Conaire' belong by right in any anthology of Irish verse. His friendship with Fallon appears to have been warm and genuine, the friendship of two poet–practitioners, even if it was clouded over later as relationships between writers so often are. When Fallon describes

166

calling on him in his Dublin workshop, he is possibly referring to the printing works of Hely Thoms in Dame Street, now vanished. (The late George Hetherington, a cultivated art patron and occasional poet, was a high-ranking executive there and a personal friend of both men; later he was active on the board of *The Irish Times*.) And the hostelry in which Fallon and Higgins drank together was almost certainly the Palace Bar in Fleet Street.

'OH, YOU must meet Higgins,' my Poet–editor said to me. We were roaming from book-barrow to book-barrow on one of those autumn mornings when the distances along the quays are composed of mist and silver, a Saturday morning, I remember, because there was a flurry and sparkle of people everywhere and a feeling of restful exhilaration, as if the city were taking deeper breaths before relaxing softly on the expanded horizon of the week-end. On such mornings the Pale of Dublin seems really to go down before the soft, peaceful invasion of sea and country; you feel the salmon nosing up the Liffey and turf barges moving in sleepily from the blue bogs. The market stalls are fruit-laden, the street corners blossom with flower-girls, the greens with dogs and ducks and children, everywhere there is a criss-cross of restlessness and bustle, a mood of light gaiety which, like those graceful Dublin distances, might come out of one's own heart. It was a day to meet a gay, delicate country poet.

I was thinking a good deal about Higgins as we strolled along the quays. His verse came out of my own country, and out of that mental country, too, where I was finding the images that excited me, those personal velocities one must touch in order to sing. And as we walked I found myself defining the velocities that inspired different poets. In Æ it was a recapitulation of other-world experience; in Yeats it seemed to be the parchment and candle of *Il Penseroso*, a cloak threaded with the signs of the Zodiac; in Seumus O'Sullivan a more human and lovable thing, such as this autumn morning when the lives of people were leaping in at the eye. And after O'Sullivan, Colum and Stephens, I came to Austin Clarke, whose verse might have been written by some vigorous Son of Learning who struck the harp while remembering the Pyx, disliking both for their sedentary implications; and then, as if by natural sympathy, to his less learned but natural brother in song, the poet I was about to meet.

To this Higgins, poetry seemed to matter as it mattered to the minor Court songsters of Elizabeth, James and Charles, a lyrical extension of the physical self in which even the muscles sought to play their part, and the poetry of ideas was deliberately discounted for the poetry of action. They are an important tribe, those lovers of living, for though they contribute nothing directly to the great inner drama of the civilising conscience, they fructify it by opposition, carrying on as they do into every new age the old faith of the Corybantian revellers, the belief in personal ecstasy, the *Gaudium veneris* to which the newer theologies seem so much smoke. Later, for we became quick friends though our ways were mostly apart, I found that Higgins, subconsciously, had come to recognise this Dionysian mask for his own. He was conventionally an untroubled Christian and the dream which illustrated for him the trend of his creative work, rather shocked him with its vivid illumination of the implications of his poetic role. We were in Kells, I think, when he told me of it. He had been very quiet as we jogged along through his own ripe country, but coming down that hilly street from the Round Tower, with children merry-making around us in the dusk, he unburdened himself. He was in an old curio shop, he dreamed, coming down a short flight of worn stone steps from the street, accompanied by his wife. There was something Parisian, something exceedingly knowing and sly about the aged Proprietor in his velveteen jacket and tasselled cap who met them in the dim hallway and escorted Mrs Higgins to the long spacious room to the right where *objets d'art* were displayed anyhow on small tables. There must have been other rooms opening from that one, for Higgins waiting passively in the hallway, was suddenly very much alone. There was a statue of a Satyr in an alcove in the shadows and he moved over to examine it. He said what struck him first was the curious nobility that seemed to underlie the conventional leer, and then as though answering his question, the statue was no longer a statue, for the eyes began to live and on its face the bronze grew out through the green with the soft hues of living flesh. Higgins became aware of many things at once, whether through speech or not he was unable to recollect, but the way of Dionysus became to him for the first time a reality. He was more amazed than afraid, for here, no longer hidden in church rhythms, in words on a parson's tongue, in Sunday-school admonitions and warnings, was the fabled figure itself before his impact on time had dwindled and Churchmen, adding horns and tail, had reduced him from Zagreus to that mediaeval devil that frightened our cradles.

The dream, now, took on something of the quality of the Temptation in the Desert. There was the same mythic framework, the same machinery of promises and worldly reward. And as a proof of its power to fulfil its promises, the figure of the god stepped from its pedestal and lifting an arm let loose a flood of roaring energies that seemed to shake the world. The while the thunder was dying away in the far voids of space, the quiet everyday voices of the curio-dealer and Mrs Higgins were heard in the next room, and the god, in some strange way, was reduced once more to a Satyr, a sly secretive figure with one ear cocked, ready for all its display of power to go underground like any other creature of the wild. But before it resumed its pedestal, it gave Higgins a long meaning glance, and implying 'you will remember I AM by this mark', laid two fingers on Higgins' wrist. At the touch, Higgins said, a wild shock of energy ran through him. And then, as the curio-dealer and Mrs Higgins came to the door, the figure wrinkled and dwindled once more into an old weathered bronze standing in an alcove.

I am no interpreter of dreams, archetypal or otherwise, but sometimes they are definitely dramatisations of the dreamer's psychic position at the moment. Jung, however, found many mythological images in the dreams of his patients which had in themselves much of the symbolic content and energy attributed to them by ancient faith. But this dream of Higgins' was, I considered, just the ordinary dramatic projection of a conflict he would not admit existed in himself, for a poet must write out of his primary inclination or be dumb, and if he be a limited poet with no large range of intellect, he must of necessity select his themes out of this inclination, even if it be as Yeats declared it, at the expense of the soul's perfection:

What theme had Homer but original sin?

All this, however, was to be in the future. I am now remembering the almost Falstaffian figure of the poet as he descended the great staircase of the printing offices where he worked, to meet two other poets out for holiday. No one would attribute psychic problems to this big man, or suspect that the mythologies were about to invade his country peace. There was an elaborate, wholesome dignity in his gradual procession earthwards. A long staircase, however, will try anyone's dignity, and Higgins, jollied along by an apt quotation from Yeats, 'the years like great black oxen tread the world', was quite human when he reached the last step. He was very like his work, I thought, dark-suited and raven-haired, with a cleverly chosen jewel-like shirt that concentrated the rich bucolic light of his face He had a very sweet smile, so sweet that the face behind it seemed to dissolve into a vague mist, timid as that fawn that trembled upon the borders of the wood. And I could see in that almost feminine softness the responsive impressionism of his work. He would never need to bother about detailed studies of objects or landscapes that interested him. Some part of him would melt and fuse with them, and reproduce them later in the flash of an image or in the drama of a phrase. And this swiftness of response, this never-ending honeymoon, was by the defect of the quality, a rare trouble to him. He was never certain that some phrase or image of his was not an echo of something he had read, and he used to go over every new poem as carefully as a seaman sounding his way to a new anchorage, shutting out everything that did not seem his very own. It was a very raw spot, this as it is with most of the poets I know, for one's worst echoes are unconscious and, when they are on the hook and fighting, always seem to be a very fine fish. I used to pull his leg about it, saying that his idiom luckily was so personal and mannered that nobody could trace a theft to him, for even Donne's line 'For God's sake hold your tongue, and let me love!' suffered so great a sea-change in its passage to County Meath, that no one would recognise it in its new guise, 'So shut your mouth and let me kiss the barmaid!'

At this time, he had little of his later certainty in himself. His juniors, better publicists than he, were making reputations as prose writers in England and America. And his traditional singing, with its country idiom and its inlay of homely imagery, was going out of fashion. It was a lonely time because the romantic, vociferous mass-produced youngsters, with slogans and signs on their arms, were manoeuvring him out of one periodical after another. Poetry was to be a definition of the time, not of the person; it must be a cast of the fluid collective shape of changing man, it was to be everything that Higgins was not, suicidal, bored, sick of a world that was nothing but 'an old bitch gone in the teeth'. In Dublin, too, it was a time of reaction. The heroic gestures of the Civil War were dying into state pensions, and patriotic reputations were being assessed in terms of business directorships. The gaudy twenties were gone, and vanishing with them as the symbolic figure of Padraic O Conaire and his donkey had vanished, was the happy-go-lucky attempt to create new art modes out of the old folk-forms. Youth wanted something bitter, something to lull the tapeworm, so it turned to Eliot and dry sherry, substituting the Thebaid for the Sally Gardens. Higgins was very much alone.

Then one day he told me Yeats had called on him, wandering in one afternoon when he happened not to be at home, cawing a little over a painting of Æ's ('He continues to paint the human figure out of his head.') and wandering away again. It was the forerunner of many visits. And soon afterwards, Higgins was asked to select twenty-five of his lyrics for a Cuala Press booklet.

I was in Dublin for much of that lovely autumn of 1933, and we spent many afternoons in Meath and Kildare. The poems were sent to the printers one at a time, and sometimes, when there was a particularly urgent SOS, a stanza or two at a time. Sitting on a ditch in the sun or in the brown depths of some village pub, a galley sheet would be discovered somehow in the accumulation of miscellaneous documents which he managed to house in his breast pocket, and there, under a side of salty bacon or a string of onions or a score of bicycle tyres, he would read me his poem. Many of the lyrics which eventually made up *Arable Holdings* were written or re-written about this time. I remember especially two gay pieces, 'The Gallivanter's Address to his Boots' and 'Faction'. Only the first stanza of 'The Gallivanter' was written when he took it along, and he was dissatisfied with that. He had promised Miss Yeats that he would deliver the poem on the following day, so every mile that took him away from the city was an added load on his conscience. Outside Chapelizod, he made me stop the car and turn back. We were to have one drink before he went home to work. And that drink produced a fairly large family, for we chose, unluckily, a popular and friendly house in the neighbourhood of Fleet Street. There as the evening wore on and the Gallivanter's adventures became richer, I caught, I think, as I had not caught before, that personal image of Higgins that beams within the exhilarating mask of his best work. He was the carefree, grotesque, wandering man of his poems, Synge's *Playboy* and Colum's 'Balladsinger' projected into a disheartened world. Every new outrageous incident we added to the peregrinations of those seven-league boots would set his huge body gurgling, and how the poem did become a reality by the following afternoon, I don't know now; but there it was, safely stowed within his overflowing breast pocket, as we strode up Grafton Street to deliver it to Miss Yeats. A new poem too, the metre speeded up by short unusual lines, composed by him in a single forenoon, a gay foam of fresh air and folksong, a memory of dying Ireland.

Certainly at this time his art was at its best. Ears had stepped in at the right time and given him heart, making him feel that he counted in a world that was giving up its personality to the keeping of the gigantic new myths. Some of us, frankly, did not feel easy about the father-and-son relationship that was growing up swiftly between those two, for the later Yeats was diamond-like in his clear-cut intensity, and Higgins, having modelled the poet in himself from his first youth on Synge and Padraic O Conaire, had so thought himself into a single pose that any attempt to whittle it down to a new conception would have brought the knife into contact with his living flesh. I know from Higgins that Yeats never tried to lay hammer and chisel on him, but no young man, no man as susceptible to the heroics as Higgins, could live long with that gilded giant and remain unimpressed. A new Higgins did emerge eventually, a Higgins whose focus on his own folk stuff had turned from inside to outside, but this was not until *Arable Holdings* had gone through the press, not until the Abbey with its problems and squabbles was draining him of his little energy, not until he was in a local way a public figure with the onus on him to live up to it. All this, combined with the work that gave him his livelihood, left him little leisure for poetry, little leisure for that daily wrangle with nothing, with one's own nihilism, out of which poetry comes.

In the two or three months preceding the publication of *Arable Holdings*, many projected poems and many half-written poems became realities, and they are the better in their intuitive rightness for their sudden births. Later, when he was preparing *The Gap of Brightness*, he was to alter some of them, but by that time had had grown away from the life that was in them, he could only impose on them a later conception of his art, substituting drama for atmosphere, seeking words with almost a physical appetite for their passionate significance and pictorial qualities. I think now of poems I saw grow stanza after stanza, poems like 'Stations' with such a delicate lifting ending as this:

> And here with light on the ebb
> And hooded while nursing
> The last faint glow in the web
> Of her bone, she seems
> A dusk-green bird in her dreams,
> Maybe the Phoenix,
> For look in the salty darkness,
> By God, she gleams.

For comparison, here is the stanza as it appears in *The Gap of Brightness*:

> And so on as twilight ebbs
> She squats less human

Cuddling a glow in her webs,
Damn it, she seems
A dusk-green bird in its dreams;
She's maybe the phoenix—
For look in the salty darkness,
By god, she gleams!

I dwell on this poem because it shows what he gained and lost in technique in the course of seven or eight years. The third stanza as rewritten for *The Gap of Brightness* concentrates the theme of the poem and improves it immensely as a dramatic statement, but the fourth stanza, where there was unusual and accurate pictorial observation, gives way to a further and unnecessary pointing of the drama. The word 'spidery' has been rammed in obviously to lead up to the word 'webs' in the last stanza, and from the new emphasis which is thereby laid on the spider quality of the image, it becomes apparent immediately that the poet who made the alteration has lost touch with his own poem. For 'web' in the earlier version is as little to be identified with spiders as the phoenix is with the Black Widow. The delicate fantasy of the first, wondering picture on which the poem depended becomes complicated and blurred. And the sound pattern has lost its lightness of texture. It demanded anything but the realism of such words as 'squats' and 'cuddling' which are too heavy, too active and pictorial, to take the faint flame of the last two lines.

And the introduction of the second expletive, which deliberately toned down wonder to the key of casual interest, leaves the poem in the air. If the poet does not choose to be impressed, why the hell should he try to impress anyone else? It seems almost as if he had come to despise his material and was condescending to it.

If those revisions are in the nature of an apology to his time for his choice of material, another instance will show his deliberate maiming of himself and his art in his effort to deal realistically with material which is in itself fantastic and grotesque. The poem 'Faction', as it appears in *Arable Holdings*, did need some slight revision because four stanzas were given to the printer before the last two were written and, with no model before him, the poet followed the rhythm, to find when the book was ready for the press that they contained eight lines each instead of seven. This, however, is really immaterial, for the last two lines of those stanzas are rhythmically the equivalent of the last line in each of the first four stanzas. The poem was important to Higgins, though he didn't think a lot of it himself, because in it he had discovered a method by which he could get in touch with the country life of his time in his own person. Up to that, although a large number of his poems are written in the first person singular, he usually spoke out of a borrowed character; he is a poor girl, or an unmarried mother, or a wandering gossoon, or a mismanaged wife, he speaks through every romantic figure but his own. In 'Faction', for once, he used folk material on his own level, and the poem, as it is printed in *Arable Holdings*, is a success because in the final stanza he allowed his fantasy the rein, turning, with a nice easy twist, the 'squat hairy stevedore' of the quarrel into that active mediaeval demon who takes bits out of the countryside here and there and leaves his hoof-tracks on the hills. It is this final hint that makes the poem a good poem; without it, it is a cock without a comb, a mere incident of versified journalism.

On that day, as we three walked out of Thom's and turned to the bookstalls on the Liffey where Higgins wanted to buy—above all things—a history of the Connaught Rangers, I sensed a good deal of what was to happen between us, but not his final severance between a poet and his real material. For a number of years he was to welcome me on my flying visits to Dublin, lumbering into the back snug of the pub where I waited for him, his huge heartiness belying the extreme sensitiveness of his nature. He would order his glass and sit down, tapping my pockets, using a phrase like 'Out with it, man, out with that babby I hear squalling!' He was always the eager critic, realistic and hard, showing no mercy to what wasn't good. The good could be better, the better best. Verse then, I think, was almost his life. You could see a phrase sinking into him like a stone into a pool. But I felt about him often that he would escape from the mental drudgery of it, if circumstances favoured, into something easier that would bring a more immediate response.

He was an active man, with farming ancestors, tied to a sedentary body, unsure of himself in those years, terrified of being what he called 'a mere poet of atmosphere,' beginning to be troubled about the impression he was making on his time. He confessed this to Æ and myself one night at Rathgar Road, and I was satisfied to see Æ bristling, for Higgins in his eyes could never be a failure. But as the reassuring peroration advanced (not as Dublin wits might have it—by way of agricultural organisation) to that mythic world wherein all poets, major and minor, have an equal footing, I noticed too that Higgins wasn't interested any longer in a mystic interpretation of his art. He wanted results, now, as a business man wants his profits or a politician a seat in the cabinet, he wanted an art by which he could batter a way through the hordes of the Philistines, poetry with bombs in every line that would make his voice the dominant noise of a noisy age.

Yet his job, as I saw it and as Æ saw it, was to do what he had set himself to do in the first place, to express the live male spirit of the country Ireland which is not always left outside the heart when men uncap themselves at the chapel door. That spirit is a limited current coinage, it is a reality that must be delivered in its own folk form, and this folk form is permissible as the imitation of fashionable techniques is not permissible because the problems propounded, social and spiritual, come out of a totally different environment. The only real provincialism is imitation.

And Higgins was doing this job well. Poems like the 'To My Blackthorn Stick', 'Repentance' and 'Faction', and the elegies, 'Padraic O Conaire' and 'Father and Son', show how close to the body he could cut the country frieze and still be himself, a person moving easily within an established convention in the way that an anonymous mediaeval stonemason might carve his own features among the wings and gargoyles of a growing cathedral. He would have been a greater poet in the end had he continued to identify himself with this first conception of his role, had he carried forward the technical discoveries he was making in such poems as 'To My Blackthorn Stick' and 'Father and Son' where his new prose rhythms dragged the folk tune into something very personal to him, and the slow line meandered till it filled its banks and was ready to marry the great glitter of the sea.

Yet, up to the end of 1934 he was doing this well. And it was around this time, I think, that he ceased to inhabit the gorgeous cattle-jobber silhouette that was so much a part of his stock-in-trade. Before him, now, was the urban future he had renounced a few years before to live in Mayo, four or five years in which he would be occupied with the politics of letters rather than with literature itself, manager of a famous dead theatre, secretary to the Irish Academy of Letters, nervous years in which he had to patch up his mask anew to meet the demands of an important middle age, years in which he finally laid aside his primary image of himself as folk poet while still clinging to its external conventions and that robust idiom that is so unsuited to the sober, in-looking attitude of our suburban time. I don't think he would ever have tuned himself to this reverie of ours where argument externally grinds on argument, where there is defeat oftener than victory, where the struggle for expression is the expression of the whole psychic man, the struggle that is to be found in the best poetry of the age but is most personal in *The Tower* and *The Winding Stair* and the later poetry of Austin Clarke, where the images glimmer in the crypts and there is terror in the faint candlelight that struggles on the altar. He was rather like the acrobat in the story who must worship in his own way; but when his gay tumbling went out of fashion, he had nothing to substitute for it.

But O it was a gay gallant fellow who lived inside the jobber's hat those times we used to wander the streets and the country roads, and who still lives within the covers of that lovely Cuala booklet he inscribed for me back in 1933.

> They'll miss his heavy stick and stride in Wicklow,
> His story-talking down Winetavern street
> Where old men sitting in the wizen daylight
> Have kept an edge upon his gentle wit;
> And women on the grassy streets of Galway

Who harken for his passing but in vain
Shall hardly tell his step as shadows vanish
Through archways of forgotten Spain.

Editor's note: The 'Poet–editor' is obviously Seumus O'Sullivan of the *Dublin Magazine*. The public house where Fallon and Higgins drank is probably the Palace Bar (still extant) in Fleet Street. The final quotation is from Higgins' 'Elegy for Padraic O Conaire'.

F.R. Higgins Reassessed

*I*N A RECENT overpopulated anthology of Irish verse, the late F.R. Higgins was dismissed as a poet who grew up in the shadow of W.B. Yeats. Which, I suppose, he did, if time alone be taken into account, together with the effects of the mature talent on the immature in a country where talent of any kind was at a premium. It could as easily be said that Higgins based himself on Colum or Hyde or Synge, on *The Love Songs of Connacht* or *Amhráin Muighe Sheola*, but if a man is a real talent the time comes when he has absorbed all influences and stands forth for what he is in himself. Poetry, after all, is not something that can be grafted from one person to another.

What was born in both Higgins and the Maestro was a rich, almost sensual, pigmentation of sound and a marvellously pictorial line, the main portion of any poet's equipment.

This (they are one) is a gift. I think all big poets have it, simply because words were sound before they made sense. It doesn't follow that a poet who happens to have it is a big poet. There is also a man's range to be taken into account, the wealth of his mind and the play of his sensibility. And the answer to the 64-dollar question, the relationship of the poetry to the poet, to his life and person: why was it necessary?

This is a question not asked very often. An amateur psychologist like myself can use it as a play. I can make a shot at answering it in respect of poets whose lives have been reviewed; I can never answer it in respect of my own self. And if one is unable to do that, it is maybe a labour of dust to pose it at all. I did, once, to some small extent use it to measure Higgins. And regretted it almost immediately. The motivation only matters to the poet himself. What concerns us is the end product.

*

A SMALL SHEAF of poems that are close to song, that could, indeed, be put to music effectively. So much, you might say, for F.R. Higgins—nowadays.

Yet even when his first or second book was reviewed—by a poet-friend of his—the final summary was that the poems were the 'songs of a country boy'. I cannot vouch for this, I can only say that Higgins himself told me so. It seems a fair summation of them to me, and yet it falls very short of truth. There was a magic verbal sophistication. If Higgins had a fellow in his kind of folk-amplification, it was García Lorca. A García Lorca who had read Roy Campbell. Take that little poem 'To My Blackthorn Stick', the last four stanzas:

> Lonesome, like me, and song-bred on Mount Nephin,
> You, also, found, that in your might
> You broke in bloom before the time of leafing
> And shocked a world with light.

> But you grew shy-eyed through glowering twilights—
> Sharing the still of night's grey brew,
> Secret and shy, while things unseen were sighing
> Their grass tunes under you.

> Manured with earth's own sweat you stretched in
>   saplings;
> Seasoned, you cored your fruit with stone;
> Then stript in fight, your strength came out of wrestling
> All winds by nature blown.

> I took that strength; my axe blow was your trumpet,
> You rose from earth, god-cleaned and strong;
> And here, as in green days you were the perch,
> You're now the prop of song.

And in the same book, *The Gap of Brightness*, the poem following which he calls 'Captain Noah'. Very little Yeats in those, rather the opposite. Even the Synge stuff, the whiskey makers *et cetera*, has become acclimatised.

> He dropped the sail and so his keel
> Was floating in response,
> Until young grasses grew
> About the ark—
> Then out went every gangway and
> Bright earth was one carouse,
> Till hoof and claw grew heavy with the dark.
> 'Twas then old Noah slept in wine,
> Full naked on the hills;
> But who'd blame that brave captain
> For his jar,
> While we sit making whiskey where
> Night on each dark pool spills
> Beatitudes from every moon
> And star.

It can be seen from those two poems how concerned he was with cutting a certain kind of figure, the parish swash-buckler, the Gallivanter, the tough boy of the locality, really in a way one hangover of the Chestertonian 'man of action' or man-of-the-open-road kind of thing, exemplified to the point of caricature by Roy Campbell, bullfighter, sailor, diver, *et cetera*. While Campbell was capable bodily of all sorts of feats, Higgins, however, was of womanish build and when I knew him stones overweight, a real G.K.C. with a velvet-napped stetson and the amble of an elephant. Maybe, applying my one-man psychological test, it was a case of the thin man screaming to shoulder man's more athletic burdens. But while it gave tone to the first poem quoted and was necessary to the structure, the attitude only interferes with the Noah poem. The hard man is dragged in willy-nilly.

The same book finishes with a poem called 'Auction', which auction is that of an old Georgian residence (mythical):

> ... miles of green wealth
> An eel-run slipped from the river's tongue,

> A house of ghosts and that among
> Gardens where even the Spring is old ...
> *Going, going, gone.*
> Now I'll knock down to this fine throng
> The spacious park—once great and grand—
> That Higgins mortgaged for a song.

I bring in this poem—which should be in every Georgian anthology—because both the best and the bad of Higgins are in it. This book, his last, is dated 1940. In 'The Dark Breed', dated 1927, he started with an assertion—

> With those bawneen men I'm one,
> In the grey dusk-fall,
> Watching the Galway land
> Sink down in distress—
> With dark men, talking of grass,
> By a loose stone wall
> In murmurs drifting and drifting
> To loneliness.

Only thirteen years between them, 1927–40, yet the whole scope of the Psyche has altered, the dream has been amended to admit our poet to the decline-and-fall saga of the Irish gentry. I don't mean this spitefully, I quote it merely to show that here was a poet writing out of a wish to be somebody else, writing, that is, in the mode of a playwright. Or a song-maker, since most songs seem to cater for wish fulfilment. So we arrive at a point of real debate: is a poem to concern itself with the facts of a situation, as the basic limitations of the poem? Or does another kind of truth emerge from the inventing of the situation, and are they both one equal to the other?

I know Yeats can be cited here, 'Crazy Jane' and all that. My inclination, however, is for a poet to face up to something in his own character, as himself and nothing plus or different. The lyric is a skin dropped, or a bubble with one's breath in it, but personally I see a poem as autobiography, of one moment in which many strata meet, or rather a moment in which the person is at full stretch from all the depths in him, and for once an identity, all his pieces stirred.

*

IT WAS ROUND the early thirties Higgins did his best work. I've quoted some; I haven't mentioned a poem much prized of its time, 'Father And Son'. This is something one gets off by heart. It is quite beautiful, if one may use the term—they go together somehow. I confess, however, that I find the poet intruding on his own grief:

> And yet I am pleased that even my reckless ways
> Are living shades of his rich calms and passions—
> Witnesses for him and for those quiet namesakes
> With whom now he is one, under yew branches;
> Yes, one in a graven silence no bird breaks.

Every age, I suppose, has certain emotive art-needs which have to be almost physically satiated before they release their hold on us. Synge and Hyde made the West of Ireland romantic. The Christy Mahon of (the first two acts of) the *Playboy* did fulfil some need in Synge himself in so far as he was a sick man in search of the fountain of life, but he was also necessary to the social scenery of the period in a way that Yeats never was. Let us say he was a timid man's projection of violence, i.e. a violence that stopped very short of actuality, and even got himself mixed up about the facts of brutality. Readers, however, have a habit of injecting the half-made, or not fully realised characters, with their own submerged wishes. If any kind of silhouette is there, they'll fill it. So the West, poetically, became populated with Christies, a new type of Christy minstrel.

Not so new in a way. The folk image of almost all the eighteenth-century Gaelic poets, except O Rathaille, is that of the Bobby Burns sort, the Irish Bull, with a Moll in every second cabin and a reputation for drink and whoremongering that finally brought the priest of the parish after him with a whip. Bad boys, Gallivanters Higgins would call them. But those were the real thing. They died young, and as a myth image they live forever.

It is important psychologically. I think every young poet must have the 'freedom of his libido', like John Donne. *Elan vital* is a requirement of life, and of life GIVING. When Higgins began writing, the Irish State was a new beginning of an ancient Ireland, there was a joy in it that gave us all sorts of lovely absurdities like revivals of the Tailteann Games, a great racial renewal even though the Civil War had quenched most of our physical-force enthusiasm. It did seem necessary for us to speak as Irishmen. If there was an Irish Thing, it required an Irish speech, a dedication to Irish subjects, *et cetera*. And obviously a special cultivation of our Irish countryside. Higgins actually left Dublin to reside in Sligo, in some near-lakeside dwelling too, bemused by his own poetic enthusiasms. He was not long back when the Yeatsian hand went out in offering him a Cuala production. After this he was to become the great man's hinge in his public (Irish) relations. If Dublin gossip were true, the mantle of Pound descended upon him also. (R.M. Smyllie showed me a Yeats poem he was about to publish with alterations in Higgins' handwriting.)

I think the Cuala book is his most representative, as it did fit the time more than the later collection which embraced it and the times had changed. This latter came too late, when his mannerisms had become inflated. And there were many 'fill-up' lines in the verse. Of course these middle years are a poet's worst time; he must make major changes in his art to correspond with his changing psyche. It is an engaging speculation to guess how Higgins would have developed in the fall and winter of life. He had made no preparations for it mentally. His scholarship was nil. He regarded all learning with suspicion. Would the 'instant' poetry of his youth have failed him? The ego become too rigid? The vanity lose its humorous edge?

*

THE POET who carries on is usually one with a working speculation apparatus, Yeats, Pound, Lowell, all with their great Gazeboes that were really projections which went from meaning to meaning and gave them room to write and a reason. Higgins had just the one side to himself when he died. But with such a verbal gift, I always have a feeling he'd have found the larger self somehow. Otherwise the waste would have seemed away out of the economy of nature. I like to think he would.

As I say, he was born with a gift and there was no transplant or graft once he'd come into it. But there was always some odd swagger, and this was an attribute to the time. Gunfighter and guerrilla had inflated the manly image. Higgins was neither, but he couldn't escape anymore than O'Casey. Even Yeats felt the attraction of the man of action (soldier) when a patrol visited his house at Kiltartan.

What still gives me room to grieve, however, was the lack of growth in the very late Higgins. I have already quoted from 'Auction', the last considerable poem he made ... splendid in its one plane, with all the good and the limitations.

> Ah, what to you this genteel grass,
> This willowed, bronzed, umbrellaed lawn
> As calm as when Palm Sunday shone
> Through aisles of elm where Stella drove
> With Doctor Swift to Evensong,
> While crows in each black chapter strove,
> *Going, going, gone.*

Editor's note: This essay formed part of a series called 'Re-assessment' that appeared in *The Irish Times*, 1972–3.

James Stephens as Wonderchild

KINGS AND THE MOON
by James Stephens (Macmillan, London)

I N *Strict Joy*, Mr James Stephens' last book of verse, it was
not difficult to perceive that the poet was in search of an
art form in which he could clarify, with the minimum of
poetic gesture, an austere and reserved attitude towards the
mystery of Life. The energetic wisdom, which in his earlier
work overflowed into lively grotesquerie and borrowed vigorous and lovely shapes from local folklore, was more subdued
and more personal, and more dependent on the shifting fluids
of rhythm than on the touch and colour of shock imagery.
Kings and the Moon would appear to be his final word on
poetic form. It is the trimmed wick. It has the ritual and
ordered brightness of candles, and like a candle-flame, it turns
brave small fine fins everyway into the great flood of the sur-
round-ing darkness. A poem-like 'Paternoster' will give an
idea of the poet's notable condensation.

> Do never pray,
> But only say
> —'O Thou'
>
> And leave it so,
> For He will know

—Somehow—

That you fall
And that you call
On Him now.

The aphorism, like Love, is the very stuff of the Lyric. In the poetry of wisdom, however, there is no rhythm of ebb and flow; systole and diastole have already done their work and are become fossilised, jewelled, cold and depersonalised. This is the great difficulty Mr Stephens has set himself to overcome. It is a difficulty which he met, when younger, by inventing characters such as Tomás An Bhuile and thrusting gnomic wisdom upon them at a crossroads public house. His present method, while it is more concentrated and direct, has not the 'entertainment value', nor, I think, the traditional significance, of the former. He employs a short, quick-changing line, sudden rhyme, and an elusive stanza-form. He has standardised his symbols—the reader will find that the Moon, the Sun, Kings, Waters, processions royal and elemental, have a certain unvaried symbolic content—and he has borrowed from poetic usage of the sixteenth and seventeenth centuries the practice of making the adjective, in capitals, serve for the noun. He succeeds, however, where others less steeped in their Donne would achieve nebulously.

Beauty is Goodness, Wisdom, and is God:
Beauty's own self is He, beauty is His!
And who, born of a dream,
And dreamily remembering dream,
Shall dream to that which wakens?
Or by what a dream recall
The unimaginable Otherwise
—Goodness, Wisdom, God—
Which—such is Beauty!

When his symbols have a more definite mental area, when their meaning has been defined and enriched by previous poetry, he is most successful. Such is the Threnos in the poem 'For the Lion of Judah':

The Swan, the Dove, the Phoenix be
In no bosom, in no tree,
In no mild of memory.

Guard, nor guide no more, but slay!
Shepherd, Pastor, Teacher, lay
Staff, and crook, and book away! ...

Noble, Wise and Kind are gone:
Men no more need muse upon
The Dove, the Phoenix, and the Swan!

—*Dublin Magazine*, April–June 1939

James Stephens: A Selection

edited by Lloyd Frankenberg. Preface by Padraic Colum
(Macmillan, London)

*J*AMES STEPHENS was the wonderchild of what has come
to be called the Irish Literary Renaissance and is, indeed,
the only true offspring of any literary size that came out of
that unique union of Eastern and Western cultures. He was
also, in more ways than one, as much a mystery-child as that
other who was discovered in a reed basket in Aegypt's lands
contagious to the Nile, and although he claimed his birthday
to be the same as that of James Joyce, both the place of his
birth and the names of his parents, their names and condition,
remain as anonymous as if he had been delivered carriage paid
from some island in Tír na nÓg. And that's the way I like to
see him, his pedigree as seasonal as a mushroom, and himself
under it hammering the golden soles he was to use in his
extravagant travels, a young head on old shoulders, an extraordinary and vivacious talent and a multi-coloured storyteller
who was the first in his time to rediscover in himself that rich
grotesquerie which is to be found in the later Bardic stories of
the twelfth and thirteenth centuries.

In Stephens the grotesque is the apple of wisdom. It was
his literary equivalent, a gamin quality that strikes sincere attitudes of rebellion even as it laughs at its own wonders. We all
have that unconscious image of ourselves which is the unborn
twin, and Stephens is his own Mac Dhoul.

> I saw them all,
> I could have laughed out loud
> To see them at their capers;
> That serious, solemn-footed, weighty crowd
> Of angels, or say resurrected drapers—
> For I was there ...
> With two weeks' whisker blackening lug to lug,
> With tattered breeks and only half a shirt,
> Swollen fit to burst with laughter at the sight
> Of those dull angels drooping left and right
> Along the towering throne, each in a scare
> To hear His foot advance
> Huge from a cloud behind, all in a trance.

This is the poem, you will remember, where Mac Dhoul bursts through the winged drapers and squats, a very imp of irreverent laughter, on the Majestic throne itself, only to be cast headlong into space, reaching the earth through a scatter of old moons to stand

> As naked as a brick.
> I'll sing the Peeler and the Goat in half a tick.

I don't know if he realised that this image was his creative fountain, but when he worked outside of it he was sentimental and even dull. Nothing really clicked. Mr Colum places more emphasis on his 'naturalism', and in a very penetrating introduction devotes much time to an analysis of the first considerable prose-work, *The Charwoman's Daughter*, a book that bored me when I was young and still bores me. It was impossible for Stephens to create a realistic character. He merely tossed off a silhouette and put a mouthpiece to it, jobbing the lot off poet-fashion to street-sing his own sort of song. Even his physical descriptions of people belong to the interior vision; they are something heard and have only the visibility of music.

When he came to retell Irish mythic stories, however, this very quality—or rather lack of it, the lack of the photographic eye—became the brightest tool in his equipment. His people became visible, his kings were royal personages at once, his queens walked like queens, and when a captain swung into the scene his breastplate clanked authentically. And there was more to it than verisimilitude suddenly achieved. There was a feeling of rightness, as if his new protagonists fitted into the pieces he offered them, but also brought their own contributions of invention, majesty and fantasy, sheer fun and genial noble spirits. The exaggerations which in real life only diminished his people, and even blew their backgrounds into smoke, were in those re-creations of an older world exactly life-size. Stephens had discovered not an art of writing that fitted his people, but a people that fitted into his talent as if they had brought it to birth of themselves.

This is one kind of writing, and not perhaps as important now as when Stephens wrote. Those 'Myths remade' were mostly done after the foundation of the new Irish Free State. They were to have the same symbolic importance as the new Irish stamps, or a new Irish coinage, but unlike those they were unfortunately not state-financed and proved economically a publisher's failure. Stephens did little else afterwards. A book or two of verse, an odd short-story collection called *Etched in Moonlight*, in which the urchin-quality is brittle and almost abashed, the fantasy bone-bright and bitter. It is the other side of the Leprechaun where wisdom has ceased to sing and caper. It is usually folly to be too wise.

And that was the way with Stephens. When he wrote out of high seriousness the result, if not exactly banal, was never exquisite, never original. His language became some sort of ordinary patter, the party pieces that reach the duller anthology. As a verse-man he was confused and verbally uninspired. Nothing condensed, and nothing is truly notable. He was a proseman who became a poet in prose; and in prose it is the poet who has all the claims to fame.

It is doubtful if Stephens's talent would ever have flowered had he not found himself in the Æ *galère*. There, hidden away from the newspapers, the gods were living entities, Manannán, the Dagda, the demi-gods of legend, no longer fabulous but famous Existences on other planes of reality, sources of power and poetry and—above all—of serious discussion. I doubt if Stephens ever took this too seriously, but he did study The Secret Doctrine and he did listen to the Master, the great

Seer and speculator himself. Æ was so singleminded and so broad in his sweep that any young man became unworldly in his presence, and perhaps in his absence inspired. Nobody, however, could have anticipated the young unknown who was to turn gods into tinkers and tinkers into gods, and so naturally that many a youngster like myself actually believed that the miracle had been accomplished.

One function of poetry is to explore the myth. The reward is the discovery of the self, not the confused everyday fellow who is blown on by every wind of fashion but the fixed image whose traffic, like that of Narcissus, passes through him into the mirror that defines his lineaments. There is no difficulty in discerning when Stephens was true to himself in this way. The work has a joy and a natural gaiety of invention, it is witty and funny at once, and at the same time heroic in mood and gesture. In other words it is right for him and for us, and an art that delivers its burden so effortlessly and with so much grace comes so near genius that I think it is bad grace to deny genius to the writer, even though the times have twisted words to other and more earthly traffic.

Mr Lloyd Frankenberg's selection is not my own, but it is a fair enough rendering of the poet and prosewriter. He gives *The Charwoman's Daughter* in full, some stories from *Here Are Ladies*—gimmicky Stephens, some of *The Demi-Gods*, some of *Deirdre* and *In The Land of Youth*, also a story from *Etched in Moonlight*. The poems are decently chosen, each book being represented, so all in all there is more than value for the money.

And all in all the genuine James Stephens comes through with a flourish, that is, if you have in your library as additional to this selection a small book called *The Crock of Gold*. And by the way, the description of the Easter Week Insurrection is reprinted also—good enough, but it doesn't seem to earn its space where the other work is so imaginatively an enlargement of and not an impingement on reality.

—*The Irish Times*, August 4th, 1962

Sean O'Casey on Himself

AUTOBIOGRAPHIES VOLS I AND II
by Sean O'Casey (Macmillan, London)

*M*R SEAN O'CASEY, a strong-headed critic himself, must have more critics than any man alive. He is not a writer with whom one agrees whole-heartedly, for if he has a case he hammers it home on our nerves. No brisk clean statement, no simple skeletal gesture here; his is a narrow-eyed, opinionated survey and once he takes a stand on something, all the chips begin to fly. The main thing, however, is that the man emerges, a man in his time, and that the time happens to be about the most interesting epoch of Irish history and the nearest to us. For the latter reason alone those half-million words have more than a personal bearing.

Not that Mr O'Casey ever really gets outside the person. He is there all the time, a cantankerous, prickly, vaunting and raw-skinned talent, touching up his own portrait, and reducing to scale the people and events of the period. His may be one of the ways of truth, as fiction in its way may be imaginative truth—the literary truth as against the literal, in which it is the writer's resonance and the reverberations inside us that matters. This is the way of the artist. And we are concerned with an artist. How does he fare?

The early scenes, the family, the mother, the suppurating slums of North Dublin in which the child O'Casey suffered all the whips and scorpions of poverty, come through in all their ravage and waste and destruction. And as a boy in that over-worked and underpaid city he discovered the other acids of society, the social mess in which he was boiled raw so that he could learn his place in the pot. This is authentic stuff, man's inhumanity to man, and if it wasn't so much overlaid with later bias and so annoyingly coloured and dubbed for political and class consumption, one would have a single mind about it. This Dublin was indeed the very city of Tribulation, God in his Heaven and the masters on the second rung to do His bidding, with them a complaisant clergy, and under them the police force where every constable had a marshalling baton in his knapsack to make sure the rest of the universe, which was one gigantic and seething slum, worked inside the uneven tenor of their wages. O'Casey's memories of those times are exact and almost factual, but he fails to see that he suffered more from every little jack-in-office and from his own fellow-workers, than he did from the actual system itself. But the system did stink, and it corrupted the people inside it; it brutalised the worker, and retained old jungle values that gave to overseer and foreman the authority of the bully and the jackboot. The soul was reserved for Sunday. The man became the job and adopted its lineaments in order to stay alive the other six days of the week.

O'Casey was in and out of jobs, and eventually, after a long spell as a navvy, became almost unemployable through illness. The reasons could be more than physical. His heart was in nothing but the books he bought from the barrows on the quays, in the other life of the mind that was unveiling itself slowly. Against all the likelihood of his rearing, Protestant Jack became Sean the Gaelic speaker, even Sean the Hurler. He wore a kilt and piped, and eventually was pulled into the secret contemplations of the Irish Republican Army. What he found there mustn't have pleased him, for later on, when he was secretary to the committee of the Irish Citizen Army, he proposed a motion that the Countess Markiewicz discontinue her association with the Irish Volunteers, or be ejected from the Citizen Army. His motion was rejected, O'Casey asked to apologise. He refused and sent in his resignation.

*

THOSE WERE the efforts of a man to find a place for himself, and I think now that this was the most important period of O'Casey's life. Certainly it was the most colourful and we could have done with more intimate detail and a closer scrutiny of the personal scenery. I'd like to know exactly what his job was in the Citizen Army, in the way of duties I mean, what his relations were to Larkin, Connolly and the rest, how close he was to the inner councils and if he was aware of the coming insurrection. But he seems to have been out of it, if he were ever really inside, when it became clear that the Army had a real war on its hands, a stand-up battle in which the members could only become the victims. Those he does mention, except the ebullient Larkin, are chopped to size. Captain White—who mentions him nowadays?—had some colour-value at the time, but gets knocked down by the secretary's red tape. Constance Markiewicz is a jiggy figure with a gun who dashed into Liberty Hall now and then with a decorative apron and a photographer at her heels. She gets slammed for lack of interest in the arts. Yet she had her value, she caught the eye of the time and directed the beam on those very conditions O'Casey was fighting. She was more then the county visiting the slum. She offered her life to it, and only her sex saved her from facing the other side of the gun when the time came.

In his treatment of the personalities of this period, indeed, O'Casey seems to be evading the real issue. I can see that the national question had given way to the social problem, that he was not happy to see Connolly involving himself in the battle of the green and red, even though—to O'Casey himself—the reasons for this are not explicit. Where he queries him are on questions of tactics, and even with the benefits of hindsight he seems wrong to me. He takes Connolly to task for manoeu-vring his tiny army in the precincts of Dublin Castle, he is a bit shocked by this needling of John Bull and the impudence of it. Yet it involved a moral victory, David with his slingstone *et cetera*, something that had to be won since boldness was the only force that this little one-rifle army could deploy anyway. His arguments are militarily correct, of course. He was right,

right, right, if only the outcome didn't show how wrong he was. As it is, I don't see how any man as deeply involved as O'Casey was shouldn't have realised the desperation of this handful of his comrades and the dedication with which they made the last great gesture. This was his world rising up against the forces that had made it.

By that time he was away out on the periphery again, and suffered Easter Week like any other citizen not a member of the Army, close enough to see the larger stores looted, closer again when he was arrested in his own home on suspicion of sniping and lodged in a big grain store for the duration, hearing—as he had predicted though no one would listen, of course—the gunboat *Helga* throwing her shells at the Liberty Hall that had been the centre of his life up to this.

*

THIS WAS some kind of end, of course, even if it was the beginning of another kind of life. It marked anyway a transition of values, the end of O'Casey as a real activist, as a man seeking in action his own fulfilment, of finding himself in events and affairs. He turned now, really, to the life of the writer, the second thoughts in which the sedentary self can have its being and justification.

After this the plays speak for him—when he allows them, his mother walks again in the mask of Juno, the old cruelties gibber again under a new face of farce, and Easter Week takes its polemic from some sort of Shavian after-thought that polices the new man as closely as the DMP in their time policed the quays of Dublin. It seems odd that in *The Plough and the Stars*, a play in which all are types and the types at home with themselves, the representative of the Citizen Army should be a vainglorious coward, and just as odd that this untypical character should—as if revenging himself on his author—never come to life, remaining to the last a mere bit of woodwork. Yet the chances are that if O'Casey hadn't resigned when he did, he too would have been thrust by the very momentum of things into the cannon's mouth like Clitheroe, if only to justify his life and convictions up to that moment, and all the stone he had quarried gone to make an heroic statue. We can spare that, of course; Valhalla's loss is Ireland's gain.

The second part of his life has not been as eventful. I do not say, like most, that he left himself behind in Dublin. A man must live, that's truism number one; that he must express himself is another. O'Casey, the Marxist, could not have had an easy time in Dublin. And the later O'Casey, in the quiet of his study, is never a man to pull his punches. But is he really a man of the people? Does the public and the private face correspond? And do all those dithyrambic pronouncements reveal him, or does he cloak, even from himself, the person he is? I keep shadow-boxing with the shadows in those two volumes. And I am irritated with discrepancies. Perhaps I am at fault, perhaps he is. Why in some (higher) middle-class flat-block in London—where he denies that Chesterton could meet THE people (capital letters, please)—does he sharpen his nib on his neighbours? He needn't live with them, nor even try to alter the outlook of some old pensioned valet who was shaped in a different mode. And why, a first-class passenger on a transatlantic liner, does he make his way into the steerage—as a visitor, spouting platitudes, a sort of inverted vicar? Why also, in a world in which we all are more winned-against than winning, does he always manage to have the last word in every little tittle-battle? And why be superior if Yeats or Æ read Wild West stories? What does he want of a writer outside of the literature? And yet when he does find a man with a real fixation, an unrelaxing person like a certain labour leader, he comes out on the other side. There are two ways—and he has rights in both.

*

THIS SORT of rigidity annoys, it has the proselytising quality of the righteous. O'Casey, frankly, is a ferocious hater. His critics are knocked for merely being themselves, poets like Higgins and Clarke who asked of the theatre what O'Casey couldn't give, as Yeats asked it—denying any greatness to Ibsen, asking the impossible you could say since the stage talks another language anyway, something of signs and portents in which it can, within the limits of the barest scenario, swap emotions with the public. If O'Casey's later plays have not had the success of the earlier, it is not because he is any the less a dramatist, but because—like Higgins and Clarke and Yeats—he has moved into the world of words and no longer throws to the crowd the blood-red stuff on which it lives.

In one way, of course, any soldier is greater than the battle. O'Casey has been through it and come out again. But, even through a half-a-million words, I don't perceive him very clearly, or maybe I should say satisfactorily, and in the round. Perhaps if he had used the simple pronoun 'I', things would have been made easier. 'I' is the capital city of the underworld in which all things happen to us, but it is also the keeper of the conscience, and the hall of mirrors that show us to ourselves as we are. In a Jack-Johnny-Sean character, O'Casey becomes some sort of dramatic composite. One feels he projects rather than lines up and questions. Yet great autobiographies are a baring of the soul, which is why they are fewer than great novels or great plays. Their business is to expose character, not to create it, moving towards some vital understanding of themselves and their motivation, which finally is both the reason and justification of life and art.

If O'Casey hasn't done that, at least he gives us enough to go on with as we read between the lines.

—*The Irish Times*, August 12th, 1963

Editor's note: DMP stands for Dublin Metropolitan Police. Fallon regarded this force as little more than the tool of the Dublin employers and the Establishment.

Synge to Kinsella

J.M. SYNGE: COLLECTED WORKS edited by Robin
Skelton. POEMS VOL. I (Oxford University Press)

DOWNSTREAM by Thomas Kinsella (Dolmen Press, Dublin;
Oxford University Press)

ANOTHER SEPTEMBER by Thomas Kinsella. Ditto.

REVIEWING SYNGE and reading Kinsella at the same
time is as much a historical as an aesthetic experience.
For one thing, modern Ireland, with the advent of the
new State, shifted to another compass-bearing; freedom, sepa-
rateness was no longer the psychological goal. That had been
achieved in the political sphere at least, and the problem for
poets who grew up with the revolution was to make poetry
out of entirely new conditions, and this in turn required
another type of Irishman.

Poets, of course, are not made overnight, nor can they
make up a face out of a situation thrust on them suddenly
from the outside. Synge, Yeats, Æ, were all Empire-Irishmen,
insofar as they lived their formative years in an Ireland dominated by England; and taking Yeats as the representative
genius of this type of Irishman, it is easy to realise that as a
fully-fashioned world figure, with an established public outside the country and with a remote and speculative poetic
material in which the average of his countrymen could not
share, he had no real need of the new native community and
could go on without it to his end, naturally and without distortion. It was different with younger men. They had to invent
a new psychological correlative and make their poetry out of

the new conditions, out of a naked country that had started to shiver in its skin.

Poetry has ceased to be important to anyone except the poet. Poems, anyway, are made against the grain of a time, ground out of it as if made on a whetstone, but they come up from the community too and the community participates in them whether it likes it or not. There is a country in every statue, a civilisation in every work of art, and eventually the work belongs to the community where it was born, even though it rejected it at its birth. And the same goes for the poet, or for any other art-worker, as it went for Joyce or even Moore, men who belonged naturally to the larger community of letters and had honed their talents on the European stone. Ireland, the Ireland of their time, had made them. They never got away from it in spirit.

Of them all Synge was the most tightly tethered, confined to Ireland not only by his material but by idiom and expression. He brought dialect to the point of art-form, and without it, as witness some early poems in this book, he was a little less than nothing. He put on importance with the cloak.

The cloak, daily, is shedding feathers; and frankly at this date I begin to suspect that Synge was an invention of Yeats, a genius that never was. But this is my middle age speaking, and I know I am being unfair, at least as far as the *Playboy* is concerned. In this play he connected with some vitality in the cottages, an eighteenth-century presence that had lived on in a thousand ballads, a swaggering joust like 'An Mangaire Súgach' or Owen Ruadh O'Sullivan that released in his own sedentary, solitary person a sort of country Donnybrook in which the cudgel-like phrases had all the resonances of the old oak. He had discovered for himself the bold peasantry their gentry's pride, the old stage Irishman little altered, but this, mark, was never an imaginary figure even if the Lever-Lover silhouette was a hit.

No doubt the country partly needed it—probably as an escape from its boredom—as back-lanes in great cities live nowadays through some Teddyboy or minor gangster. The important thing about Synge is that he exalted virility in a literature that lacked it. Being what he was, of course, he hedged and whittled down, accommodation the comic spirit evading the doom, but he went as far as the time allowed him, and even further—as witness the riot that received his work. It would take another country generation to release politically what he had foreshadowed in letters. Then those mild feuders who had besieged the Abbey stage would stare aghast as barony after barony threw up those half-glimpsed guerrillas who were to bring the older drama to an end.

Was he a poet? Mr Skelton gives us every opportunity to answer this for ourselves, even to verses ground out of near-school days to which the poet himself had refused publication:

> 'Fair flower,' said I, 'thou all alone
> Thy days up here are spending.
> Now listening to the sad winds' moan.
> And now before them bending ...'

Compare this with the verse of the latest Irish poet of any quality, with Thomas Kinsella's tact with words.

> Down the church gravel where the bridal car
> Gleams at the gate among the waifs and strays
> And women of Milewater, formal wear
> And Fashion's joke hats wink in the breeze.
> Past, the hushed progress under sprays of broom
> And choirs of altar lilies, when all eyes
> Went brimming with her and the white-lipped groom
> Brought her to kneel beside him. Past, the sighs.

There is a world between those two quotations, of sensibility and art, but of talent too. Where Synge insisted on introducing the brutal into literature, on delivering himself in a batter of cudgels, Kinsella refines on the thing observed by imaginative verbs and double-edged adjectives. 'Brimming' has the double image of tears and mirror and is the sort of use that defines a talent. The reportage turns into poetry.

What of the stronger Synge, the mature writer? Synge obviously worked with great difficulty, and while facility may be a curse, a little of it is the blessing of the Gods and an authentic sign of inspiration. In almost every poem of Synge's, we feel the difficulty rather than the inspiration. He is seeking in the lyric a drama that mere verbal order and discipline are unable to give, whereas Kinsella, a true poet, finds the poet's order of drama in the very kick of the words. A lyric, oddly, is anything but an emotional gust, and it is certainly no immediate vehicle of desire. It rarely rises out of the immediate occasion, indeed, it takes its own time as its chronology was that of another heart than the poet's and its plasm definitely its own. In other words its business, if it has any at all, is to create emotion in the poet rather than express anything he is feeling at the moment, not vice versa as the professors of universities would have it. Take this thing of Synge's:

> Yet I lie alone with my depth of desire
> No daughter of men would I choose for my mate
> I have learned loving and lived to require
> A woman the Lord had not strength to create.

A large and ornate saying, a swagger and inflation, a stage inflection to hit off a rebellious speech. Examine it, however, as poetry, not for content. Ask how can anybody lie with a 'depth', for instance, or how does one learn 'loving'? Even the word 'require' seems wrong, because it is poetically inadequate. The whole stanza somehow falls apart as if built on some expediency of emotion. It's a letting-off of steam, the smoking rump of rhetoric, not the chilled wine that bubbles up when the cork comes off. Synge, of course, killed off some of those poems himself, or Yeats did in the first selection made for the Cuala Press, but I am glad in more ways than one for a chance to examine the poet afresh. It puts both the man and his time into perspective. A good book, indeed, dealing with the climatic changes of the last fifty years, the years between the sensibilities of Synge and Kinsella, is something that should be tackled without delay by some native intelligence. We've had enough of Yeats and Joyce. What we need is the shifting background, the pressures on the poetic psyche of the new Ireland, the poets in the presence of a new dilemma.

*

ELEVEN-CHILDED and happily-married Laura was Petrarch's pure paragon and Platonic love, yet he lived with a mistress while he wrote his virginal sonnets and begot two children outside the law. His poetry for all that is authentic, living on as poetry, not as history and ephemera. I bring him in because Synge found some affinity in him and yet jotted down whatever happened to himself emotionally as some wayward caress or body-blow from the divine Muse. What he was after really was some dramatic utterance that would enlarge the ego. Such as this often-quoted little playlet:

> I asked if I got sick and died, would you
> With my black funeral go walking, too,
> If you'd stand close to hear them talk or pray
> While I'm let down in that steep bank of clay,
> And, No, you said, for if you saw a crew
> Of living idiots pressing round that new
> Oak-coffin—they alive, I dead beneath
> That board—you'd rave and rend them with your teeth.

A comment this, savage and sweeping, that had learned its authenticity from the middle Yeats, but even in its very simplicity one feels that lack of a real poet's craftsmanship. There's a syntax muddled at source, and it's knocked together out of clichés, too. I can't see Kinsella, for instance, shoving in the additional 'That board' having already realised the image in the coffin. I can't see him either, or, indeed, any modern Irishman, writing verses like 'Seven dog-days we let pass / Naming Queens in Glenmacnass,' yet with pieces like 'Beg-Innish', 'The Passing of The Shee', and 'Danny', it has passed into Irish anthologies, marking the change in poetic sensibility between the Twilight poets and later poets such as Austin Clarke and F.R. Higgins. Synge, indeed, was the natural poet-father of F.R. Higgins, a fine lyricist at his best, a romantic who ushered in the new Irish State but whose capital city was in Connemara or Erris Head, out in the blue with Paul Henry. It is extraordinary now, looking back, to see how large a shadow Synge did cast over following generations, in conjunction, of course, with Kiltartan and the Abbey Yeats and the *Love Songs of Connacht*. And it is difficult to see that it marched hand-in-hand psychologically with the creation of the new Irish State—which required a new front, a new Establishment with father-figures in Senate and Dáil who would insure the homely virtues of field and fair, all to be thrown up quickly out of the very soil that had harboured rebels for several hundred years.

Higgins' verse, indeed, prolonged the Synge oration, emphasising the racial origins of the poet to distinguish him from English poets writing in English, and as far as he could make it, it had the strut and swagger of eighteenth-century peasant poets though what Gaelic he had came from Mrs Costello's *Amhráin Muighe Sheola*, a collection of folksongs from the neighbourhood of Tuam and Headford. Austin Clarke, too, was emphatic about the Irish difference, knitting his verse into Gaelic patterns, discovering in the Irish Catholic conscience a drama that required Gaelic modes of expression. Where Higgins was expansive Clarke was repressive, making a monk-like art more conscious of the fires and hails of Purgatory than of the sunlighted flesh it fended off. But the country, on the whole, was in the sort of psychic mess that needs no poetry. The poet was suspect as a person, he didn't conform, he rang his bell for a non-existent congregation since his pieties were those of his art and his allegiances elsewhere. What I would like to emphasise is that both Higgins and Clarke made a definite poetic effort to come to terms with the community, even limiting themselves to do so, and that it was the community itself that rejected them as poets, moving away as it did from the idealism of its beginnings into the modern maelstrom where Race is only another front for the Pound sterling.

Poets who followed moved with the State, keeping pace with a new audience. For poetic purposes London is the capital of Ireland, Kinsella more influenced by Auden than by the Irish sagas he translates. I find this natural and appropriate. A poet nowadays has only an audience of poets. He is not conscious anymore of writing for enlightened souls down in Ballydehob. He is unwilling to limit his sensibility to the togas of Merrion street. He uses language nowadays in a way that is no different from that of an English poet. And he makes the same sort of use of his material. In other words, his attitude and his approach are understood immediately. They correspond to a general corpus and have a common sensibility. They need not be 'translated' any more because the themes are everyday, the people ordinary and urban. In those attitudes Kinsella moves with assurance. The first poem, 'Downstream', is a lovely water-colour of a Zola-esque figure, a delicate use of blunt images as fertile as a farmyard. He is happiest in the thing seen, something he can dissolve and bring to birth again luminously in description. 'Cover Her Face', for instance, concerns itself with the obsequies of a girl and is ennobled in a casual way by a very discreet use of the new literary language:

> Her cracked sweet laugh. Such gossamers as hold—
> Friends, family—all fortuitous conjunction—
> Sever with bitter whispers; with untold
> Peace shrivel to their anchors in extinction.
> There, newly trembling, others grope for function.

As a successor to the first book *Another September*, it fulfils the promise in most ways. The Auden note has gone, something more native to the man remains, knotty, problematic, and often most lucid and illuminating. There is a person behind the poems, oddly discreet as if he held his hand, fearing the personal splash between himself and ordinary meanings. Yet the main poem, the name poem that titles the book, never seems to get anywhere special. Woods and water incommode, it lapses into mere description, the painter's function, it shrills up with such phrases as 'swanned into flight', 'arches worn by the sublime', it ceases to be more than a night jaunt on a river long before it ends, though certainly there are magnificences scattered throughout. It doesn't matter, the main thing being that the book as a whole is a sound job, in a modern idiom that should have no difficulties internationally.

But as I say there is room for the other book, one to span critically the fifty-odd years that lie between Synge and Kinsella. It is extraordinary to read Petrarch in Kiltartan nowadays. One wonders at the failure not alone in sensibility, but in art. It is like a war-piper trying a Chopin Nocturne, each translation tramping bare-kneed and with a tartan swirl out of the gilded room where a lyre sings a lady. It just shows you how a theory can work out in practice and that a great poet like Yeats could be as blind as another, even in his own art-world. Perhaps a good critical book would show the reason why.

—*The Irish Times*, October 20th, 1962

Ibsen and Synge

IBSEN: COLLECTED WORKS, VOLS II AND IV
(Oxford University Press)

THE PLAYS AND POEMS OF SYNGE
edited and with a preface by T.R. Henn (Methuen, London)

I SUPPOSE one of the differences between Ibsen and other dramatists—modern dramatists—is that between the professional and the inspired amateur. He weathered the stage in most capacities, he wrote and produced himself, he measured all kinds of audiences, and when he eventually emerged as a master he had that combination of basic and filtered understanding that becomes a sort of second sight. We are all impressed with his social and communal understanding, and by his 'group' psychology, his way of blasting fissures in the ground and moral fronts of provincial towns, and by his pre-Freudian feel for the occulting secretion in the Unconscious where guilt labours away to make its jewel out of sin. He was a social dramatist of great power, and to become such he had to use the world in which he lived, but the community framework he used was never so much concerned with the situation as with the people it embraced and destroyed and regenerated. He was a poet first and foremost and all the rest was framework, what Yeats might call the stilts.

It is almost amusing, at this date, to see how largely he was misunderstood by the England of Archer, and in suffragette times admired for all the wrong things. *A Doll's House* was one of the popular Abbey plays at one period; the frame was the thing and the Pankhurst argument, not the odd and overwhelming Ibsen woman whose passions anyway were uncontainable by anything less than death. This is the omnivorous creature who blew her head off in *Hedda Gabler* and who in one way or another assaults all the civilities from her first appearance in the dramatist's mind.

Beside this woman Goneril and her weird sister are lightweight makeshifts, their passions ordinary and of the flesh; they drift into crime, compelled by accidents of greed or power, they are made and coloured by the immediate situation in which they find themselves, and they are on top with almost unlimited planes of action. Ibsen's women, on the contrary, like the middleclass lady of his time, like women everywhere in our Western civilisation, were bound in straitjackets and attitudes too small for self-expression; the provinces had them in its grip, they carried all the sideboard silver on their rebellious backs. They were secondary citizens in their own households, who had only the eunuch techniques of the harem at their disposal. Yet all this does not explain them. They were unique in that they did not belong to the earth at all. They are just the romantic woman whose basic meal is the male.

We can see them more plainly nowadays when we have arrived at something approaching their degree of *Angst*. Their dissatisfaction really is one with the human skeleton which cannot contain them. Love seems the theme, love unrequited, love impossible, that burns them up beyond the sticking point, love that turns bitter beyond anguish so that it becomes another thing, another withering faculty that unlooses the demonic. Ibsen's woman is a devil who has unsexed herself, a sort of natural force that looks over all boundaries and fences for space enough to destroy itself and all its incumbent world. This is not of the order of nature, and it is almost out of the range of naturalistic drama—indeed, I really think it so and if it belongs anywhere it is to the poet's imagination alone, where woman is an idea that flays around her with electricity, the unappeasable goddess whose touch is both marriage and death.

This woman was early in Ibsen's plays, in Hjordis in the *Vikings of Helgeland*, for instance, in which a primitive community seems to give a natural state and a remote background where the imagination can tolerate her. But even there she is recognisable as Hedda Gabler, love-destroyed and destroying, too large for any mere skeleton of human bone. This is the real Ibsen, and this Volume II of the new collection of Ibsen is well worth the printing if only for this play alone. In it, I think, is the real genius of the poet. With *Love's Comedy* and *The Pretenders* it combines to make up the volume.

Emperor and Galilean has always seemed to me an unaccountable sideshow in the master's progression. He thought a lot of it himself, however, and he is there in individual scenes in a glib and jibing shorthand that shows his quality. Messrs McFarlane and Graham Orton, too, give alternate versions of various scenes that bring us inside the workshop, but this is not the play in which we ask for them where so many of the greater works could yield us better fruit. In any labour of love, however—and where else could labour be better applied?—the worker will cater to the beloved, and we are obliged to the scholarship that produces such a well-edited and splendidly translated monument to the first master of the modern stage.

*

SYNGE'S WORLD, after Ibsen's, seems like the last and diminished cadence of a great gale in an island chimney. He got very near to cottage life, and anybody who reads the Aran essays can see how close he was in observation and feeling. The play in which all of this discovers itself in a form simple and unadorned is *Riders to the Sea*, a play almost unstageable now because we have lost, in our self-consciousness, the dramatic and barbarous climax of the *caoine* on which he relied finally for his full effect.

Dr Henn, who edits this volume of Synge's collected plays and poems, writes a general introduction to the playwright which includes a section on the language of the plays and Synge's rhythmical speech, and then goes on to introduce each play separately with hints on the method of production. This is excellent, and both practical and scholarly. It is also a very fine summary of Synge.

His remarks on rhythm I find extremely interesting. Some years ago, in working it out for a broadcast, I discovered it had an iambic basis that wandered at will, and that this unacknowledged verse-structure made all the difficulties that early actors complained of before they came to Kiltartan terms with it. Synge owed nothing to Kiltartan, however, but much to the *Love Songs of Connacht*, and to play him with any kind of accent is to barbarise a work of art. In actual fact, these plays are as remote and conventional as ballet; a natural production destroys a dimension and ruins all those silent reaches that surround the statuesque with the simple properties of space. Turn *The Tinker's Wedding* into ballet-movement, for example, and you have a remoteness which brings real play into the play, the delightful impishness will come out lightly and without the immediate offensiveness which the first audience found in the *Playboy*. This was never a matter of local morals at all; the quarrel lay in the taste of the time and in the unimaginative production of what was really a *jeu d'esprit*. The play demands the secret dance and the hieratic gesture, and sometimes the broad wink of the music-hall. In a fumbling way, by incidental music and ballad, young and modern Ireland has understood this, but unfortunately at the same time misunderstood the size of the playwright and the distance he expected to exist between himself and an audience. As it is, in the one production I saw, Gilbert and Sullivan had taken over the wings and were standing in the footlights.

Somehow, in all those years, I have felt that nobody has really given Synge the sort of production he requires. His dialogue is what one might call a stylistic arrangement, he demands overtones and a lightness of exaggeration, you must feel the dance in the way that his lovely flickering irony is a dance and a release. It is, of course, another thing in *Deirdre*, where the weight of tragedy dragged at his syllables and life exists only one step from the grave.

By the way, Dr Henn, Edward Martyn was not a Mayo landowner but had his estate in Tullyra, Co. Galway, and Lady Gregory's famous Coole happens to be in Galway too. Indeed, if we include Yeats' affiliations with Sligo in the set-up, the Irish Revival may be said to have its origin west of the Shannon.

—*The Irish Times*, December 28th, 1963

Editor's note: The third last paragraph probably alludes to the Synge-based musical *The Heart's a Wonder*, highly successful in its day.

George Bernard Shaw's Dublin Roots

SHAW AND THE NINETEENTH-CENTURY THEATRE
by Martin Meisel (Oxford University Press)

S HAW HAS seemed to me always a simplification of a
man of genius. The energies are there, and the worldwide roll, and the vast social engagement, everything, or
almost everything, that matters. And all this directed by a vital
and vivifying intelligence, as sharp-sided as a diamond cutter.
Yet something lacks, something one hardly notices, something
one doesn't really care to notice if one falls for the shock-tactics
and the gay, deliberate sophistries. For myself I'd hate to ask
the last impertinent question: what is the difference between
Shaw and a man of genius?

Professor Meisel does not pose the question, but goes a
long way towards answering it, simply by sorting the plays
into their categories (Shaw did this) and then breaking down
construction and character till the basic association with the
prototype becomes apparent. Shaw was not original at any
stage of his career, at least in the making of something new.
His novelty was in using the old and the tried and in tricking
his prototype into new dimensions. His heroes were arguments
that wore masks.

He was steeped, of course, in the melodramas of the time.
Indeed, Dublin made him, not one hundred yards from O'Con-

nell Bridge, the Royal and the Queen's, the bravura acting that made him say later to a critic, 'you are right in saying that my plays require a special technique of acting and, in particular, great virtuosity in sudden transitions of mood that seem to the ordinary actor to be transitions from one "line" of character to another'. What is not very evident is that there was also an operatic basis to the casts of his plays, what Professor Meisel calls a musical-rhetorical notation. In a way, he wrote opera without music. There was undoubtedly in these old plays an unmistakeable coincidence of dramatic line and operatic voice. Indeed, 'since the operatic and dramatic stages shared stories and materials', Professor Meisel can stereotype the correspondence to make his conclusions overwhelming.

Not that Shaw ever made a mystery of his art. His writings and letters are strewn with explanations.

In selecting the cast no regard should be given to whether the actors understand the play or not ... but their ages and personalities should be suitable, and their voices should not be unlike. The four principals should be soprano, alto, tenor and bass. Vocal contrast is of the greatest importance ...

All through his long career, he seemed to act on those principles. And the great speeches are written to some unheard accompaniement, spaced for music, and as carefully compact of speech as any operatic quartet. This, I think, enabled him to carry off situations no other dramatist would dare. He relied on older patterns to carry him, adding his own liveliness and sense of timing. And at all this he was marvellous.

Why then do we hesitate to bestow on him the final accolade? Is it that the idea is not so important as the person, the reason less than the heart, the brilliant sophistry no substitute for feeling? Speculation is perhaps a private affair. And as stage argument, for all its trappings, is just one soapbox talking to another. The major part of the human being is not involved. We are in the presence of a remorseless commentator, a witty purveyor of the day's attitudes, a ballet of opinions standing on their heads, with all the accustomed scenery turning inside out.

As a work of reference this book is superb, as an analysis of Shaw it is even better. Nothing as well documented has come my way for a long time, but where the book really shines is in the recreation of the older stage, the stage of Boucicault and the Adelphi. It is Shaw plus the time plus the background, and a book for any Shavian shelf.

—*The Irish Times*, 1964

A Batch of Poets, Mostly Minor

POEMS OF KATHERINE TYNAN

POEMS OF SAMUEL FERGUSON

POEMS FROM THE IRISH BY DOUGLAS HYDE

POEMS OF JOSEPH CAMPBELL

THE 1916 POETS: P.H. PEARSE,
JOSEPH M. PLUNKETT, THOMAS MACDONAGH

THREE PLAYS BY PADRAIC COLUM

(all Alan Figgis Ltd, Dublin, for An Chomhairle Ealaíon)

*T*HE LESSER poets in any generation usually sink into the general broth of the time; and the older the time the lesser the individual taste or special bouquet. As far as posterity is concerned, indeed, they only last if the time is vintage, such as the Elizabethan or Jacobean. Nothing is so trivial as, for instance, a Victorian anthology, nothing so faded—and nothing so unnecessary. So if I say that all except a tiny percentage of Katherine Tynan's poems should be allowed to subsidise their own survival, and that they really aren't an Arts Council charity, I am not speaking as a rate-payer, but as a critic with a pain in his neck.

> The rain gropes with delicate pushing fingers
> At the dry lips of the small things, dying of pain,
> Gives of her best. 'Twas but a dream! She tarries
>   and lingers.
> The thirsty death is upon them. Hasten O Rain.

This is abomination in any language or period; to resuscitate it is not to do a national service. And this is not the worst by any means. The whole of the Tynan work is the particular cliché of her time, and not particularly honest cliché—since it was not a particularly honest time, nor Katherine Tynan a particularly honest writer. I could quote *ad lib.*, but move on instead to one of the few genuine writers we have, Samuel Ferguson. Yeats found him a bit dry, but used him both technically and psychologically, and indeed—when it came to a matter of choice—put him far and away ahead of the other Anglo–Irish poets. Take the opening of 'The Vengeance of the Welshmen of Tirawley':

> Scorna Bay, the Barrett's bailiff, lewd and lame,
> To lift the Lynott's taxes when he came,
> Rudely drew a young maid to him;
> Then the Lynotts rose and slew him,
> And in Tubber-na-Scorney threw him—
> Small your blame,
> Sons of Lynott!
> Sing the vengeance of the Welshmen of Tirawley.

The difference, indeed, is not depth but kind, a world of difference. Ferguson had a grand male sweep for one thing, but he had also an interest in Irish poetry and in Irish history, which served as a sieve to his sensibility. He was never very much caught up with the themes of his time. He had no success in what he called 'the great centres of criticism in England'—which do not allow for the local anyway, for the odd rhythms of native speech, or for the historical overtones. He is, accordingly, a poet in the second-best sense, meaning one who does not translate fully into the literacy of other communities, but who commands all the attention of his countrymen for other than lyrical reasons. I can see nobody translate as well from the Irish, for instance, or anybody find his poetic self the larger for the translation. Ferguson was no great original, but the effect he left after him was that of an original, an original with flavour and taste who was to lend to a young and infirm movement a backing of scholarship that was to serve in lieu of the usual literary tradition. Only Yeats knew that the Irish literary tradition had to be built up from the ground, Ferguson being most of the ground, and an indication of the rest. 'My business is', he stated, 'to do what I can in the formation of a characteristic school of letters for my own country.' He did that, I think.

*

DOUGLAS HYDE'S value is much the same. The literature left is not so valuable, or so varied; the enterprise not as monumental. Yet Hyde, in that sort of magical way of innovators, is more of an original intelligence, if one can allow the word to a life that reached out by instinct, seeking nothing but the simple pleasure of the unpossessed. Hyde, I think, was more happy to declaim than to declare, yet life thrust on him the continual affirmation of his nationality, of his Irishness, and in the end tailored him to a sort of deadwood Mick, a figurehead that had no meaning at all to the first ebullience of the homespun youth who went among the mowers for his songs. One cannot say definitely who really was responsible for what is called the Celtic Renaissance, but the folk mode was Hyde's, and all the Connacht lovesong idiom that went into the *Playboy* and later into the poems of F.R. Higgins. Hyde was a prodigal, and unstudied. His brush flashed and the paint flew. He threw off stuff on the instant that was almost perfect, so very nearly perfect, indeed, that it is only on occasion that one's critical faculty lodges a complaint—the first stanza usually being by far better than the last.

I feel all Galway in this little book, a western idiom, and to me it is timeless, as if the only school Hyde founded was a hedge school. Joseph Campbell on the other hand, a far more sophisticated poet, has dated, dying into his time, and it really isn't fair. Campbell could build a lyric into the effects of drama, he was a balladmaker with his homelier turns of phrase, a folk-singer one might say—by adoption, yet his world is always a world that has just passed by, the world we call the Good Old Days. I think he ached after a country simplicity. He and Colum could be twins, folksy and mannered, early twentieth century when very little good verse seems to have been written, when the social scene was already fragmentary. It is not Campbell's fault that he could set himself to write the poem of the type as in 'Irishry', where each poem is a sort of tiny prose essay on the various people who could be found in any country parish of the time. There is the Farmer, the Wood Gatherer, the Turfman, the Whelk Gatherer, the Labourer, *et cetera*. Those are works of consciousness, prose-schemed, rather than the haphazard gifts that come tumbling down the mountainside. The strange thing is how often they do come off, often with the help of a refrain:

> The cart is yoked before the door,
> And time will let us dance no more.
> Come, Fiddler, now and play for me
> 'FAREWELL TO BARN AND STACK AND TREE'.

What does come through is the climate of those early Irish Revival days, the period peace of a dedicated Ireland. I think that the time was one in which the poet's attitudes arranged themselves, when the poet became politician–historian–socialist, an amalgam of all that was good in the new revolution, but an amalgam that delayed the arrival of the real poet until it almost was too late. In his latter days, and perhaps only really in his old age, did Joseph Campbell attempt to get inside the stuff that truly concerned him.

*

THE EASTER WEEK poets are Pearse, J.M. Plunkett and Thomas MacDonagh. I think the order of names should be reversed, for MacDonagh seems to me to have more relevance than the others, and a more natural and direct speech. Pearse always seems to have a public oration in mind. Even when the subject is sensuous the mind is dry, the speech uncalled for, and the whole poet redeemed only by his death. As a craftsman, too, he lacked ear and grace:

> I have not garnered gold;
> The fame I found hath perished;

> In love I got but grief
> That withered my life.

Pearse, as a lyricist, never worked in the double-edged metaphor, or in the fine-grained word that had not been overlaid with romantic meanings. 'A Song for Mary Magdalene' is an instance. This clumsy Rossetti hangover could have significance as a psychological pointer, but never as verse. And 'Renunciation', a much-quoted poem, I find nauseous. All in all, the poetry was in his life, not in his words.

*

THREE PLAYS by Padraic Colum, introduced by a remarkable and condensed history of the early beginnings of the pre-Abbey Irish drama in which the author was one of the brightest and most particular stars. The plays I read long ago, in library editions—for they had been out of print even before my time, at least I think so. The odd thing is that the plays now appear to me as something-old-something-new, almost as if I hadn't read them at all. Anyway, enough has been said about them in all our literary histories for the past fifty years, so I pass them on without further comment. They gave the tone to a lot that came after them. Like every good thing their parasites have eaten the heart and meaning out of them. But as history they have as much validity as *The Playboy Of The Western World*.

All those books are subsidised by An Chomhairle Ealaíon, published by Allen Figgis and printed by Browne & Nolan to be sold at 10/6. I suppose I'd better put in a growl before some other busybody does, but I do think the paper used should have been better quality. Each page is shadowed by the print on the obverse side. Otherwise, the books are handy pocket-size—if you do use pockets for such literary purpose—and are pleasant to handle and to read.

—*The Irish Times*, November 24th, 1963

Graves and Pound

ROBERT GRAVES: COLLECTED POEMS 1965
(Cassell, London)

EZRA POUND: POET AS SCULPTOR by Donald Davie
(Routledge & Kegan Paul, London)

*T*O BE A poet in youth is, in Yeats' phrase, to sing in a marrowbone. It is a natural process, the pith becomes vocal of itself, and there are no problems except talent. Later on, as the prose body of life compacts, the difficulty of remaining a poet will begin, and the range of a talent show itself. In many poets it wilts. And in many more it dies. In some, like Yeats, it achieves a major resurrection, a miracle I think that owes itself to a body of 'poetic' material. In Yeats this, of course, was the mythic story of the soul, its transits and changes. In Robert Graves, more consciously, it is a belief in the mythic mother symbolised as Muse. It doesn't very much matter if either has a factual reality. Poetic belief is not a religion. It is only a sort of working hypothesis, a sort of *via sacra*.

So we have Graves as alive at seventy as at twenty. But unlike Yeats, unchanging. He writes still with the pressures of twenty-one. His love of poetry has the clamour of a youth; and is almost as uninvolved.

I used to have a theory, when I had theories, that a poet seeks emotion in verse rather than releases it. There is a feeling that one should feel, or must, and that otherwise there is nothing very much in this life anyway. A talent is mostly narcissistic, a compulsion to identify a passion with one's own lineaments, and I have never really believed that one gets rid of a load of emotion simply by writing it, or singing it. If we are in a feeling state, writing is the last thing one does about it. Simply to be alive is enough.

So I take most of Mr Graves' late love poems as a kind of jousting, as a challenge to the accumulating years, as a poetic foil to the wasting body. It is magnificent. It is gay as youth, and as sad in its disenchantments. It could only happen when there is a Muse-belief in woman, 'Eternal beauty wandering on its way', when a woman is just the flesh for the great shadow, Venus Anadyomene in transit. The poet has no daughters, only mistresses. And they in turn are simply the representatives of the Muse.

This is a very romantic view certainly, but it has at least the benefit of tradition and is in itself a relic of an older religion. It is also in the pattern of poetic experience. And it is almost amusing to note how the disillusioned poets of the thirties reflect it nowadays. No one, of course, except Mr Graves has allowed it to dominate their thinking, or their technique. Indeed, I feel that he has deliberately restricted himself in order to fit into it. He has accepted, in a time of technical experiment, a way of versemaking that is very nearly academical, he excludes about ten-tenths of what went into Eliot or Pound, he doesn't seem to confront a world, a modern world, in a total way. He has all the docility of a received religion.

The main thing is that a very large number of Mr Graves's poems are good work by any standard. Whether he is what is called a major poet is something else, something that only the very junior members of the fraternity can decide. Only they can tell us, in their own work, whether or not he has created a new climate for them. To myself it seems rather as if he were a magnificent summary of the old, a Georgian at large, wilful and skilful, and eternally young.

*

IT IS ANOTHER story with Ezra Pound. I know no more perceptive critic than Dr Davie, and this treatise—it reads like a series of separate essays or lectures—does justice to one of the most complex figures of our time, a poet who travelled in every direction but that of Mr Graves, and was probably the only one who could be good and bad at the same time. They did have a common starting point, love of tradition, but in Pound's case this meant recreating it in new form. When Dr Davie asserts that 'when Pound is writing at his best we seem to have perceptions succeeding one another at unusual speed at the same time as the syllables succeed one another unusually slowly,' we strike one of those basic facts that are the property of the great critic.

Nobody, of course, ran the gamut of the Isms like Pound, and still remained himself in all guises and disguises. And nobody tried as much, or learned as much. The main thing about him, as far as I am concerned, is that he tried to get everything into a poem. Even simple facts were miracles, the daily miracles of life.

This comes out especially in his translations, a word that doesn't suit him at all, for he was after something else, something not simple or literal, but a curious amalgam of poet, translator, time, place, and possible reader. Plus the Joker, plus the gamin. On this Dr Davie is very good, answering his own question—and the question of a lot of academics—as to why a poet should 'contrive the effect of translating carelessly when, in fact he is doing something else'. He is not after 'deliberate nobility' as Yeats said he was, but

If he is sure that there is more to his subject (more, perhaps, to any subject) than he got out of it, or ever could get out of it, if he believes that all the wine never can be got into the bowl or into any bowl, then, like Michelangelo, leaving some portion of the stone unworked in his sculptures, the poet will deliberately seek an effect of improvisation, of haste and rough edges. For only in this way can he be true to his sense of the inexhaustibility of the human and non-human nature he is working with, a sense that makes him feel not noble, but humble. And the same reason will make him use rhythms which seem, or are, uncontrollable, not to be measured ... in order to compass the unforeseen which inexhaustible nature necessarily and continually provides.

Writing a generation before Graves, Pound felt the full

European brunt of the loosening verseline and oddly seems younger now than his junior. It is, however, to another point that I would like to draw attention, a disconcerting judgement on a poet's place, *qua* poet, in society, which on reflection I must agree with entirely. Dr Davie is speaking of a remark made about Pound by William Carlos Williams, that 'he really lived the poet as few of us had the nerve to live that exalted reality in our time', and then goes on to add that the implications of this after 1939 diminished for all time the figure of the poet as a member of society. For, when Pound was released from the mental asylum in which he was detained as unfit to plead and received the Bollingen Prize for Poetry in 1949,

this was enormously to the credit of American society, but it did nothing to vindicate the exalted reality of living the poet's life ... it meant in effect that it recognised an absolute discontinuity between the life of the poet and the life of the man. Undoubtedly, at the present moment of history it is the most humane, and to that degree the most civilised arrangement possible. Still, the privilege that it extends to the artist is the privilege of the pariah ... To be on the safe side, society will treat him from the first as pathologically irresponsible in everything beyond mere connoisseurship and expertise in his craft'. For Giorgio Bocca's question to Pound is unanswerable. 'How is it you who merited fame as a seer did not see?'

Pound has made it impossible for any one any longer to exalt the poet into a seer. This is what Pound has done to the concept of the poetic vocation; and, challenged with it, all he can say is: 'I'll split his face with my fists.'

SO WE ARE back to Plato and the poet's exclusion from the ideal Republic. And perhaps to Seanchan's fast on the King's Threshold, which may diminish the poet, but not the poetry. Anybody taking pains, *et cetera*, can be a social figure.

—*The Irish Times*, 1965

Graves and the Muse: Oxford Addresses on Poetry

by Robert Graves (Cassell, London)

M R GRAVES, in a complimentary sense, might be called the most eminent Victorian of the nineteen-sixties. He has the magnificent dedication of the full-bodied man of genius, the inner certainty of major inspiration, and some talent for throwing over his time a gigantic if unrepresentative silhouette. And at all times he has the ability to command respect, this in person and in *persona*.

He is, of course, first and always a poet, a poet who has written novels as a task, as a historian's task, but even in those he was using a poetic divining rod as if it were just another tool in the scholar's equipment, for he is—among all the other things that he is—a classical scholar, not the kind who adorns a common room but an independent fieldman who uncovers his own Troy only as a springboard to further speculation. And his speculation is a joy. He can reason hugely upon a straw and deduce a Paradise from a mushroom. And of course he is a master of the synthesis, a great rationalising intelligence who oddly enough has made the myths once more a current shorthand—and this at a time when poetry had come to lack all inner resonance, when it had dwindled to a mouth or two and had no belief in anything, even in its own origin. Graves, I think, has asserted all its ancient dignities. Its rights are another thing.

So his appointment as Professor of Poetry at Oxford University was one of those delightful jolts against the common rub of his time that even the most reverend universities have to suffer now and then. It could also be an omen of things to come, of changes which are shifts of the psyche rather than merely transitory fashions. He comes, of course, like his own oaken hero, with a cudgel and is in no two minds about laying it about him. And it seems to me he challenges not only the literary opinions of our day, but the traditional concepts in which State and Church exist. In asserting the supremacy of the Muse and her immediate inspiration, and the validity of the ancient Poetic Theme, he topples most of the illustrious figures who propped our schooldays, but also—and here is the magnificent inconsequence of the lover-poet—the basic formulae in which we have at least our contemporary being. More than Virgil must hit the dust if the Poetic Theme takes social form. It will require a new kind of man, and certainly a new sort of woman.

That, however, refers to us, the conditioned Westerners. The poet's exaltation of the female is no new thing and is present in all genuine poems, poems that Mr Graves calls Muse poems. Those are composed at the back of the mind; an unaccountable product of a trance in which the emotions of love, fear, anger or grief are profoundly engaged, though at the same time profoundly disciplined; in which intuitive thought reigns supralogically, and personal rhythm subdues metre to its purpose. In such poems the presence of the Muse is felt immediately and almost sensibly, as if by some direct contact and is something like a supernatural experience. What he calls Apollonian poetry, on the contrary, 'is composed in the forepart of the mind ... always on a preconceived plan, and derived from a close knowledge of rhetoric, prosody, classical example, and contemporary fashion'. In other words, the reasons serve social ends rather than inner necessities. They are the masqueraders of the verse-form.

Oddly enough, there are as many bad poems made in the one order as in the other, and yet there is a difference that any poet will recognise.

IN HIS FIRST lecture Mr Graves affirms the difference, taking as his example of the dedicated poet, John Skelton, Poet Laureate in the fifteenth century, who in his old age called himself 'the British Catullus'. He doesn't seem to fill the bill completely, to me at any rate, and I rather suspect that Mr Graves chose him as much for his appealing eccentricity as for his excellent poetry. He was a gorgeous character, an unruly subordinate and an entirely whole man who at the same time wasn't entirely unaware of where his own interests lay. And indeed, for a man in orders his interests were more lay than clerical. So it's not exactly logical to exalt him above Donne, whom Mr Graves takes to task because

he used love-poems as a means of seduction. He persuaded himself, at times, of his love's absoluteness; yet when the flame had died down, declared that the spiritual identity of lovers was an illusion. His poems yield no portraits of individual women; their bright eyes always reflect his own passionate image.

Now all this seems to mean that a poet should affirm consciously the poetic logic of the Unconscious and no poetic logic of the conscious. But first, if he is a Reasoner like Donne, he must discover it; and after, seek in life or literature some confirmation of it before he can entrust to it, as mere intuition, all the main drives of his life. Donne was an honest sensualist and it seems to me he was never a dishonest poet. He was, after all, a piece of seventeenth-century time, more widely read than most, but the Ugarit Epic was not discovered until 1926, and it is unlikely that he could have formulated the Poetic Theme, as deduced by Mr Graves, even with such assistance as that could afford him. Indeed, I am positive he would have regarded it as offensive. The Goddess had to make her way through his sleep, but she was certainly present when many, or most, of his poems came to life.

The Poetic Theme itself derives from Middle East vegetation cults and

originally concerned a seasonal war between the spirit of growth and the demon of drought. It seems that at the barley harvest, when the blazing Palestinian sun had dried up all grass and herbs, Anatha, incarnate in a priestess-queen, annually ordered the crucifixion of her sacred consort as a means of placating the Demon of Drought; then took the executioner into her bed until the autumn rains should come—after which she destroyed him, chose another sacred king; in theory, the crucified man risen from the dead.

This is the basic pattern of the attitudes inherent in all Muse poems, submission to the woman as goddess, 'but only THE woman, the royal woman, an incarnation of the Goddess, gifted with her "Kra", who (he assures himself) is waiting somewhere to restore the lost mysteries of mankind'.

The theme is an old one. It is the basis of many stories— 'Diarmuid and Gráinne', 'Deirdre', to mention some Irish tales, deal with it explicitly; it is also, well-hidden under a cloak of farce, the theme of 'The Vision of Mac Conglinne'. Indeed, it seems to be definitely reflected in poetic psychology. Whether it may be translated into a social concept one day is another thing. Its last fling Westwards seems to have been among the Troubadours, and nobody seems to be quite certain how it worked even then in a most diluted and stylised form, though there is a marvellous story how the jealous Count of Castel–Rousillon murdered Guillem de Capestang, causing his own Countess to commit suicide by serving up for supper the uncooked heart of the poor love–singer.

In one sense, of course, all poets are barbarous, meaning when they are possessed, when they inhabit their own words and move through them in the order of some old rhythmic dance. This, usually, is a stumbling and fleeting experience, interspersed with shots of the real and unmixed wine, and it is understandable to feel within it some presence other than the mere self. Identifying this presence as that of the Muse Goddess is probably the most startling contribution to the poetic corpus since the twelfth century.

It brings, at least, some excitement to a world without Gods. It gives reasons for making poems, and for continuing to make them. So Robert Graves, well past sixty, flourishes like a youth, and writes just as immediately, always catching fire. It seems that in limiting himself to some definite conception of the Universe, as against the poet with no *idée fixe* or faith, he has found the autumnal reserve that masses the fruit on the bough. It is one of the values of tradition, but it is only the gift of the single-minded. And of an affirming soul.

*

THREE SHORT addresses to other groups at Oxford complete the book. One deals with a shoddy medal presented to him as gold by the National Poetry Society of America, this serving merely as a prop to a large disquisition on the use of gold. I suspect a merry piece of poet's waggery. Another explains the word 'Bakara', which he defines as a sort of aura of use that some personal and prized possessions assume in time like a special virtue. To illustrate this he mentions the *King James Bible* as against the *New English Bible* (what I call the Montgomery Version). The latter translation is 'carefully purged of all Bakara'. Though this has sold by the million, the verdict of the British countryside is: 'We don't like this book. The old one was holier.'

Once there was a tumbler who did his circus act in honour of the Virgin. It was an act of worship and dedication that wider meanings and greater perceptions could belong to this poet. He has simplified all the complexities of art into the simplest of glosses and he is about the only person in writing with whom I am entirely in sympathy.

—*The Irish Times*, May 17th, 1962

IV
General Book Reviews

EDITOR'S NOTE: Though he sometimes claimed to detest book-reviewing as a distracting, unrewarding and badly paid chore, Padraic Fallon nevertheless did a great deal of it over more than four decades. (In fact, after a prolonged non-reviewing spell, he was liable to ask various literary editors of his acquaintance for more books to send him.)

The selection that follows does not claim to be anything except a fairly representative cross-section of his regular reviewing output; it is not held together by any central thread or theme. Previous sections of this book have grouped together various lengthy essay–reviews dealing with a common topic or a chosen writer. The following one merely includes a number chosen almost at random from the files of the *Dublin Magazine* and *The Irish Times*. Short, casual or wholly outdated pieces have generally been ignored. However, allowing duly for the disparate nature of the subject matter, the range of interests and the intellectual grasp displayed speak for themselves.

A Half-Day's Ride

by Padraic Colum (Macmillan, London)

I HAVE been trying for some time to explain to myself why
Mr Colum's prosework, even that slight part of it which is
journalistic in origin, should have a certain rare air of distinction which seldom visits the more glittering essayists.
Reading him, I find I am not concerned with manner, with
words or their combinations or even—though he strikes out
many happy coins—with images; it is the attitude, the viewpoint that takes me, the eye that selects aspects and events
from, the life around him at the moment and traces their kin-
ship to what matters, to what is timeless to him. Here I assure
myself lies his charm; and thinking around it I remember
young poems that took flight among the old permanencies so
I turn to 'Wild Earth', and there with 'The Plougher', 'A
Drover', 'The Old Woman of the Roads', I find 'The Furrow
and the Hearth':

> Who will bring the red fire
> Unto a new hearth?
> Who will lay the wide stone
> On the waste of the earth?
>
> There's clay for the making
> Moist in the pit;
> There are horses to trample
> The rushes through it.

I speak unto him
Who in dead of the night
Sees the red streaks
In the ash deep and white;

While around him he hears
Men stir in their rest,
And the stir of the babe
That is close to the breast!

He shall arise,
He shall go forth alone,
Lay stone on the earth,
And bring fire to stone.

There, I conclude, is the bone that shapes his attitude. With it, as flesh with the bone, goes a great love of those small communities that are near to the soil, self-contained, with their own handiwork, their own stories, songs and music, their hereditary occupations, hereditary costumes. Their comfortable 'poverty' by shutting away multiplicity can endow familiar things with special intimacy. There is a crowded family life, with great comings and goings, and the child growing up—but let Mr Colum suggest his world:

Here sits a child watching a woman knitting. The flame on the hearth rises and sinks down; there are shadows on the walls; the clock ticks loudly; the cat drags her kittens about. A man comes in with a load of wood, and a friendly or quarrelsome discussion begins between him and the knitter. These are types that the child will remember, that he will discover in every literature. As he listens to them he learns about human history and human relationships. Rhymes, fables ... conjugations and declensions, become part of what he guesses at. He knows about the world as man first knew about it—as myth.

While he considers such communities, so related to some religious or metaphysical idea as to deepen and enhance the inner life, to be the nurses of civilisations, he sees them really, I think, as symbols of or perhaps in themselves the flowers of an ideal civilisation where a man—as he says in a fine appraisal of Robert Burns—finds a poem when his plough-share turns up a daisy's root or a mouse's nest. The tragic sense of life would not be absent there. Those who strive toe to toe with nature know it soon, and with the discovery dignity is lent to life. There is no hiding from death, no attempt at evading the realisation of it by externalising thought; it is accepted, final, as much a part of living as air and food. Life stripped thus is a finely personal thing, and Mr Colum may well ruminate on the strange madness of Mr Henry Ford, who would impose some mechanical system on its surface where the individual, drawn from his own depths, would become a cypher blowing around an artificial centre. Secure in his own centre, Mr Colum may range the world with profit.

The most elaborate essay in the book, 'Island Days', will be remembered by readers of the *Dublin Magazine* for its delicate evocations of the South Sea Islands. The part dealing with Hawaiian poetry is especially memorable as showing a stage in the evolution—or rather devolution—of poetry from magic. But the best thing in the book is the vignette of Hans Andersen. The subject is a particularly happy one, the boy Andersen growing in just such a life as our essayist would wish.

The people he came from had in those days a life of their own; they had their stories, songs and music, their hereditary occupations and costumes. Little towns were not then dependencies on the metropolis. Andersen was born in the little town of Odense. It is only twenty-two miles from Copenhagen, but Copenhagen in those days seemed to be in another country. There was a little theatre in the town where plays were produced in German; it was possible for a boy to grow up in Odense with a passion for and some knowledge of the theatre and the sort of poetry that belongs to the theatre, and at the same time to have his connection with a local and popular life that had its own distinctive literature, its own distinctive tradition.

It is among such phenomena he would have children grow, a contemporary pool in the stream of tradition that half remembering its own bright origin in primal fountains, spreads itself almost by instinct in ancient patterns. And he stresses so much the value to the young inner life of accumulated creations of folk imagination that, here, I would alter my earlier conclusion by fusing with it an element that derives from the folklorist in him. It is his absorption in, his knowledge of the ancient moulds and forms, his learned love, in fact, of those small antique blossoms that have renewed themselves into our time that gives him his fine poise, his especial quality of charm.

In *A Half-Day's Ride* we do not find the full colour of Mr Colum's mind; for that we must go to his verse. But we get the bird footing the nest's edge between flights carelessly and casually, as befits one to whom both elements are native, and are grateful for the opportunity of studying him. Although there is an apparent readiness for flight throughout the book, he can write lightly, sometimes almost frivolously. The eye is always alert and the fancy correspondingly atiptoe; a magpie in a cage outside a shop 'can whistle and say "hillo", but his accomplishment has made him socially difficult. He sits sulky and apart like a neglected altar in a public house.' Only a poet of his calibre, indeed, could stay so comfortably atiptoe.

—*Dublin Magazine*, July–September 1933

Taurine Province

by Roy Campbell (Desmond Harmsworth, London)

*I*N THIS ESSAY Mr Campbell does some violent butting
in defence of the ancient and heroic art of Tauromachy. It
is rather regrettable, I think, that he should think it worth
while to lower his head and kick up his heels at such windmills
as 'the kind of man who wears woollen underpants, carries
horrible little black umbrellas, is afraid of germs, and objects
to almost anything in life, especially to anything that surpasses
him in valour or skill.' The 'potbellied draper who has made a
fortune' and 'Lord Dash and Lady Blank, who can off and
wound fifty antelope which, escaping, die in agony a few days
after', as representing the Lowest Common Denominator of
'the most vulgar and degrading spirit which is active in modern life, that bastard of decadent Protestantism which expresses itself vicariously sometimes as Humanitarianism, as Socialism, as Fabianism, as Sportsmanship, or as Vegetarianism' are
scarcely worth butting.

It is equally unnecessary, too, I would suggest, in a book
of this kind to trample the china shop in search of the H.C.D.
They long ago have been cursed by Apollo and frozen in their
own abstractions, and in kindness it should be remembered
that the wine that was too strong for them filled bright phials
for Shelley and many another. Its workings, too, while generally a nuisance in so far as it makes John Citizen more
engrossed in his neighbour's moral welfare than in his own—

giving us censorships, vigilance societies and their like—has some fair deeds to its credit, such as child-welfare homes, hospitals, limitation of working hours, and is perhaps in its best aspects a necessity of industrial civilisation.

A curious corollary to Mr Campbell's hatred of abstractions is that he has come to see abstractions as individuals; Big Business is Mr Drage and Mr Pelman, the prophets of democracy have funny little bodies, ugly faces and miserable shuffling legs. And a strange corollary is that his own hatred by the natural perversion of many mirrors is itself turned to an abstraction. The result is that in this book—in which a man of equal talent with no obsession but love of his subject would have given us such uninterruptedly fine description, that we could catch as much of the beauty of it as would fall into words—there is a series of jumping starts, a continually digressing middle and an ending which, as containing the *raison d'être* of the book—the elaborate and civilised choreography of bullfighting—is far, far too hurried. And that is a pity, for the best defence of Tauromachy (if defence it needs) is to rediscover it, like some antique statue, against its native background. It is not unfair to it—it doesn't need a tourist's appreciation—but to the tourist, who in this case is the reader, that the images of a bright pagan civilisation it evokes should be made broken and jumpy by the emergence of a different and opposite series—strange bastards of Eastern metaphysic.

Had Mr Campbell kept his compass point to the south, he would have made a fine book about a fine subject. As it is there are such hints in it of such ancient myth, old airs of gold still lazing somewhere in our day, that the heart stirs sometimes as though on the brink of bright discovery. It is regrettable that he chooses such moments to set his phobias ballooning.

—*Dublin Magazine*, October–December 1933

Collected Poems, 1909–1935

by T.S. Eliot (Faber & Faber, London)

Selected Poems

With an Essay on her own Poetry, by Edith Sitwell
(Duckworth, London)

WHILE Mr Eliot may not be said to embody in himself any great movement in literature, he will be more interesting, I fancy, to the literary historian than the greater poets of our time. Poetry in him ceases to be local, and becomes not international but expatriate, a wanderer driven to evacuate the traditional household not by the assaults of a new age, but by the incessant siege laid on his spirit by the old. We have come to that point—all cultures reach it eventually—in which every natural attitude seems to be afflicted by an ancestry. 'Is there anything whereof it may be said, "See, this is new?" It hath been already of old time, which was before us.' The one new thing we may have is the viewpoint implicit in the point of time which we have reached.

It is Eliot's virtue to have found this contemporaneity and, for at least one decade between 1909–35, to have related it to the accumulated genius of the centuries by injecting his own music with such a serum of allusion that many times seem to live in the echoes. This, normally, might be classed as plagiarism, especially when he enriches his own imagery by visitations to the armouries of others. In Eliot it is something not at all wayward; it is directed and in full accordance with the

weary, ironic intellect which recognises all gambits as old gambits, but finds pleasure, newness of attitude, in shuffling them
about, making combinations of old poets and later counters of
thought, transposing all to the confused present and leaving it
there with a comment more tired than ironic. It is a poetry in
which other poets are used as currency; and, because Eliot has
fine technical mastery of his medium, the currency will be
admitted as legal enough.

From 'Prufrock' in 1917 to 'The Hollow Men' in 1925
we have, I think, the Eliot who speaks for his time in-so-far as
any one poet may speak for it. He is there the confused wanderer in wasting cities, the expatriate, Baedeker in hand, seeking a soul-refuge from the explored disharmonies of his own
age, very weary of the spiritual malaise that seems like Time
rotting ...

> I should have been a pair of ragged claws
> Scuttling across the floors of silent seas ...

He is the heir of dead cultures, the emptiness left when
the fire goes out of the heroic gesture and the arm fails.

> I grow old ... I grow old ...
> I shall wear the bottoms of my trousers rolled.

Because the spirit has known greater modes and multiples
of values, there is a devastating indeision which leaves action
out of the question; and a terrifying nostalgia ...

> We have lingered in the chambers of the sea
> By sea-girls wreathed with seaweed red and brown,
> Till human voices wake us, and we drown.

Webster's gloom, Laforgue's pillory, the Parisian sharp-
ness of Gautier helped to make his manner in 'Prufrock' that
of the mature man. I am not quite sure if *The Waste Land*
(1922) shows any advance in technical excellence. But, spiritually it marks, I think, his peak. The man meets life for one
whirling moment and yields to it 'the awful dating of a
moment's surrender' and afterwards admits that 'by this, and
this only, we have existed'. 'The Hollow Men', however, seems

to retract this. Mixed with despair in this poem are memories of supplicating litanies which develop afterwards in 'Ash Wednesday' and choruses from 'The Rock' into a very determined effort to praise God. The verse becomes saturated with a ritual quality. We become aware that there is no longer any great 'action' or struggle for harmony in the soul of the poet. He has found it, and—may I say it—become dull. Prufrock's voice was firm and definite as he slipped Hamlet-wise between the pros and cons for living: turned churchgoer, there are many times when his voice is little but a pious drone. Still, the time to sleep is when the battle is over; and for one decade, at least there was magnificent war in Mr Eliot's soul.

*

IT IS VERY easy to label Miss Sitwell's work as outmoded Baroque, as a fanciful façade, or just 'escape', and be entirely wrong. She is, I like to think, one of the most individual writers of this age, and certainly one of the most sensitive. Her genius is strangely aural and visual at the same time. Miss Sitwell has eyes for even the tiniest wordfall. She can prolong the reasonable and the sensuous meaning of a thing till the image, buoyed up by sound, makes a perfect thing in the consciousness.

> How shall I know you from the other long
> Anguishing grave-worms? I can but foretell
> The worm where once the kiss clung, and that
> Last less chasm-deep farewell.

The falling wave is here both sight and sound and meaning at once. The image is complete.

For a poet to be great it is not necessary that he should add anything new to the thought of his time. It is not even necessary that he point out to individuals of his type a way of adjusting themselves to their time. But it is necessary that he dramatise his personal conflict in characters that all of us can help from our experience to fill with the semblance of life; he lives in his hearers. Miss Sitwell has her own complete world and makes liaison with the common world of everyday more in music than in a shared experience of living. Like de la Mare, she builds in the folk-imagination.

The really extraordinary thing about Miss Sitwell is her varied music and her mastery of it. I have noted the combined sight-and-sound motive already; I would draw attention now to the architectural values implicit in it. Her longer poems are an achievement in form and would do credit to the Augustan age that has influenced her. I think especially of 'Gold Coast Customs'—a poem that I cannot quite fathom because of its privacy.

If Mr Eliot may be said to have spoken for the procession of the spirit through a certain period of time, Miss Sitwell may be said with equal truth to be the voice of a mode of mind necessary for all times. She is the momentary withdrawal, the state of grace in which the world may seem, after all, to have been created for purposes of beauty. The darker imagery and the taut music of 'Gold Coast Customs' show that she is no stranger to pain; and show, too, that she is alive to the rottenness of the practical ethic of the day. Her gift, however, to the world is that of a good fairy, a flickering wit and light feet to meet the young moon on equal terms.

—*Dublin Magazine*, January–March 1937

The Green Fool

by Patrick Kavanagh (Michael Joseph, London)

*I*NTIMATE CONTACT with any people is likely to persuade one that the theories of the anthropologists are a sort of inflated currency, and that there is an unfathomable difference between scientific and psychic content, and between the conventions that arrange life and life as it is actually lived. Mr Patrick Kavanagh, a young poet well known to contributors of the *Dublin Magazine*, tells of his life in a county of little hills somewhere between Carrickmacross and Dundalk, and the patterns of country life which he unfolds, while they may have little anthropological interest, have a human value which is measurable only in terms of actual living. His book is not fine literature, if one sights it through a literary lens, but out of it there drifts, literally, the sights and sounds of the Monaghan farmlands, and a people whose very bloodbeat seems to come out of the soil.

Mr Kavanagh, one of a large family, was born in Mucker, a townland in the vicinity of Carrickmacross. His father was a shoemaker, his mother a careful, wise woman who would impose on her poet son the bread-and-butter ideology of her farming blood. Farmers, however, are born, not made; and Mr Kavanagh, though he was unaware of his function for many years after leaving school, was born, definitely, a poet. Poetry is one way of adjusting the psychic scales in one's favour. In a community where values are hardheaded but not intellectual,

hearty but not of the heart, our poet was not the shining light
he would have been in a more urbane section of society; and
while he entered fully into the life of the neighbourhood—it
would have been impossible, indeed, to escape it—he was, even
to his own thinking, not exactly of his environment. It was just
that difference between himself and his neighbours which
enables him, now, to keep things at imaginative distance, and
to tell of them with an unprejudiced objectivity which is
humorous, likeable and charmingly lyrical.

Luckily, however, he had plenty of time to take part in the
life about him before he awakened to his poetic gift. The
scenes and the people he describes for us are part of an experience that does not suffer from any literary self-consciousness
whatsoever. They are the juice of life.

In Mucker, and the neighbouring townlands, there was
very little of the traditional lore which is supposed to be the
peculiar heritage of the Irish countryman. There were fragments, faint relics, retained doubtfully in degraded forms.
Even the Ladyday pilgrimage to the holy well was practised in
the face of mockery ...

The horse moved off. We were going on Pilgrimage ... 'Let's go the
Bohar Bhwee,' someone suggested. It was the pilgrim's road that
twisted by quiet fields away from the clever villages that laughed at
ancient holiness ... All the vicinity of the well was packed with pilgrims. Like the mediaeval pilgrims very probably; some were going
around on their bare knees making the stations, some others were
doing a bit of courting under the pilgrim cloak. There was a rowdy
element, too, pegging clods at the prayers and shouting. A few knots
of men were arguing politics. I overheard two fellows making a deal
about a horse ...

This decadence of folk-belief may mark the advent of a
new epoch in mystical history, in the mystical history of Ireland where religion has been positive so long because definite
places have been associated traditionally with natural miracle.
In the folk an older religion than Christianity is dying rapidly;
and it seems that the folk, who know many gods instinctively
through the forces of the earth, are both loath and not loath
to get themselves rid of the burthen. One wonders how they

will react to the more reasoned Catholicism of the future, and the Anglican Catholic incense of the Chester-Belloc following.

Mr Kavanagh, however, though he is entitled to the poet's dispensation, rules out religion as a topic. Actually his earliest poems are, in time, somewhere B.C. Ploughing a field, lazing on a hillside while his horses crop the headland, he is involved in that outbreathing of Deity which the ancients called Pan ...

> I find a star-lovely art
> In a dark sod;
> Joy that is timeless! O heart,
> That knows God.

Only in verse does he transcend his rural Ireland. In prose he is of the people, realistic and hardheaded, a man with two eyes in his head, and a faculty for fine generous, lively conversation. A delightful book.

—*Dublin Magazine*, October–December 1938

Old Galway. The History of a Norman Colony in Ireland

by M.D. O'Sullivan, M.A. (W. Heffer & Sons, Cambridge)

O NE OF the real values of history is the sense of world perspective it gives; and the fault of most, indeed of all, local histories is that this is lacking in them. A multitudinous minutiae of detail, all those entrancing casual footnotes to the everyday people of the past, seem to be the *raison d'être* of the local genre, but Professor O'Sullivan in this fine book has shown how the local eddy may be magnified, and at the same time pinpricked on the great living chart of the whole. In *Old Galway*, detail is not lacking; it is various, pro-longed, and carefully recorded; but, unlike Hardiman who saw Galway in its isolation on the western seaboard, Professor O'Sullivan sees events and happenings there as something that dovetailed daily into European life. We who see a world strat-egy in action to-day, can appreciate this, but the labour of the historian who translates it into terms of plain cause and effect must be tremendous, for history is not politics or economics or religions in their separate manifestations, or a façade of dom-inating personalities, but the movement of life itself as it is deflected and inflected by man. So if we are to have something that approaches to a complete picture, all human activities must come under the eye of the historian.

In this book we have, nominally, a picture of a unique

mediaeval city, but actually it is much more than that. The city was a Norman colony with a far and uncertain base in the English court at London, and with a constantly disturbed and often actively hostile hinterland at its back to which it was both trade-mouth and symbol of political domination. So the picture to be whole must be, too, a picture of Ireland as a whole and this picture again be expanded into the European Time of the epoch, in order that the forces which played upon the city, built it and finally killed it, may be shown in their true relationship. This task Professor O'Sullivan set herself to do, and she has done it with great credit to herself and honour to her university.

Galway, the city, was founded by a group of Norman gentlemen who settled there to carve up with the pen what the fighting knights before them had taken by the sword. Professor O'Sullivan seems to credit to their reputedly gentle blood the architectural beauty which the city later borrowed from Spain and La Rochelle, but architecture was the popular art of the period and an appreciation of the beauty of utility is the common attribute of all merchants who have a surplus of money in their pockets. Where their Norman genius made itself really apparent was in the organisation of the feudal life of the city and their manipulation of the proletariat within the walls and the hordes of strange countrymen without. On the latter their prosperity depended, yet they kept aloof from them, and rarely married among them, never even accepted them as clergy, for with the hammerhead independence of their race they got a local control over church appointments by Papal Bull so that their lawful archbishop, usually a man of Irish blood, had only nominal authority over them. In all they were almost as self-contained a mediaeval community as there was, with a charter from the King of England that exceeded in its independence even that of Drogheda, for to the kings of England who more often than not were preoccupied with large and continental enterprises, their independence represented a counterbalance to the independence of the unruly de Burgos.

In Professor O'Sullivan's hands, history that is narrow and local assumes an extraordinarily wide significance. One realises the impact of great happenings the more by studying the effects in miniature on a small city-state such as Galway. There, surely, Man made a royal attempt to cope with life, a narrow, concentrated, passionate effort that succeeded for a time because it was exclusive, an accurate expression of mediaeval Europe and a counterpoint in political economy of the scholastic. This is history as professors in Irish universities should write it. Let them do it soon, for, compared to most countries, the back-garden of our past is very poorly cultivated.

—*Dublin Magazine*, April–June 1943

As the Crow Flies

A Lyric Play for the Air by Austin Clarke
(The Bridge Press, Templeogue, Dublin,
Williams & Norgate, London)

THAT AUSTIN CLARKE should reach back to the seventh century for this play is no novelty in the history of art, though the almost unanimous trend of the later schools is to take the immediate present as being the only part of Time that matters, the present tense of a verb that has no past. This, of course, is a ridiculous limitation, for worlds that vanish historically seem to recur again and again in art as if through some law of psychic necessity. Whatever excites a poet to creation would seem to have modern significance because it has psychic significance, and very often this is the clearer and more defined for being removed from the immediate naturalism of everyday.

This new play in verse, an old folk story adapted to dramatic form, has all the 'murderous innocence' of Clarke's later work. Externally, it derives from that Celtic Romanesque vision of Ireland which he described not long ago in this magazine, a world, like a mediaeval map, peopled by voids and holy guesswork where the Gaelic imagination was moulding in itself, in the manner of a miracle play, the first striking elements of the new European learning. What was, however, a simple tale in the mouth of the annalist suffers in Clarke a seachange into something almost terrible—the more stark, I

think, because some of the naïve overlay of the folk tale is
retained with its grotesquerie and sly wild humour. It is not
until the climax comes with terrifying suddenness, and life is
stripped of all the pleasant romantic hazes that humanise it,
that we realise that this is a vision of the world, the old riddle
of the universe that is the beginning and the end of all thought.

In different ways, in different plays, he has touched on
this before, leaving himself uninvolved like a schoolmaster
who throws a problem at his pupils and never questions their
answers. In this play there is no miracle or no accident that
faith might name as miracle. The schoolmaster, for once, cor-
rects the answers. And the answer is bleaker than death itself.
The annals with apparent innocence hide an analogue as
deadly as ruthless intellect. We invent Gods for forefathers,
dress appetites in silk, and make our beds in prophetic heavens, but what is the reality? Listen to the Salmon of Assaroe,
that mythic figure who has lived many times and was once
known as Fintan, who

> saw a deluge
> Destroy in rage the ancient world
> And millions perish in the surge
> Hugeing above each mountain refuge.
> I could not keep by subterfuge
> My mortal shape. Yet I escaped
> Into another consciousness
> That did not know me. I lived on.
> Men called me blessed. In the west
> I prophesied to Partholan,
> Divined the arts but knew no rest.

Fintan, answering the Eagle, who in this play is a symbol
of happy-going unthinking man, is the intellect speaking within
its life experience.

> How can you guess,
> Poor bird, dressing your carrion meat
> With highflown feet, that every creature
> We know is eaten by disease
> Or violent blow! We are unseasoned,

Unsensed, unearthed, riddle-diddled
By what is hidden from the reason.
How can the forethought of defilement
Be reconciled with any faith
That teaches mortals to be mild?
A thousand years I waited, prayed
And all my fears were only answered
By agony of ignorance.
How must reality be named
If carnal being is so shamed?

The play, then, with its bird-masks and monks, lyrical as
birdmusic and as simple-seeming, with its Shannon setting and
green glimpses of the natural earth, and its astonishing and
magnificent speech, is the poet in all his trappings, but with
the poet now, in a definite equal partnership, goes that eternal
questioner, the questing, querying, unresting intellect, Clerk to
the Court of Reason, who will bring everything before his tri-
bunal and insist that a decision be given. The result of the partnership is a brilliant clarity of technique where every lyrical
impulse finds room. Fintan in his Salmon-form can declare the
unfinal end:

The very plague-pit in my breast
Widened with time. How can I find
In all the ages I have known
The dreadful thought that slowly brought
My consciousness beneath those waters
Where memory unrolls the mind
In chronicles of war, greed, slaughter—
Unchanging misery of mankind!

but while he is telling of time, the blackbird on the bough,
with all the egoism of a star performer, is, in very human fashion, dazzling itself with day-dream.

In little cells behind a cashel,
Patric, no handbell gives a glad sound.
But knowledge is found among the branches.
Listen! The song that shakes my feathers
Will thong the leather of your satchels.

This little play, though made for the air, should give some imaginative producer a job after his own heart, if he were able to gather the necessary verse-speakers. On the air, it was a triumph.

—*Dublin Magazine*, January–March 1944

Lucky Poet. A Self-Study in Literature and Political Ideas

by Hugh MacDiarmid (Christopher Murray Grieve)
(Methuen, London)

THIS IS NOT a book, but a personality. It begins with a frontispiece of a slender man in kilts, poised like a dancer or a lightweight boxer, but I think there was a rapier there too, a dazzling thing with a blue point, which the unimaginative camera failed to register. For this, Ladies and Gentlemen, is one of Scotland's Elect. Two hundred years ago he would have carried a sword among European courts, the bane of English espionage, and serenaded a queen with one side of his mouth while with the other side he cajoled from the King, her husband, an expedition strong enough to free his native Scotland. And had he succeeded, the Bonnie Prince, of a certainty, would have beheaded him later on. For he is that kind. He would have concerned himself with awkward things like reform, shorn the great nobles of their privileges, and insisted that the poor should share in all other things as well as in the privilege of dying for their country. And one fine day he would find himself climbing the high road to a hempen necktie, or die in some sham brawl with a dagger in his side. He is, I repeat, just that kind of man.

But now, when real adventuring is an intellectual and no longer a purely physical affair, when world ideas are the world's courts, he is still a Scot, but a Scot of that large tradition whose heritage is to be a citizen of the world; and those appreciations of himself, both as person and writer, which he sheds all over this book, can be regarded in the light of letters of introduction from his peers to his public. They crop up from all corners of the universe, but certainly the most exact and imaginative estimate of him is that of a fellow countryman who called himself Lewis Grassic Gibbon, a young writer who died young. This, or part of it, I quote because, coming from an intimate, I do not think it could be bettered:

He seems to have done, seen, and read everything. He launched the Scottish P.E.N. He launched the ship of Scottish Nationalism. Probably he invented the Celts, staged the rising of William Wallace, led a schiltroun at Falkirk, and wrote Dunbar's poetry for him. At the moment he is in the Faroe Islands; the Faroes will probably declare their Independence, cast off from Denmark, and elect him Archon for life.

Between whiles of reforming the world and chastising the English (by some slight accident he was missing from the battle of Flodden, and has been making up for it ever since) he writes, in collaboration with his 'distant cousin', Hugh MacDiarmid, the only poetry Scotland has produced in the last three hundred years, stuff unexpected and beautiful, mellow and keen. The 'Hymns to Lenin' are among the world's most magnificent hymns to the high verities of life. He has shown the Scottish speech capable of dealing, tremendously and vividly, with the utmost extremes of passion and pity. All good art is propaganda, and Grieve, ex officio or otherwise, is a splendid propagandist. Paradoxically, his weakness in prose is his delight in word manipulation. He might refer to an adversary as a negligible person; instead he refers to him as, say, a 'negligible, nefarious, knock-knee'd nonentity'. Like bringing up the tumbrils and guillotine to execute a rat.

And from this extract you may begin to realise what I meant when I said that this was not a book, but a personality. For myself, not having met him in the flesh, I am not quite certain that he is not all myth, even though he squares up at me from the frontispiece, pelts me with quotations, and invites me to read him as he would invite me to a bull-fight in which, as it happens, I am the bull, he the matador, dangling his subject and whisking it briskly away as I butt in for a good gore. No, I am not at all certain he is in the flesh, though he has all his flesh-alibis ready for inspection, of course. He can show that he was born in Langholm, in Dumfriesshire, on August 11th, 1894, of solid and pleasant parents, and that he used the magnificent library of that small burgh to great and enduring effect; but I have a fancy myself that he was born of a conspiracy and a round-table conference where Marx and Engels were a bit bored by Rabbie Burns, and where the Irish Representatives lost him to the Scottish Representatives, which was our loss but Grieve-MacDiarmid's gain. For certainly, had we won him, he would have spent very many years in English gaols, caused riots in the Dáil during the Treaty Debates, and ever since been a man on the run; that is, if he had not died in the Post Office, or ousted Pearse, and then he would be, as the other lonely unpensioned are, a pious memory—and a marble bust.

He is, as I have said, just that kind of man.

This very many-sidedness, however, which he glories in, has its drawbacks. In Ireland, we had our Pearse and Mac-Donagh, our Hyde, Yeats, Griffith and de Valera. It is outside one man's compass to roll those figures, like history, into one person. Outside of Scotland, Hugh MacDiarmid is known only for his poetry—the other things are local and incidental, what one might call 'character values', and for a poet of his quality it is surely a waste of time and valuable energy to concentrate upon the figure he cuts locally. The *petit bourgeoisie* are the same in all countries except Russia. MacDiarmid's poetry is a headline of what the real Scotland may produce in the future if, like Ireland, it remembers its ancient and separate culture. Such poetry calls for a single heart and no byeways. Unfortunately for MacDiarmid, he is a Pathfinder who must, of necessity, quarrel about a right-of-way, and with an empire of bourgeois space around him, he must stand on the top of his voice to get any kind of hearing. There are silences that can choke a poet. The danger is that continued protest may externalise a man and stay him psychically in a single gesture, so that what is real in him goes to feed that phantom—the figure one cuts in the eyes of the world. Hugh MacDiarmid, to put it plainly, is too much concerned with himself as a world figure.

And this latter is of real importance since it has touched his later poetry. He would take the whole world of knowledge as his work, and slap you with a sackful of 'facts' as solidly as any two-guinea textbook. The long extracts he quotes from recent work are fantasies of allusion, a marvellous display of downright scholarship or merely omnivorous reading, impressive certainly as a *tour de force* but—may I say it?—dull as poetry. Facts cannot be used for their own sake, or for the sake of showing the extent of one's reading. Poetry has its own structure, facts are important there as all accuracies are, but in the poetry they are so twisted and strained imaginatively as to become other than themselves. The trouble, and the art, is to use them in just that wise.

There are two books to follow this. I, for one, await them with the greatest impatience. And what a present they would make for some of our anti-Irish Revivalists, if one could find any of them sufficiently sensitive to real cultural values to be influenced enough to realise that real civilisation is the product of many local cultures flourishing and thriving within their separate race areas. The trouble is that most people are lazy and uneager to apply themselves for any length of time to anything that needs a stirring brain. In Ireland, with the road clear ahead, we are finding this, for after twenty years of something very like freedom, the old hoary Tory voice, telling the old hoary story of empire, is as loud and impatient as ever.

—*Dublin Magazine*, April–June 1944

The Hungry Grass

by Donagh MacDonagh (Faber & Faber, London)

DONAGH MACDONAGH, for a poet, has the clear and uncomplicated personality that makes for natural harmonies, so one expects from him a rich speech and a technique of elaboration like Synge. He depends for his effects on a body of accepted opinion that he can dazzle just because he shares it. In other words, he is the traditional lyricist, an intelligence that simplifies; not a temperament, like Eliot, that in the process of solving one problem must create a dozen others. This is a ruthless type of talent, an enlarged kind of common sense, it takes its material from the everyday and prefers to concern itself with the immediate façade rather than the psychic shadows that haunt the intellect. It is the sudden art of the impression, the leaping gesture and the comment. It is an art that has its losses and its gains. It is concrete and glad and sad and very definite, but it will not appease my sense of the mystery on the bestial floor.

I will not go to it for the stone faces of oracles, or for lamp and mask and sacred darkness.

On the other hand, however, I find it is a part of my daily mood and of the more untroubled side of my consciousness; and if I have a quarrel with it at all it is not that it isn't what it could not be, but that the poet, technically, is not aware of his own powers. For outside of his variations on traditional Gaelic themes, Mr MacDonagh has failed to take advantage of

A Poet's Journal and Other Writings 1934-1974

his own temperament. Instead of exaggerating the native element in himself, something after the fashion of Clarke or Higgins, he has strait-jacketed most of his stuff in the anonymous English manner of the middle thirties.

So, in large portions of this book, the matter pulls against the manner and there are major discrepancies between style and temperament. To Auden his catalogue, Spender his ponderous commonplace. Let me say immediately that my remarks apply to early stuff, all middle thirties, when Eliot was dominant in the house of Faber and the cust of the house was illuminated by a chorus of ascending *Poètes Manqués* who, in their celebrated habits of black and yellow, were ranked in every Dublin bookshop of the last decade. The elegy on Charlie Donnelly has all the bulbous plaster of the Faber idiom, but then it is dated 1937, and the poet since then has moved considerably towards his proper centre of gravity. Unimaginably different is the spare and powerful poem that opens the book, the title poem he calls 'The Hungry Grass'. I will quote two stanzas—with a purpose.

> Here in a year when poison from the air
> First withered in despair the growth of spring
> Some skull-faced wretch whom nettle could not save
> Crept on four bones to his last scattering.
>
> Crept, and the shrivelled heart which drove his thought
> Towards platters brought in hospitality
> Burst as the wizened eyes measured the miles
> Like dizzy walls forbidding him the city.

This gets to the point at once. But the last line does not belong to the milieu, and it seems to me that the poet has allowed his earlier manner to substitute for something more striking and appropriate.

The Irish pieces come headlong out of another world and are gesturing and unusual in a book with this imprint. One swallows them wholesale—in one gulp gulp like raw whiskey. In poetry, it is being drunk that matters first. The rest is criticism.

I do think the poet would have been better advised to have left most of his early stuff in the expensive anonymity of

256

his Cuala booklet. He has outgrown it. The later work is so curt and so free of clique-markings that it just mocks the lumbering and somewhat pretentious lines that a young poet wrote before he found himself. He was unluckier than most Irish poets of the past half-century, for the centre seems to have fallen out of Dublin literary life just about the time he started writing—which is a curious anomaly when one considers the quality of the poets who lived there. Perhaps Yeats, as remote in Rathfarnham as the old man of the Sidhe, should have done more than read an odd Abbey play. Hasn't Eliot said something about the poet carrying on the struggle for the maintenance of a living language and its strength and subtlety and quality of feeling? I feel he must do more than that, or at least do some of it by word of mouth.

It is the local that matters in the long run; and while I have ceased to give a damn for folk-ways that exist no longer, I consider an Irish poet is an idiot if he doesn't have some equivalents to English as she is spoken in Ireland. MacDonagh is well into the process of doing this, perhaps because of his work on street-ballads and folksong, and I expect his next book will something closer to his personality. This, for all its early faults, has a lot one can delight in.

—*Dublin Magazine*, January–March 1947

The Life of the Virgin Mary

by Rainer Maria Rilke, translated by Stephen Spender
(Vision Press, London)

*T*HIS CYCLE of poems, with the exception of two, was written by Rilke in January, 1912, but, Stephen Spender tells us in his introduction, they had been contemplated as far back as 1900 when Rilke had been shown some sketches for religious paintings by the artist Heinrich Vogeler, which gave him the idea of doing a book on the Virgin, with Vogeler to do the illustrations. When Vogeler reminded him of this in 1912, the poems would seem to have composed themselves in his subconscious and to be ready and waiting, for the 'little work' as he says himself, 'was presented to him'.

The poems are not very important and are the creatures of a manner rather than of a man. The first poem, for instance, would be striking if we did not remember similar phrases in which the car is put before the horse to obtain an effect of verbal wisdom. Let me quote the opening stanza:

O, what it must have cost the angels then not to
suddenly break out singing, as though into tears,
because they knew: to-night the mother is about to
be born to the boy, the One now soon to appear.

The momentary effect of this is successful. But after a moment or two we realise it is the success of the habitual wit, the slickness of the inverted cliché, and instead of accepting the poem we start looking the gift horse in the mouth. Rilke has made a style out of sensibility; equally he has made a sensibility out of a style, and where the two don't fall pat, as in a very great deal of his work, the effect is that of posturing and insincerity, of a man who has to work up a passion by simulating it. I think his own fluency fitted too well his private image of himself as a man of extremely delicate feelings. But was he? Psychologically, I don't believe he was more of a mess than another poet, but where another poet attempts to find himself through his poems, Rilke evades analysis by throwing himself into the air from every quivering tendril. How much of this delicate agony is invention?

'The Life of the Virgin Mary' is not an answer, but an indication. He dwells on the steps of his approach, enlarges the externals of art, but the temple is never exactly where he points; he is more concerned with the wording of his prophecy than with the truth of it. And yet what a wording! Mr Spender is most moved by the simpler poems, but Rilke is never very good when he is simple; it is only through elaboration that he reaches a simplifying image, and it is through the image he becomes a poet. It is a triumph of art over artificiality.

I do not believe in Rilke as a poet of feeling. He has too many defences in depth. His quiverings are the quiverings of the nerves. But when he builds his pyre carefully, however, when he lays stick by stick, something escapes when the match is struck, something that seeks the air like eagle or dove. Take that elaborate poem, 'The Presentation of Mary in the Temple'. Here the Temple is created like a vast ceremonial, columns, galleries, crescents, towers appear within you, and then—

> She, though, approached and raised
> Her eyes to take in all this scene.
> (A child she was, a small girl among women.)
> Self-confidently then, she stepped serene
> Up to the pampered pomp which stood aside;
> So much had all men built already been
> Outweighed by the praise

Within her heart. And by her longing
To give herself up to the inner signs.
Her parents thought that she was being taken
By the jewel-breasted one, the overwhelming,
To whom they reached her. Yet she went through all
And forth from every hand, small as she was
And into her fate, higher than the hall,
Prepared already, and higher than the house.

This is Rilke's achievement, an achievement that is not feeling but a description of the processes of feeling. I do not find it in poems praised by Mr Spender, such as 'Before the Passion', where the grief seems to me a literary grief. Simple sorrow, indeed, was quite outside Rilke's imagining.

The German text is given along with Mr Spender's translation, and no one can quarrel with the translator. He has done his part very well.

—*Dublin Magazine*, April–June 1952

The Man Who Was Shakespeare

by Calvin Hoffman (Max Parrish, London)

ON MAY 20th, 1593, Christopher Marlowe was arraigned before the Queen's Council on charges of atheism. Some day between that and May 30th, he was in the country house of Thomas Walsingham, and in Deptford on May 30th, where in a house of public resort he met his death at the hands of one Ingram Frizer, who according to the evidence given at the coroner's inquest on June 1st (which cleared him), stabbed the playwright in self-defence.

Mr Hoffman's thesis is that the man thus stabbed was not Marlowe, but some person unknown who had been lured there and killed, identified and buried as Marlowe by Marlowe's friends, so that the playwright, in serious trouble for his opinions, could escape to the Continent and assume another and safer identity. To bolster his argument, he proves that the man who struck the fatal blow was a creature of Thomas Walsingham, that the man named Nicholas Skeres was a rascal of the same service, and the third, Robert Paley, a person employed constantly and questionably in businesses of a higher order by the same Walsingham. Paley, indeed, was a business front for Walsingham and his lady in many deals and it has been proved that he had just returned from one of these on the day he went to Deptford.

All this is in evidence, and factually correct. The information offered at the preliminary hearing of Marlowe's trial is available also. It was proffered by the police spy Richard Baines and contains this interesting paragraph:

He saith likewise that he hath quoted a number of contrarieties out of the Scriptures which he hath given to some great men who in convenient time shall be named. When these things shall be called in question, the witnesses shall be produced.

Now let us see what Mr Hoffman makes of all this.

Walsingham, he avers, was a patron of Marlowe's and a protector. The friendship between them was of a homosexual nature. They were lovers. Walsingham deliberately arranged the killing of a stranger on May 30th, suborned the Queen's coroner, supplying his own bravos to do the killing and to identify the body as Marlowe's. In other words, a very shrewd and unscrupulous businessman, a married man too, was to put his head in a noose and his reputation into the hands of three scoundrels who could inform on him at any time. And for what—for love, even if it were homosexual love, of his fellow-man?

He could have loved and admired the genius of Marlowe to distraction, certainly. But on the evidence, the connection between them was that Marlowe at some time did some secret service work and that this Walsingham was his contact with the Queen's Council. There is nothing whatsoever to show that Walsingham had the smallest interest in the arts. He seems to have been purely a most mercenary man, an Elizabethan gangster, even to the hired cut-throats he employed. If he regarded Marlowe at all, it was only as one of the Frizers and Skeres and Paleys whom he used in his own way.

So, as his ways were those of darkness, it would not have been to his profit or reputation if Marlowe had been questioned thoroughly on his life and associations before the Queen's Council. He could have received a tip to that effect. It seems he had much profit from information received through some member or members of the same council.

This being known to us, let us read the characters into the situation. This indicates that Walsingham had Marlowe murdered to shut him up. The presence of Robert Paley, weary as he must have been after his return from The Netherlands, shows that he considered it of urgent importance.

Another point. Had Marlowe escaped to Europe, his presence there could not have been hidden from the British Secret Service. It can be seen from those records how thoroughly wide-spread was this secret web and how closely the actions of British travellers were regarded. So, though Marlowe seems to have had enough talent to have written the later Shakespeare—*Edward the Second* for instance is more fluent than the historical opus of the Master—it seems on the face of it that he had no opportunity to do so.

I would like to think that he did live on into Lear and Othello and Hamlet and Antony, and that this Shakespeare mystery had been solved finally. For certainly there is a mystery. And so many mysterious hints that point to it. There is the 1616 quarto of *Faustus*, for instance, so wonderfully amended from that of 1604 as to be almost a new play in its maturity. Who altered it for the printing? Who invented the new Papal scenes and introduced Benvolio, Martino, and Frederick? And into scenes that have all the art of Shakespeare. And a new sense of Europe.

The puzzle must go on. And this book may be only another tale of Hoffman. But if life were just sensational literature, I confess I could fall easily for the Marlowe–Shakespeare figure. The talents are on the one large level. And Marlowe, after all, was the great initiator.

—*Dublin Magazine*, April–June 1956

The Little Monasteries

Poems translated from the Irish by Frank O'Connor
(Dolmen Press, Dublin)

TRANSLATION is one thing, the bare literal bone, the skeleton meaning; a metrical translation is another thing entirely and must be one of the most difficult tasks a poet can set himself. He can approach it in different ways. He can imitate the stylistic devices, the word patterns, the sounds and syllables and involve himself completely in the metrical structure, or he may take the gist and prose-meaning of the poem and make of it an original poem of his own.

The first is always unsatisfactory. The genius of one language does not transfer to another. The metrical gears of each do not mesh easily. The syllabic and the stress will not compound, and all sorts of padding devices are pressed into use. Most metrical translations from the Latin and Greek flop into this category. They remain academic excrescences.

Mr O'Connor adopts the other mode, shelves the ornament and shells the meaning, keeping—I think—to the main stanzaic structure only in regard to the number of lines in each. He is thus free to make his own poem on a given theme, and it is on those terms he must be judged.

I'd be dishonest if I said I liked them. Here's one, 'Advice To Lovers'.

The way to get on with a girl
Is to drift like a man in a mist,
Happy enough to be caught,
Happy to be dismissed.

Glad to be out of her way,
Glad to rejoin her in bed,
Equally grieved or gay
To learn that she's living or dead.

It's not the trite thought here that hurts, or the girl's-album handling, but the blatant rhythm and the vulgar monotony. There's a juke-box in the house.

To stop here, however, would not be fair to the author, who in other fields is a master. He can pull out a good phrase and wring things for the drama in them. He can make his point, and generally he does. But the verse all the time is on the boiling point of declamation. Those are verses to read with resounding thumps. The internal disciplines of the poet, the wavering needles that tempt the North, are simply not there. Mr O'Connor supplies the drama at the expense of the poetic body.

The first poem loses least:

Fall is no man's travelling time
Tasks are heavy, husbandmen
Heed the low light, lingering less.
Lightly their young from the deer ...

Here there is some attempt at an equivalent pattern, some matching of the original poem but it is not in the word-form of 1963. It seems somehow to summarise a century of translators. It doesn't ring from a new man. The workman shows through it and all the other workmen who went before him.

Maybe I'm hard. But I think of Pound and Propertius, and how the one swotted out of the other a marvellous and modern poem. I suppose the difference is that Pound is a poet.
—*The Irish Times*, June 1st, 1963

Plays by Jean Giraudoux, Vol. I

THE TIGER AT THE GATES, JUDITH, DUEL OF ANGELS
Translated by Christopher Fry (Methuen, London)

Plays by Eugene Ionesco, Vol. V

EXIT THE KING, THE MOTOR SHOW, FOURSOME
(Calder, Edinburgh)

MOYTURA by Padraic Colum (Dolmen Press, Dublin)

*T*HE NATURALISTIC play seems to have died on some-body's hands. What with Ionesco's discovery of the ceremony of Innocence, Genet's harping to its anarchy and the Old Guard, including Monsieur Jean Giraudoux, still emphasising its original sin, not to speak of the monolithic Brecht who bestrides it like a rather lopsided colossus, the stage to-day has become as varied and shameless as a southern seaport, not so much a clash of cultures, but like a multiple store offering its items dispassionately and without favour.

This, of course, throws open new doors into old themes: Realism, Naturalism, as modes, have yielded whatever they had to give long ago. They had limited the stage, too. Even its physical size, I think, was diminished to cope with urban subjects. A back wall cut off from the world, and the wings where movement generates turned static, and it seems to me that all this compression and boxwork reduced the people, reduced them in all ways, because it demanded only certain themes and a very narrow and specialised treatment to cover them.

266

Giraudoux escapes from the box by making his people some magic inches larger than life. God-in-the-machine too is taken for granted; you can have all Olympus as backdrop if necessary and not be self-conscious about it, and brightness falling from the air. A scene in *Judith*, for instance, sees a drunken guard turn into a god—or angel—for as long as it is necessary to solve the knotted plot. I am all for that. It flatters us spatially, like a fairy-tale or a heroic story, but it is also a trick of technique which is part of the gesture of a theme in which man is always larger than his physical body. Giraudoux takes it for granted that the emotions are literate and that the passions have received the gift of tongues, so his stage spreads to accommodate a dialogue which is possible only on the highest levels. He is not so much concerned with appearances as with the thing that sustains them, and he is not concerned with man at all, but with the idea of man.

This literacy is always exciting. There is a wholeness about it that does not take stupidity as the norm. Thought, indeed, has as much place as feeling or emotion, is actually emotion too and as portion of a dramatic situation can add another dimension. No-one, of course, will believe that Judith's collision with Holofernes could ever have happened in precisely those terms, but what does happen is much more important and, as far as I can see, is dramatic enough. The theatre, however, is the test, and here *Judith* had some measure of success. So, too, had *The Tiger at the Gates* and *Duel of Angels*, each—as all—with the Giraudoux cachet of flavoured argument while some cardboard Rome went up in flames.

*

EUGENE IONESCO has made a ritual of the Absurd. *Exit the King, The Motor Show*, and *Foursome* are no exceptions. The king could be anybody, a royalty, a person, or just the principle of life. He is dying by a process of diminution, which in this case seems a gradual stripping away of all illusion. Indeed, the play is, I fancy, an attempt to dramatise the actual process of dying; and effectively too—if one can enter into the mode. Ionesco plays, however, are not for the printed page. They require the weight of the actor to add live body and reason, or the semblance of reason, to the train of trivialities that fire up to a sort of non-compos climax where logic, at last, seems to sit in judgment on itself. The worst thing about the Theatre of the Absurd, of course, is that a trifle can pass for a masterpiece and nobody be much wiser. A lot depends on the *voyeur*. Caught up in some Bacchic bathos, he will see a symbol in everything—and everything in symbol.

The theatre has a life of its own and the sort of rules that go with it. Plays like Ionesco's are delightful and marvellous extravagances. To me they seem to be irradiations of the older Italian theatre of the haphazard, the Commedia del Arte, the *Noh* play of its time. They use negatives to ensure the positive, but at the same time they take for granted that the logical and reasonable lend them standard and measure just by existing. What they lack, and this, I suppose, is not a basic weakness in the theatre any more, is a literate language—words that have the connotation of poetry, that forward the action but enhance it as if lending another dimension.

*

PADRAIC COLUM has chosen to crystallise an incident from the life of Sir William Wilde. I heard this play broadcast from Radio Éireann and was very much impressed: Colum uses a poised native idiom that reflects his time, which is effective and always economical.

—*The Irish Times*, October 19th, 1963

New Poems, Rainer Maria Rilke

German Text with a Translation, Introduction and Notes by
J.B. Leishman (Hogarth Press, London)

WITH THIS BOOK, Mr J.B. Leishman has to come
to the end of a long labour of love. Rilke is not the
easiest poet to re-arrange in English form. Rhyming
schemes, expected in the German, clamour at an English ear;
indeed, one has a feeling of a gambling machine gone mad—
one of those that spill a jackpot all over the floor at the turn
of a handle. Mr Leishman, needless to say, is vastly ingenious,
or else he has supplied himself with a terrific rhyming dictionary, but in addition to all this he has marvellous daring and
is without a qualm in the world, and I don't think any other
translator of Rilke has managed half so well.

It is not for this rhythmic effects, however, that Rilke is
important. In all the poems, even the slightest, is the skeleton
of imagery, an articulating conceit that makes the poem as visible as sculpture. He may have learned this from Rodin, which
I doubt—since the quality is a gift of nature and not the application of an art, but it seems to me to be an almost painterly
quality left over from the Impressionist painters. He did study
the painters; and from them, I suppose, he learned to look in
a very special way, but he carried the actual impression over
into something else. The image, like the sick man in the Bible,
took up its bed and walked, walked into a life of its own.

This can be marvellously exciting. When St Christopher is

called the 'Master of bridges and their stony strides', one recognises the rightness of Art and the exhilaration (and also the genius of an accommodating translator), but one senses also that the process belongs to the timeless world of myth, to that special art-world in which Rilke lived and had his being. And into which, on his own terms, he translated the actual world.

Thus he gives movement to every object and a heart to stone. A flight of steps in Versailles turns into pacing royalty, and yet can retain its identity of kind. Sensation refines itself but thrusts itself upon us oddly as merely another problem, as if somehow the eye, suddenly, was achieving second-sight.

At this period, 1905/6/7, Rilke was working to a plan, a sort of poem-a-day plan, the inner eye working on the outer eye its own embroidery of meaning, startlingly new and very rarely mechanical. He may fetch forth now and then some obviously highflown conceit, or he may vapourise an object— talk it out of the reasonable world, but usually he assumes it as another body only when it has time to divulge its own actuality. I know no other poet with this gift, although it is supposed to be one of the steps towards Buddha-hood in the eastern parts of the globe. It is, however, not so much 'understanding' the object with Rilke as embracing it with the myth-making mind-understanding its very special 'Spatial' quality, its place in the world plus its place in the world-mind.

Most of the poems translated here by Mr Leishman show the poet defining his own limits. One poem—I'd like to quote it for many reasons if I had the space—seems to anticipate the sonnet form he made famous later on. It's about an island in the North Sea, and I mention it because it embodies—for me— the entire scope of the man, and the process of his art, what one might call a typical Rilke poem, impressions thrown not on a calmly reflecting mind, but on waves of sensation in which things live actively. I'd better quote an illustration.

> As though it lay within some
> lunar crater's
> Outthrust, each farm's surrounded by a dyke.
> And garths are costumed by
> their cultivators

The same way and, like orphans,
combed alike

By that storm-wind, so roughly
educating
And cowing for days on end
with perishings.
One sits inside the house then,
Contemplating
In mirrors hung aslant what
far-fetched things

Stand on the dresser. And
When day is done
One son will draw from his
accordion
Before the door a sound that
seems to weep—
Such in some foreign port, it
Reached his ears—

And huge and almost threaten-
ingly appears
On that surrounding dyke one
of the sheep.

It is extraordinary here how effective is the use of the mirrors
aslant and the epithet 'far-fetched', which alters the whole sensation of the place at a stroke. The whole poem vibrates.

In addition to translating, Mr Leishman contributes a
notable preface to the poems. He makes the point I make
above about the image–simile, to him, a poetic device, but
declares that the innermost secret of Rilke's poetry 'is to be
found, not in its imagery, but in its syntax and rhythms'. What
is important is that in a short space he puts the poet and his
poetry in perspective as a European and as a German poet,
and at the same time details the influences that broadly helped
him to find himself. He is to be congratulated on achieving the
work of a lifetime.

—The Irish Times, 1964

The Esdaile Notebook

A book of early poems by Percy Bysshe Shelley
edited by Kenneth Neill Cameron (Faber & Faber, London)

ALL ART is mostly rebellion. And every young man with a quarrel is really one of the unacknowledged legislators of mankind; Percy Bysshe Shelley the Onlie Begetter of the angry young man.

Shelley's youthful assurance seems now a sort of Eden innocence. At sixteen he was in full blast as a political agitator, and in correspondence with great names. He never stayed put in his study, like most writers learning their trade. He had huge concepts of right and wrong, and almost before he was out of the shell he was trundling those about the world, a great baggage of Platonic metaphor. It is not often a poet is born with a social vision of that kind. Yet every great poet inherits some kind of 'great gazebo,' a personal structure in which he works out his relationship to things like Dante, like Yeats; and while this may be—and it usually is—arbitrary and even artificial, it is a simplification satisfactory enough to allow him to stand inside it and get on with his real work.

I think it was Jung who said that a man's status depends on his conception of the universe, and if we measure Shelley in those terms he was a great man. *The Esdaile Notebook*, a collection of poems written between the age of sixteen and twenty-one, of which about forty were never published before, while it adds little or nothing to his reputation as a poet, is of importance accordingly. All, as he says himself, breathed 'hatred to government and religion'. He meant established religion, not the unceasing process that begets gods who die in their formal establishment and figureheads. He was a poet in love with an ideal universe in which uninhibited man lived out of his life freely, and in which no social compromises were required of him. He died almost as young as the day he was born. And yet, and in the meantime, from this magnificent and youthful dialectic, he achieved great verse.

There is very little in *The Esdaile Notebook* to promise this greatness. And in saying that, I could be wrong. One would need to be sixteen, in the reign of Castlereagh, to feel all that it tried to convey.

> Full many a mind with radiant genius fraught
> Is taught the dark scowl of misery to bear;
> How many a great soul has often sought
> To stem the sad torrent of wild despair.
> 'Twould not be Earth's laws were given
> To stand between Man, God and Heaven,
> To teach him where to seek and truly find
> That lasting comfort, peace of mind.

Even his love in those years was rhetorical—to us I mean, in this age. It has the painful inflation of a universal naturenote. And yet this attitude, later, gives us some of his most mature and appealing poems. The person did not alter but the art improved. I doubt, indeed, if he ever grew up, in our terms. It wasn't necessary. If he distributed himself in Fabian pamphlets, Ariel was always rocking the inkwell. He needed both of his worlds to be in equilibrium.

One needn't explain any poet really, for the main thing, the poetry, will always escape the label. But Shelley's 'Socialism' has always seemed to me his personal balance between his vision of the world and the guilt of the well-born. He couldn't use the one until the other had been assuaged, or crow till the dunghill was all roses.

The *Notebook* is edited by Kenneth Neill Cameron with all the painstaking miracle of American scholarship. He places every poem in its time and place, detailing Shelley's movements and his activities. He was under police watch part of the time. His manservant, an Irishman called Daniel Healey, was arrested for distributing *Declaration of Rights*, a pamphlet written in Dublin. Indeed, his Irish sympathies were most remarkably liberal for anybody except a practising revolutionary. If he did write in Dublin a poem hailing the Mexican revolution of 1812, he also wrote 'The Tombs', a tribute to the men of Ninety-eight:

> All that could sanctify the meanest deeds
> All that might give a manner and a form

Somehow all this activity brings him close to our time once again. One sees the liberal lineage still at work, banning the bomb and seeking the peace of the world. Shelley after all is part of our age and lives politically as well as poetically. And if the shapes of things are a little different, the new Bogeys are the old ones up to date. One likes to think of him in there and tilting, Eros with a pamphlet, Ariel with a blowpipe. And he died young enough to make a modern hero.

—*The Irish Times*, 1964

Poetic Love

by J.B. Broadbent (Chatto and Windus, London)

*E*ROS is the four-letter God who never dies. His many and various faces are in themselves phases of history or civilisation. When Mr J.B. Broadbent had the idea of seeking him out in the utterances of the poets, English poets mainly, from the Renaissance on, he had to preface the Divinity by a preliminary chapter dealing with Christianity and Platonism, and with the nimbus that transferred itself from the Arabic to the Troubadour country, Provence; and to cite Augustine and Paul in the process, and even Boethius who, telling the tale of Orpheus and Eurydice in the sixth century, asked rhetorically, 'Who lays down the law to Lovers?' It is, however, from the Renaissance onwards that he chiefly cites his scriptures, with Amour Courtois, and that priest of Love, Andreas Capellanus, a courtly fellow who seems to have forgotten his tonsure in his lovelocks and forsaken Calvary for the boudoir. Capellanus codified the aches and stresses of Troubadour love till passion itself must have died of ceremony. And of course it did. A balloon can only take so much hot air.

But real emotion there was. And the inflation, or the attitude, of Troubadour love which increased the value of the object, was doubtless necessary in semi-barbarous times when women had little social value. Even to a poet all women outside the charmed circle of birth could be used regardless. Only the canon was holy. And the worshipped woman never profaned.

Needless to say a wife was, in consequence, never the worshipped woman. Motto, no wife is a Muse.

Vassalage, Mariolatry, there are many names for this psychological conditioning. The Arab Court poets sang of it, taking it for granted that true love was the reunion of souls separated at creation. Then there was the new Platonism, which saw in earthly love only a reflection of what cannot be fully incarnated, reinforced the attitude. It went into Dante and created Beatrice. And Beatrice became angelic. Petrarch devoured it too. He loved at such a distance that he never saw his inamorata more than once or twice during all the years of his sonneteering; the lady in the meantime producing child after child to her lawful spouse. It is all very confusing. And yet, as they say, not so. It has all the attraction of a psychological stasis in which some kind of rose may bloom upon a cross. It also expresses the duality that does exist between body and soul.

Mr Broadbent opens with a significant quotation from Donne, the greatest of the Metaphysicals, who took the Petrarchan mood into much greater depths of feeling. In Donne love was an energy that had to find room in a Christian ethic. It followed too that God was somewhere inside the emotion of love, profane love. This is the quotation.

> Her pure and eloquent blood
> Spoke in her cheeks, and so distinctly wrought,
> That one might almost say, her body thought

This conspiracy of soul and body, the urgent need of one for the other, Mr Broadbent calls associated sensibility. Upon it he bases his theme, tracing it from the Italian Renaissance through Chaucer, Wyatt, Surrey, Spenser, Ronsard and the Pléiade, Shakespeare—of course, and Sidney to Donne and his imitators and the metaphysical decadence in Cowley, Herrick, the Cavaliers, the Augustans and the pornographer Rochester. It is a sweeping survey, but surprisingly rich in detail and quotation, for it leaps from the past to the current, takes in quick gulps of Lawrence, Yeats and Eliot, and switches on to some younger men, just to define difference in rhythm and syntax. Mr Broadbent shows superb knowledge of the poet's craft as well as intense cultivation of his source poets. And his scholarship is such he can plump bits of Mr Eliot's 'Burnt Norton' or 'Little Gidding' into Herrick and Herbert and Shakespeare, making a point of the different uses of poetic material.

He is concerned chiefly to display the values of Associated Sensibility. What Donne said about the body 'thinking' is 'what all the most approved Western poetry tries to say. The desire to say it springs from the tension that is felt between body and mind, and in a series of other dualities—action and idea, love and law.' In such dualities the tension is the poetry. It holds both sexes together in a flowing hermaphrodite figure, the house of Eros in which opposites meet. And find their temporary or transitory solution.

Nothing, of course, is permanent, or valid for any time except its own. Ronsard and Petrarch and Dante yielded the stuff that Spenser and Sidney used up, and that the younger Shakespeare—more true to them in spirit than the others—finally transfigured. In Donne it came into a priest's hands, and the war between lover and cleric created another kind of tension. Donne was the realist of his time. He gave love a desperate body of flesh, it sweated and groaned in a new constriction. It disjointed his metres and over-rode his rhythms. He was beyond his time because he has lasted fervently into ours. He was more of his time than—say—Herbert. And more Christian because he never burned his more profane verse, as Herbert did. He was the true man, carrying the true cross. And possibly he crucified himself upon it, admitting everything but countenancing nothing outside his vision of Christ. Mr Broadbent distinguishes him from the Romantics that came later by saying that unlike them he did not see soul and body in equal balance. That could only come when a perfect life was perfected in death, becoming a psychosomatic whole like angels. Perfection to him was a 'rigid hierarchy with the soul in Command'.

Analysis of this sort is usually heavy-handed. Mr Broadbent, however, has all the bright currency of our time. And a gift for the phrase. In introducing his section on Shakespeare's sonnets, he can say 'one is often baffled by the heavy Tudor air of public intimacy', which does illustrate my own feelings exactly. And then he can go on:

Although we may have insight, the sonnets are so much working models of what they are about that they remain deeply private. They are about the metaphysics of love—the meaning of erotic words, erotic situations; but they are much more impersonal than Metaphysical poems.

Very few can get right down like this—as quickly. It compels our respect immediately. His summary of Spencer is equally relevant, and Sidney. He picks up what is essentially the 'climate' of the poet's thought, and then measures the technical achievement, how much he got out of himself in terms of the time.

I have omitted the real wit of Mr Broadbent's commentary. When he says 'The Augustans associated Hobbes' state of nature with the Civil War,' he has said almost all that need be said about that particular bit of sensibility. When he says of Pope's women, 'it is clear that the goodness Chloe lacks is prudential,' he has said all that's necessary about that particular aspect of Mr Pope. And so on. He drops those little jewels so casually that one almost ignores their rightness. All this in a chapter on the Sentimental Decadence, in which The Sermon on the Mount is shown to have a commercial basis—in Pope.

Pope's century indeed was an all-time low in regard to the true Poetic Love. But then Mr Broadbent feels that the tensions are now with tragedy and the novel. Exit us, and our lessened strophes. Our dithyrambs are old hat.

It could be true. I mean it could be correct, but hope it is not true. After all, the great media are for audiences or readers of millions nowadays. And can we say that a poet with an audience of a couple of hundred is representative any longer? Can a dense lyric compete with a pop-song? If it can't, of what importance is it?

I really can't answer my own question. But I believe that poets will never cease to make poems. And I believe they will be dense with the chary wisdom of the solitary, as ever. And in their own semi-divine way, the only true reflection of their time. And perhaps of Mr Broadbent's thesis, for Poetic Love will always be with us, even though its tensions are only those of our age, the age of the Bomb.

—*The Irish Times*, 1965

Nationalism in Modern Anglo-Irish Poetry

by Richard J. Loftus (University of Wisconsin Press)

NATIONALISM to most Irishmen has a political, and perhaps a militant, implication. We are still too near the propaganda and the guns to be objective about it. Professor Loftus, however, is sufficiently remote, both in time and feeling and in place, to give the word a different connotation. He allows it to embrace racial feeling and what we might call our cultural heritage, so that looming behind the word are the old epics and mythology as well as all the rebellions and defeats that make up our history.

His approach to our later poets is thus a bit different from any Irishman who has lived through the last fifty years of Irish history. I don't think many of us would regard Yeats, Æ, Stephens, Colum, Austin Clarke, or F.R. Higgins as nationalist poets. They were just Irish poets, poets who happened to be alive when things worried up to a climax that found some kind of political solution. Their verse was seldom activist and very rarely propaganda, as that of Thomas Davis and the Young Irelanders was. They were caught up, of course, in some vision of the past. At least Yeats was, as were Stephens, Colum, and Clarke. Æ's verse could have been made in any other country he lived in. They were the fabric of vision, and the native nomenclature he used for his gods and heroes fails to bring them home to the Irish hills.

So the best essay in this book is on the three political figures McDonagh, Pearse, and Plunkett, at least it is the most true to his thesis, and of those he puts Plunkett first as both craftsman and thinker. The fact remains, however, that none of them excels as poets, or stands out enough to be considered with the others Professor Loftus includes. MacDonagh was excellent in Gaelic translation, finding for the Irish a rich, lively idiom that was most unlike the academical speech he took to his own thought. In Yeats' opinion he would have made himself into a fine poet had he lived, for he had an unresting mind and a wide intelligence as well as the other qualities that make up a poet, sensibility and energy. Plunkett, on the contrary, never got out of the sacristy in his verse. And with Pearse one felt always the sword or the pike, or even the gibbet, was on the next landing overhead. It was a sort of preparation for martyrdom mostly, and when it did consider life it did so with sentiment, not with sensibility.

Yeats, of course, is the mountain view and major pinnacle, the poet who touched everything and made it his. Professor Loftus, however, makes no mention of the poet's profession of faith: 'Know that I would accounted be / True brother of that Minstrelsy / Who sang to sweeten Ireland's wrong'. Not that it matters. What does matter is that where he was most fiercely nationalist, say in *Cathleen Ni Houlihan*, he used it as a theme for art purposes. Even in his Blueshirt days, he remained a poet.

This is the norm in every land and poets write for the few, for their peers if you like, or for those who speak their language. Most poets use the Philistine for counterpoint, aware of their own size and of their limited social significance as odd and single voices lost in the great cacophony of the Establishment. To Yeats, however, Poet meant Prophet and unacknowledged legislator for mankind. He did extrude from his proper function on occasion, as when he wished to give to Ireland a new order of worship, with its HQ on Lough Key, and Maud Gonne the priestess of The Golden Dawn. This might go down in California; I hesitate to think how the Bishop of Elphin would regard it. Or the Archbishop of Canterbury. Posterity, however, will allow it as the surplus of his genius, even though it refuses to be so kind to Shelley.

Professor Loftus sees Colum as exemplifying the Philistine attitudes of the majority, and his work accordingly as sentimental. He sees Colum as involved with Griffith, whom he regards as the arch-Philistine of the time, the man who left the Abbey after the *Playboy* rioting, *et cetera*. He disparages him also for what he calls his peasant outlook, and at the same time is at pains to prove that his outlook was not peasant but suburban, or small town. But Colum was—and is—just himself, a poet writing in a mode that came naturally to his hand. There is no excess in him, no wild surplus, he is sparse and neat and cunning with what he has, and if his tools are small he uses them with care and precision. He is the realist of the period. And this, I think, because he took the people seriously and went among them like a proseman to absorb them as persons. I prefer to see him as the passive receiver and as the truthful recorder of what he saw. His verse got down to the people, which is an achievement for such delicate stuff, and I am quite sure that if he avoided any head-on impacts with the popular sentiments, it was not because the community limited him, or influenced him, but simply because he was a man of the people. The one spirit moved them.

Professor Loftus has prejudices of his own. When he decries Colum for his praise of sparseness and frugality, he is speaking from the armchair of an opulent community 'that never looked out of the eye of a saint'. There is a dignity in having nothing and being something. The labourer who praised his spade as if it were a Crusader's sword had a point Professor Loftus may have missed. Indeed, a lot of men get more from little than from much. Colum was putting this point forward when one of his characters is made to say that a man with a few books may know more than a man with an academy. After all, the libraries of the world, with the help of a computer, will not produce a real poem. And—excluding original sin—what had Homer but 'Bog Wisdom'? And some tradition of verse-making.

I don't, of course, take the attitude that a library is not of inestimable value to any poet who lives to use it. But most poets, whether they live long or short, have a habit of dying young. They find other solutions outside the Muse. F.R. Higgins, however, is debatable and a much better poet than Professor Loftus allows. He had a rare verbal gift, for one thing, and when he used the rein, an imagery unusually imaginative.

It was hit or miss, certainly, and I see now mostly miss, with lumps of bad taste that leave some poems beyond salvaging. But Professor Loftus should go over the good things again and put Higgins more into perspective, historical perspective. The Irish 'Troubles' did mainly represent a peasant uprising, and put a premium on physical qualities. Higgins with his exuberance and swagger was the poetical equivalent of the gaitered guerrilla. He was also just one remove from the country boy, with all the psychological nostalgia of the uprooted. But he was no conformist, except in rebellion. He didn't take his morals from Colum, but from the *Amhráin Muighe Sheola*, a collection of folksong made by a lady in Tuam, Co. Galway, remarkable for its earthy breadth. I notice no mention of it in Professor Loftus's reading.

I think Professor Loftus is wrong, too, in assessing the influence of Yeats on Higgins. One poem he mentions as being based on 'Sailing To Byzantium' was actually written before Yeats' poem appeared. (I think he can check that from the *Spectator* files.) Later there was influence, when the mutual friendship ripened, but I think it was to the advantage of both, except that the elder man was the more prolific and the quicker of the two to make use of things. There used to be a slanderous story current at the time that Yeats was the unsleeping partner of the firm Yeats, Higgins and Gogarty, meaning, I think, that the old man's new lease of exuberant life originated in the vigorous interchanges of those two constant visitors. Perhaps we owe them a great national debt.

I am glad Professor Loftus takes Austin Clarke at his real value as a poet. He is mistaken, however, in saying he is not appreciated in his own country. Only a few people matter poetically in any country. I can't see Eliot, for instance, hitting it off in Bradford. Or Ezra Pound in Chicago—or in the Pentagon. Indeed, I don't feel altogether happy in his summary of our local attitudes. Sean O'Casey, for instance, was not driven out of the country because he was a Marxist. At the time he left Communism had not become a bad word, and I doubt if anybody knew his affiliations anyway. He was a 'Connollyite', a former Liberty Hall man, and that was very respectable after Easter Week. And didn't he, in *The Plough and the Stars*, poke fun at the thing?

Another addition to Professor Loftus's reading should be the *Dublin Magazine*, edited by the poet Seumus O'Sullivan, who printed contributions from Yeats, Æ, Colum, Clarke, Higgins and James Stephens. To be frank, I think this book is just a little off the beam, not much, and mainly in accent. But then, perhaps my own taste could be a bit too local.

—*The Irish Times*, February 1963

V
Verse Chronicles 1956-8

EDITOR'S NOTE: The last dying years of the *Dublin Magazine*, Fallon wrote a quarterly 'Verse Chronicle' that covered a wide range of contemporary poets: Irish, English, Scottish, American, etc. The versions that appear here have in some cases been cut or truncated, partly for space reasons and partly because a number of the poets he reviewed are now quite forgotten and scarcely deserve resurrection at this late stage. However, there is still abundant matter to interest poetry-readers of today, and Fallon's approach is sometimes trenchant but usually generous. Frequently he goes well beyond the compass of book-reviewing as such, to launch some observation or speculation of much wider relevance or validity.

The first two pieces were not actually headed 'Verse Chronicle' when they first appeared, since that title was not used until the third in the series and was continued after that. However, obviously they belong with the rest and are printed here in that chronological order.

After Seumus O'Sullivan's death in March 1958, the *Dublin Magazine* to all intents ceased publication. Spasmodic attempts made later to revive it did not last long, since the days of the old-style literary magazine seem to be numbered and publications such as the *New York Times Review of Books* have taken over much of its function. Fallon himself, in the months immediately after its editor's demise, approached several influential or moneyed people with the suggestion that they might finance future issues; however, none of this came to anything. But in any case the magazine was O'Sullivan's own, unique creation and so perhaps was best left to die with him.

Verse Chronicle I

ANCIENT LIGHTS: POEMS & SATIRES
by Austin Clarke (Bridge Press, Dublin)

THE ARCHAEOLOGY OF LOVE
by Richard Murphy (Dolmen Press, Dublin)

COLLECTED POEMS
by Bryan Guinness (Heinemann, London)

BRIDE OF REASON
by Donald Davie (Fantasy Press)

SONG AT THE YEAR'S TURNING
by R.S. Thomas (Rupert Hart-Davis, London)

A WAY OF LOOKING
by Elizabeth Jennings (André Deutsch, London)

TWENTY YEARS ago Irish poets were more concerned
with Gaelic verse techniques and with a local subject-
matter than they are today. The change is personified in
the Master of the Old, Mr Austin Clarke, and in Richard Murphy, the professor of the new. Both have points in their favour.

Mr Clarke, of course, does not stand or fall by this booklet, and in the corpus of his work it will have the effect of the
smaller sideshow as against the three great rings. He is not naturally a neat knifeman, having used the larger cutlery of the
romantic cavalry commander, and I do not think the smaller
suit of the satirist keeps his elbows in. He refines too much for
the fun to be effective, and he should learn of Swift not to be
slow when it comes to hard clouting. After all, satire is not a
Dublin whisper in the ear, it consists of the ribald and the

robust protest, and one clamorous line that is quotable outside of context can easily—or possibly at least—have as much effect on a populace as an election campaign. Satire is, after all, an art of publicity.

But there is wit. And into Mr Clarke's wit always intrudes the double truism of life. Here is a tiny squib on women's fashions in which three different things are implied perfectly, the thundering of mediaeval morality, the middle-aged morality of the pater-familias, and the simple morality of Eve's latest daughters:

> Now they have taken off their stockings
> And bared the big toe like a monk,
> Warned by the figuring of thin frock
> And belt, modesty must look up
> Only to meet so pure a glance
> The ancient sermon will not fit,
> Since right and wrong though self-important,
> Forget the long and short of it.

Marriage, with its problems of Catholic birth control, causes another flight of tiny arrows, barbed and pretty, but the odd thing is that it is the pin-cushion we pity; the target has not been elaborated enough, and—hush—not sufficiently elevated for those delicate *pointilliste* things. He should have called the tune by title 'I'll Sweat by Moonlight', and hit the thing broader on the beam. But there is this queer mastery of the line in all that comes from Austin Clarke's hand. It is only in the total effect of the tilting that we recognise he is making his art out of miniature nowadays. But then, those are the jottings on the edge of the page, the passing glossary on life in this new Republic of Ireland.

Mr Richard Murphy, my second Irish poet, owes nothing to the neo-Yeatsian school, nothing to the metric of the Gaelic, and in subject matter, be the landscape ever so local, he thrusts upon it an alien rhythm of distance. His idiom rides not alone but in that large company that started in the thirties with the publication of the first Auden. He is, accordingly, speaking in a kind of collective tongue, which is no great harm, but the limitations of this are that he just fails to be as a person distinctive and definite as an individual poet should be. The cloak keeps him muted.

I go over one particular poem of his again and again, 'The Philosopher and the Birds', which he made in memory of Wittgenstein at Rossroe. In many ways it is solid and satisfying, but my poetic memory nags at phrases like 'time's rain eroded the root since Eden' and 'fantasies rebelled though annihilated'. A very little work would bring this poem into the constant of memory, just as the doffing of his current cloak will make this poet sizes larger. It is all there, the size, the material, and the man.

Another Irishman. It comes as a surprise to find that Bryan Guinness has been writing for such a long time. Those poems, period 1927–55, have a companionable pictorial quality one has ceased to expect from modern verse. Poets there are of all conditions and degrees, the Great Raveners not at all being those who give their names to the hearth, and for myself anyway I can find a place for the man on tiptoe who can bring me a welcome from the quiet and thoughtless moment. Many of those poems could go easily into the simple cry of song-music, being stripped to that potency by the singleness of the feeling. Take 'Love in a Crowd'.

> She held me in the chattering crowd
> That gapes about us like a shroud.
> She would not let me say the words
> That choke my heart in bitter curds.
> She would not let me tell my love
> That rots to see the light above.
> Here it remains in buried lust
> That, by its nature, heavenward must.
> Here, stifled by its own sweet breath,
> Love, coffined in the heart breeds death.
> Oh, curse the hundred-pointed ears
> That clip my tongue with listening shears.
> For, left alone, with eloquence
> My love would so inspire my sense
> That her bright eyes must weep to hear
> And save me with a single tear.

Dr Davie, so well-known as a critic, makes his first appearance as a poet; and without cap and gown and a reason for everything is nevertheless a figure that in its restraint and reining still inspires some awe. If there is reason in pedagoguery, however, it is to be found here, though the massed traditional effect can throw up beyond artifice the real whole and poetic structure, so that the feeling is of the modern landscape rather than the clipped yew of the eighteenth-century quadrangle. Most poets come into their talents on the footprints of the preceding generation, they do not love poetry but a certain kind of poetry, meaning some technique that released them into words before they brought their own individual qualifications to bear on their matter. Dr Davie, on the contrary, seems to love the metric and definite patterns given to the language by the genius of its older versifiers, and metrically his intentions seem to be to consolidate those rather than invent others. That is all right, too, since his particular talent seems to fit.

All of his poems, or almost all, seem to have a quality of enormous aptness. Wit, in its eighteenth-century application of the term, is the shaper of each. But for that very reason, the poet seems often to be outside the poem, in the Brecht manner of playmaking. There is some disassociation, if I may put it that way, and at a time when we expect absolute fusion between a man and his poem, it is sometimes disconcerting. I do not say that poems are made of feelings, but I think the best poems must use feelings if the fable is to be effective; and to use feelings is to appear to be the feelings we use, to embody them, as the phrase has it. One real reason for this is that there is always present and ready to be called upon by the poet a corpus of emotion which is not to be disdained simply because it is not the response required by the intellectual structure of the poem. Response necessarily is a mixed affair, and emotion or feeling of any kind usually finds the shadow of a corollary somewhere in the head. In other words, in seeking its reason for being moved, it approaches the poem from another, if secondary, direction, and the answer it gives to the poem may exist in this mere seeking for a reply to itself.

And this, I fancy, has been put better, and in his own way, by Dr Davie.

I'd have the spark that leaps upon the gun
By one short fuse, electrically clear;
And all be done before you've well begun.
(It is reverberations that you hear.)

I'm doing this book badly because I feel behind this poet
a critic enormously wise and who knows exactly where he is
going. Its main strength, however, as I see it, lies in quite a
small number of poems where the poet is excited beyond himself by his own imagery. One poem I remember after several
years, since I came upon it first in some periodical, which he
calls 'Poem as Abstract'. Here is the second part of it:

No trowelled matron but a rigger's mate,
The pile-high poet has no time to brood.
He steps the mast; it does not germinate.

Not for ingestion but to frame the air
He flies the spar that even winter's tree
In green ambition cannot grow so spare.

The orange dangles, drops, and comes again.
To make a fruit he has to be a fruit,
A globe of pulp about a pip of pain.

But tiptoe cages lofted in a day
(To make a grid he has to make a grid)
Have come unprecedented, and to stay.

If poems make a style, a way of walking
With enterprise, should not a poet's gait
Be counties wide, his stride, the pylons stalking?

Another book, nearest to us in theme with its mountain
landscapes and lost small villages, is a book from Wales by
R.S. Thomas, a young clergyman, many of whose poems have
appeared in the *Dublin Magazine*. Mr Thomas bears the brunt
of personal loneliness in a community where his pastoral
duties have forced upon him a traditional and figured mask.
His business, as the people see it, is to be above them, a sort
of invocation-maker at need, one who legalises their love-beds,

opens some unseen and unbelievable gateway for them at life's end, and in between times baptises their offspring and officiates for them of a Sunday. He is expected to hector and to heat, but not to intrude, not to interfere. He is expected to be officially deaf and blind, to be always an office and never a person.

But a sacred kingship of that kind demands absolute belief all round: his office has scored great welts on this poet. His ministry has become his theme and it is harsh and dominating, and very single. The poet, however, in spite of the exceptions who have worn the holy orders with the laurel entwined, is at heart a very lay person; and in this poet, too, can be seen the saving grace of sympathy with what some call original sin—meaning how the body inclines to its most natural appetites. Coming to a parish, he discovered a people; and fighting for the over-soul in them, he found also the older under-pinning, the primal person who thinks only in terms of the barest requisites, food, houseroom, fire and woman, and generally in that order of needs.

> There is anger in his voice often, and the hectoring of a
>   parson's pain.
> I know now, many a time since
> Hurt by your spite or guile that is more sharp
> Than stinging hail and treacherous
> As white frost forming after a day
> Of smiling warmth, that your uncouthness has
> No kinship with the earth, where all is forgiven,
> All is requited in the seasonal round
> Of sun and rain, healing the year's scars.

I could tell the poet, of course, that his image of the peasant is biased by his mission and by his own romantic necessities, which bid him live up to the landscape and be lyrical. A hard grind may wear away a man's nose for the obvious beauties of things, but in the limited vocabulary of the sensations all men are more or less at home, and a ploughman on a fine day may be ploughing an altogether different furrow from the one under his feet, one to which there are no words nor even the hint of a pictorial image. I think the wordless allow the subconscious to do their thinking for them, such as it is, while with the mind they engage their local world where is their habitation and their names. Mr Thomas catches a hint of this also in one of the best lyrics in the book.

> Scarcely a street, too few houses
> To merit the title ...
> This last outpost of time past.
>
> So little happens; the black dog
> Cracking his fleas in the hot sun
> Is history. Yet the girl who crosses
> From door to door moves to a scale
> Beyond the bland day's two dimensions.
>
> Stay, then, village, for round you spins
> On slow axis a world as vast
> And meaningful as any poised
> By great Plato's solitary mind.

Another way of poetry is *A Way of Looking*, a book by Elizabeth Jennings, whose work I have been meeting here and there in various periodicals with great pleasure. Her method divides the world like a lens, and what we see is outlined firmly and exactly determined. Thought, indeed with its concomitant feelings, is a kind of divulged landscape, and complex because of analysis rather than appearance. In the name poem of the book, Miss Jennings makes her point.

> It is the association after all
> We seek, we would retrace our thoughts to find
> The thought of which this landscape is the image,
> Then pay the thoughts and not the landscape homage.
> It is as if the tree and waterfall
> Had their first roots and source within the mind.
>
> But something plays a trick upon the scene:
> A different kind of light, a stranger colour
> Flows down on the appropriated view.
> Nothing within the mind fits. This is new.
> Thought and reflection must begin again
> To fit the image and to make it true.

Formally, too, the woman makes way towards the lover. There are delicate areas of footsteps in such a poem as 'Tribute':

> Sometimes the tall poem leans across the page
> And the whole world seems near
> And none else is necessary then ...
>
> Are you remote, then, when words play their part
>
> With a fine arrogance within the poem?
> Will the words keep all else outside my heart,
> Even you, my test of life and gauge?
> No, for you are that place where poems find room,
> The tall abundant shadow on my page.

Since Laura Riding, indeed, there has been no woman-poet as promising. This is water stilled to take the large images of what passes to and fro. No man dares to be passive in such a way.

—*Dublin Magazine*, April–June 1956

Verse Chronicle II

RAGHLEY, O RAGHLEY by Robin Wilson

OXFORD POETRY, 1955 (Fantasy Press)

THIS AND THAT by Gordon Wharton (Fantasy Press)

FANTASY POETS D. Mitchell; H.S. Eveling; Mark Holloway
(Fantasy Press)

THE DOLMEN CHAPBOOK (Dolmen Press, Dublin)

ONE FOOT IN EDEN by Edwin Muir (Faber & Faber, London)

BREAD RATHER THAN BLOSSOMS
by D.J. Enright (Secker & Warburg, London)

POETRY: A MAGAZINE. Editor, Henry Rago (Chicago)

THE TALENTS this quarter are wry, dry, but trimmed to the new order of the conservative that reserves its sparkle for the careful eye and the discerning. Verse once again is seeking the common language of the myth, and there seems to me to be an increase in grace and depth, but—and perhaps as a consequence—some diminishment of range and everyday vitality. I don't know which is the more valuable.

Take a poem from one issue of *Poetry* for instance, one that comes late to me, February, 1956, the poem 'Salome' by James Merrill, a theme that should have worn itself out in many five-fingered exercises, but which under the thumb of this young poet comes green in its background of the mosaic, curiously modern in pattern as if an old fact had refashioned itself for current scrutiny. This poem is in three short parts, which are only rhythmically related, and the two last parts are only different burdens of comment on the first part of which I quote:

> No wonder shaggy saint, breast deep in Jordan's
>   Reflected gliding gardens,
> That you assumed their swift compulsions sacred,
> Nor that, dreaming you drank, so cool the water,
> Regeneration, of which the first taste maddens,
> You let spill on the naked
> Stranger a pure and tripled mitre.
>
> Nor that later, brooding on the sacrament
>   Of flowing streams you went
> Back where none flow, and went in a new dread
> Of water's claspings, whose rapt robe, whose crown
> Make beggar and prince alike magnificent
>   A dry voice inside said
> Life is a pool in which we drown.
>
> Finally, then, small wonder the small king,
>   Your captor, slavering
> In a gold litter, bitten to the bone
> By what shall be, pretended not to hear
> His veiled wild daughter sinuous on a string
>   Of motives not her own
> Summon your executioner.

This poem is so full of distinction that I hesitate to pin it to any special type of kind of poem. Let us say, instead, that it is the kind of poem to which many current poems aspire to. But let us add also that it is definitely not what has come to be regarded as Romantic poetry, because the theme is one of those emotive things that stir of themselves, that have a certain mythic value. The word 'Romantic' has now accrued some derogatory sense that applies no longer to the poetic theme; for its opposite, Realist, has gathered its own discredited meanings also, and the one nowadays counterbalances the other among the discards.

    Things have reached the stage, indeed, when all poetry is respectable in kind and a poet can take his themes out of himself and his bent. It is remarkable that once again we are almost where we were in 1850. The Tennysonian returns in its own way, proving—in its own way too—that the myth is a necessity to the poet, its psychological shorthand a part of his natural equipment.

This new book of Edwin Muir's for instance, Orpheus, Abraham, Oedipus, Telemachos, the heroes, Prometheus, all have a figurative value beyond the moving mind. They are psychological peaks in a shifting telescope, mounts of some kind of transfiguration. They both fix a landscape and populate it. They are vast originals, the prime aborigines of the psyche. It would seem, indeed, that they transmit certain modes of apprehension which make the poet a kind of archaic priest, one who officiates on different levels of mind where the energies have another necessary logic, the unacknowledged legislator of mankind passing through himself, as through some old stone-faced oracle, the constant message that takes its particular form and shape from the poet's own person. Mr Muir has not the verbal range—or do I mean the new type of equipment?—which makes the Merrill poem I have quoted a many-mirrored entertainment in addition to its other qualities. He is exact in a pictorial sense, but the pictures come slowly out of his words, not poetically, without detail, but in the Tennysonian manner of accumulation. Often, however, the signal phrase which is the authentic poetic shorthand lights his way. As in this poem on Animals:

> They do not live in the world,
> Are not in time and space.
> From birth to death hurled
> No word do they have, not one
> To plant a foot upon …

It is a kind of hierarchic house he builds, and he moves slowly within acknowledging all the Elders. I confess I miss something.

Like that poet in D.J. Enright's new book. Mad Poet, he calls him:

> He dances on his naked native toe.
> And stars and blots and jottings sport about his head,

Read or unread his works lie in a silken pile,
Beneath the unpacific sky he dances, while
The autumn pine drops leaves of thought about his head.

Mr Enright balances on an idiom that may slither fatally,
or just sprout him to the pinnacle. It does one as often as the
other, and while the first is regrettable both very definitely add
entertainment value to his gorgeous quality. I know I will
reread this book many times and not for any clear motive or
any definite purpose, but simply for the daring and individual
ways of the poet. 'Tea Ceremony', for instance, is already a
part of my personal cosmos.

Robin Wilson's poems most Irish people know, some of
them, anthology pieces, being a part of our make-up, for all
the yearly Yeatsian influence that in time he worked off.
R.N.D. Wilson took no great bite of the golden apple, his was
a small accurate voice and a sharp accurate eye:

A boy who brings the boat to shore
And balanced on his head
A basket like a salver dripping
With its precious dead.

Into this accuracy, however, something, as in the quotation, intrudes, here the Salome motif, but in other poems
something in imagery almost alien to the simple theme. His
most special quality, indeed, was imagistic, the picture going
deep into the metaphor. Like this:

A hand upon his shoulder
froze like a ghost,
and the bleached tree of winter
was a whipping post.

Not a large breath, as I have said, but the linnet is notable even
when the great blackbird dominates the evening. I think particularly of the elegy for Lyle Donaghy, his fellow-poet who
also died young. The gods must have loved them both.

If a university is a trend of the times, Oxford poetry of
1955 is an embellishment of the opening of this review. Here
are poems from many youthful hands, many of them deriving

their impetus from the classical theme, from the first gazebo, from the old worlds where literature was a commentary on the Gods. Here are poems on Hector, Theseus, on Atlas, the Phoenix, Daphne, and all in the most impeccably regular verse-forms, the old wearing its new with a difference. It sounds stuffy, but the minds working inside those strict forms are to my thinking bolder, and more individual of tongue and thought, than at any time for the past thirty years. There was only one Auden after all, the others of his term being reflected lights; but in this small book collected from some nineteen poets nearly all speak individually. If the talents last into what is called maturity, the times will be rich indeed. Influences, naturally; echoes, rarely; the achievement is a more than one-planed poetry and a return to the normal language of the Muse, which is suggestive and over-toned and which attends on euphony once more:

> The monster moth, the furry voyager of night
> Has stumbled into a storm of light
> My lamp's cyclonic circle ...

Which brings me to a bunch of *Poetry* magazines, left on the shelf for some considerable time but not forgotten, dipped into more than occasionally, especially one that often hits my mood, May 1956, containing selections in translation of some modern Japanese poets:

> Waving sad fins
> A woman bathing is truly like a fish.
> Her skin swims out smoothly
> And has a quiet and erotic odour.
> So by the hot drainage from the bathroom
> Are green grasses that spring oddly in winter
> And project their shadows on the lonely sky.

And a poem called 'Birth':

> One day when spring rain fell heavily,
> My mother bore me.
> My father was scraping snow on a tall mountain.
> Snakes were delighted and coiled in wide circles.

The river, with hammered spine, lay stretched out.
My mother, her chest thrown out, bending her
　　body like a bow,
Walked dauntlessly.

I have more, but little room, alas, for this large and ever-rolling American mill that rarely seems to repeat even its poets. Poetry, indeed, has continental richness of content and it is good that it is able to carry on in those money-times. But our own press doesn't do too badly. Here is the Dolmen Press with a Chapbook Miscellany and a ripe ballad from Arland Ussher, poems from Thomas Kinsella and others, and drawings from various hands. This rivals the old Cuala series, edited by Higgins and Yeats, and the only thing now left undone is to get Jack B. Yeats into the series. That would link it up with genius gone and make this but a new turn of the old wheel. May I make the suggestion, Mr Editor?

　　　　　　　　　　—*Dublin Magazine*, July–September 1956

Verse Chronicle III

SEVEN CENTURIES OF POETRY
edited A.N. Jeffares (Longmans, Green & Co, London)

NEW LINES edited by Robert Conquest
(Macmillan, London)

NEW POEMS, 1956. A P.E.N. ANTHOLOGY
(Michael Joseph, London)

A WORD CARVED ON A SILL by John Wain
(Routledge & Kegan Paul, London)

GOOD VERSE must always drag itself through stanzas of question marks, answering some in its limited way, but leaving the reader too to frame himself from his own replies. We never know really what we ask of poetry, and when a good poet puts us into his question-time, there is no one to gong us when we come up with the near-miss or with the irrelevant and ridiculous. Mr John Wain has a capacity for making me feel wrong from the start. Yet I must regard *A Word Carved on a Sill* as at least one voice that does not cry from a wilderness. The prophecy may be petty, but the stuff somehow seems to be waiting on the poet as silences wait on a man until he switches off the engine and lets things do their work for him. Putting it into critic's cliché, I don't think this poet has found his theme, the whole knit of man and time.

The authentic poem, I fancy, never has one tongue in its cheek. It must believe in its own rhetoric, though the content of one poem may contradict another. Mr Wain's reasons for not writing orthodox nature poetry, if there is such a thing as orthodox nature poetry which is not merely decorative verse, are just reasons for writing the nature poem he prints under that title:

> The January sky is deep and calm.
> The mountain sprawls in comfort, and the sea
> Sleeps in the crook of an enormous arm.
>
> And nature from a simple recipe—
> Rocks, water, mist, a sunlit winter's day—
> Has brewed a cup whose strength has dizzied me.
>
> So little beauty is enough to pay;
> The heart so soon yields up its store of lore,
> And where you love you cannot break away.

So much for relevant nature, the thing that got into the picture and behind it, but the poet goes on:

> So sages never found it hard to prove
> Nor prophets to declare in metaphor
> That God and Nature must be hand in glove.
>
> And this became the basis of their lore.
> Then later poets found it easy going
> To give the public what they bargained for.
>
> And like a spectacled curator showing
> The wares of his museum to the crowd
> They yearly waxed more eloquent and knowing ...

Feeling, of course, there must be, and inherited, since the skeleton alters little inside any specified number of centuries; so we need not expect Mr Wain to acknowledge a stimulus much differently from—say—Tennyson. He may amend an idiom and be merely an accompaniment to a tradition, as I judge him to be, but at times he is playing the man in the picture gallery, I-know-nothing-about-pictures-but-I-like-this-one, and that is not an attitude one expects from the artist. It is a playing down to lower levels.

The fact is that the art of throwaway is difficult, and is only another artifice. And you've got to have something good to throw away before it is effective. The elegiac verses to a college porter, for instance, seem to me to be a lapse in literary

taste. And for all the good things in the book, I find the poems
lack definition of attitude. Somewhere in the making of most
of them something has slipped, like a face or a shoulder, but
the slip actually is that the two languages used by the poet
have not yet become shadows of each other.

It is the time of the young. Mr Wain is one of nine young
poets gathered in selection in a new anthology called *New
Lines*, the editor being a young poet himself, Robert Conquest.
Of Mr Conquest it could be said that he, more than most, has
given his verse a sort of critical occupation, as if Art was a
theme and not a way. Out of his own seven poems in *New
Lines*, there are three that dial their references to the art of
poetry. Too many, Mr Conquest, when there is still original sin
and all the decent archives of this post-Eden and architectural
flesh ...

> Now darkness falls. And poems attempt
> Light reconciling done and dreamt.
> I do not find it in the rash
> Disruption of the lightning flash.
>
> Those vivid rigours stun the verse
> And neural structure still prefers
> The moon beneath whose moderate light
> The great seas glitter in the bight.

It is one way of putting style together, neat, accurate and
clipped after the manner of one who reduces spacious thinking
to the point of aphorism. Poetry is more than ideas about
other poems or conclusions, studied or artful, about the possible meeting-places of the ideal and the actual; it is more than
talking Art—which is the commonplace business of the critic
or even the philosopher. While I can knock out a pleasant half-
hour with those delicate jaunts of the editor, I come to the conclusion that he knows all the corridors but has ignored the
rooms, the living-rooms and the great basement kitchen where
all the work is going on.

Of those nine poets, who stands out for honours to
come? A major question, my masters, and where all are expert
users of the referring phrase that brings more than one level to

the surface of experience, I could not dare to wager on the sur-
vivor who will be the winner. Make no mistake about it, those
nine race for the eventual honour. But if I try to remember
poems that hit the memorable, it is one short poem by John
Holloway that comes up, 'Journey through The Night', which
in most ways is neither bright nor clever verbally, one that slip-
slides gently into the gesture of drama and so may not fit the
theorems of the pure lyricists. Then there is D.J. Enright,
always a delight in his unexpectedness. His interests—and
contours—go much beyond the verbal—

> And the Laughing Hyena, cavalier of evil, as volcanic
>   as the rest
> Elegant in a flowered gown, a face like a bomb-burst,
> Featured with fangs and built about a rigid laugh,
> Ever moving, like a pond's surface where a corpse
>   has sunk ...

There is a certain solidity even in this picturesque and high
kick-of-the-heels. Here is a person pinching his gods and his
gear into a world-shape and pushing them into the market-
place to dance into high seriousness.

And what about Donald Davie? There is equipment
enough for ten poets in this one alone and a rhetorical wit that
he handfasts steadily to restrain abundance. And that in itself
maybe is some sort of stricture, for it is never enough to consolidate a culture. A poet should make one. Dr Davie says such
wise things that we realise that the body has not had its full
share in the speech. Let me quote 'Rejoinder to a Critic', which
could be a reply to myself in my present state of mind.

> You may be right: 'How can I dare to feel?'
> May be the only question I can pose,
> 'And haply by abstruse research to steal
> From my own nature all the natural man'
> My sole resource. And I do not suppose
> That others may not have a better plan.
>
> And yet I'll quote again, and gloss it too
> (You know by now my liking for collage):
> Donne could be daring, but he never knew,

When he inquired, 'Who's injured by my love?'
Love's radioactive fallout on a large
Expanse around the point it bursts above.

'Alas, alas, who's injured by my love?'
And recent history answered: Half Japan!
Not love, but hate? Well, both are versions of
The 'feeling' that you dare me to. Be dumb!
Appear concerned only to make it scan.
How dare we now be anything but numb?

Which is asking us to lay down our arms before the cannon-ball shoots off our legs. Provided things live, it doesn't matter very much if they don't scan.

And Mr Thom Gunn, more than interesting, a talent authentic in its vitality, gifted too with the simplicity that gives its real task to the metaphor ...

Now it is fog, I walk
Contained within my coat;
No castle more cut off
By reason of its moat:
Only the sentry's cough,
The mercenaries talk.

Miss Elizabeth Jennings takes a crystal rather than a looking-glass as her symbol, and those mutations in clarity that are her poems have some affinity with the watercolour, and always seem to be at barely one remove from some troubling emotion. She is a cool poet, however, and translates the spectator into a mild standstill where he can recollect rather than collect himself from a delicate fluency that has flown around him from the distances. Someone has said that emotion has really no part in art at all, and that the Aesthetic are conclusions arrived at in tranquility, simply by moving away the obstacles to understanding; I feel that is what Miss Jennings does all the time. I see better for having read her, or think I do, so those poems are legitimate in their way, and—let me say it without reservation and old-fashionedly—lovely and thinking pieces of workmanship.

THE P.E.N. anthology for 1956, edited by Stephen Spender, Elizabeth Jennings and Dannie Abse, comprises poems from forty-six poets, from the late Walter de la Mare to Mr Abse himself. It will bring the usual recriminations for inclusion and non-inclusion, and indeed it is difficult to see why fifty per cent of the stuff was printed at all. A book not to be compared for quality with 'New Lines', which at least is a book that has been thoroughly vetted. It is relieved, certainly, by good work—in their middle-sorts—from Auden and Louis MacNeice and from a young poet, Philip Larkin, whom I omitted to draw attention to in my note on *New Lines*. Larkin has that undervalued art we call entertainment, which means there is more than verbal interest to his poems. He goes for his themes to his life, like a prose writer, and knows what hurts him into song. I think he has the reservoir for a lot of good work to come.

Another anthology, *Seven Centuries of Poetry*, selected by A.N. Jeffares, sweeps us from the fifteen hundreds to the present day, including among the current poets, Austin Clarke and Robert Farren—neither at his best. This poem of Clarke's, however, demonstrates the gay virility of his work in the twenties; it is a Jack Yeats in colour and content.

What more is there to be said of such a treasure galleon? From Shakespeare on through the whole galaxy. Perhaps there is more concentration on the eighteenth century than is usual, though I am not one to agree with the editor that 'few people realise its richness until they have themselves passed from the romantic subjectivity of adolescence into what may be some degree of rationality, some greater social consciousness'.

Do I detect here conscious or unconscious criticism of the real content of most worthwhile poetry? 'Appear concerned only to make it scan.' A fear of raptures. A putting of the poet's shoulder to the great wheel of logical social thinking, which, by the way, changes from season to season. The poetry of the thirties should be the poet's reply to this falsification of his business. The editor, however, has done his work well and his selection should help students on the royal journey beyond the purple.

—*Dublin Magazine*, October–December 1956

Verse Chronicle IV

NIGHT THOUGHTS
by David Gascoyne (André Deutsch, London)

POEMS by Elizabeth Bishop (Chatto & Windus, London)

TIME IS A SQUIRREL by Rhoda Coghill
(Published for the author at The Dolmen Press, Dublin)

THE FABER BOOK OF MODERN AMERICAN VERSE
edited W. H. Auden (Faber & Faber, London)

POETRY NOW edited G.S. Frazer
(Faber & Faber)

'NORMALLY,' says Mr Auden in introducing this new anthology of modern American verse,

in comparing the poetry of two cultures, the obvious and easiest point at which to start is with a comparison of the peculiar characteristics, grammatical, rhetorical, rhythmical, of their respective languages, for even the most formal and elevated styles of poetry are more conditioned by the spoken tongue, the language really used by the men of that country, than by anything else. In the case of British and American poetry, however, this is the most subtle difference of all and the hardest to define ... What the secret of the difference is, I cannot put my finger on: William Carlos Williams, who has thought more than most about this problem, says that 'Pace is one of its most important manifestations' and to this one might add another, Pitch.

The poems gathered together in this magnificent selection, then, are not exactly what an American poet of equal standing to Mr Auden would select, though my fancy is that

Mr Auden includes a good deal that strictly does not come within the terms of his own British sensibility. In the case of some poets, however, he has transferred to me at least some new interest. I am one of those to whom Mr Carlos Williams has had little to say up to this, yet on the strength of one poem in this book I have made the magical contact, which in its way is the discovery of a climate. 'To Daphne and Virginia' is in its detail almost as imageless as a piece of music, but out of it comes the main image of a poem, the message of sensibility, and I realise why this poet has escaped my net heretofore. I have been looking for different qualities in the poet, for the pictorial element which under inevitable poetic stresses is pushed into image and symbol line by line, and which this poet does not use at all or very seldom.

Wallace Stevens is another difference, however, and this anthology does not solve it for me. Even the collected volume of this poet's work seemed to be in many minds about him, each with its own manner within the main and somewhat too designed *modus* of the man. The poems selected do not happen to be poems I like and I am left wondering if I have been admiring Stevens for what might be called his unAmerican activities, poems which are nearer to our European sensibility than others. Much of his work, to my own mind, has not reached the clarification of the real thing, the simplification that silences difficulties, and I still consider that this side of him is represented too emphatically by the selection of later stuff made in this book.

The major names are all represented except T.S. Eliot and Laura Riding, who for reasons of her own did not contribute, and I consider the nuances of this anthology lack something by her absence. The eldest poet of the eighty-one represented is Edwin Arlington Robinson, who was born in 1869, and the youngest is Anthony Hecht, born in 1922. In between those years is three-quarters of a century of wilful experience, and on eighty-one different wavelengths. To see it as a sort of unity is possible, but for myself I prefer to see it in terms of the person and the variety of the individual contribution. Two widely different styles of approach there are, however, the folksy and the rhetorical, and if we take Robert Frost as one, or ee cummings, and John Crowe Ransome or Wallace Stevens as the opposite pole, we find most American verse inclining towards one or the other. Both modes are exciting, though Frost has always seemed garrulous to me and his simplicity verging on the phoney; but then plain speech is the most difficult of all and is, indeed, one of those abstractions in itself which are merely theories of an ideal.

The fact is that there is no poetic language but the poet and that this anthology is a magnificent explication of the difficulties and the successes of modern American poets.

*

Poetry Now is an anthology of the younger British poets with some inclusions from Ireland, good poems from Thomas Kinsella and Richard Murphy, Ewart Milne, W.R. Rodgers and Maurice Craig. Mr Kinsella's poem, 'Baggot Street Deserta', has an intriguing young-man theme:

> A cigarette. The moon. A sigh
> Of educated boredom. What,
> Dear world, is the matter? What's to be thought,
> What's to be done? All that I
> Am sure of in this jaded night
> Is the slow explosion of my pulse
> In a wrist with poet's cramp, a tight
> Beat tapping out endless calls
> Into the dark, as the alien
> Garrison in my own blood
> Keeps constant contact with the main
> Mystery, not to be understood.

There is a too-fashionable imagery here, but redeemed by the last image I quote, and it seems to me the poem inhabits its time and place and possesses the final quality of any real thing.

One of Mr Richard Murphy's poems I selected for special mention in a poetry review for this magazine not long ago, and I am glad to meet it here again. The other poem, 'The Archaeology of Love', has a more generalised idiom, and all the personal catches do not seem to snap into place with the same finality.

About the selection as a whole no one can grumble. Some I can ponder on with that sweet feeling of adding to a hoard or broadening out beyond an experience. If I mention Terence Tiller especially, it is for the kind of double-planed imagery he manages. I take a stanza of his poem, 'Beggar', to demonstrate:

> Old as a coat on a chair; and his crushed hand
> as unexpressive as a bird's face, held
> out like an offering, symbol of the blind,
> he gropes our noise for charity. You could build
> his long-deserted face up out of sand,
> or bear his weakness as a child ...
>
> As if a mask, a tattered blanket, should
> live for a little before falling, when
> the body leaves it; so briefly in his dead
> feathers of rags, and rags of body, and in
> his crumpled mind, the awful and afraid
> stirs and pretends to be a man.

Good poems from Donald Davie, Thomas Blackburn, D.J. Enright and other fine poets enliven what is rather a lumpy book. There is much that could profitably be left out, but on the other hand it is better to err on one side than the other.

Miss Rhoda Coghill's little book, *Time is a Squirrel*, does not, I think, on the whole enlarge the clear-cut effect of her last book which was notable for a direct pictorial quality and a painterly eye. For instance, I find the opening of the first poem vastly uninteresting poetically—

> In a bowl, in a leaning ash-tree's roots,
> water brims where the twisting roots writhe
> like a young reptile's limbs. In this pool
> water springs unheard, springs underwater,
> in a continual gravelly gush
> and circular fall of sand.
> The creeping water thinly threads a way
> between lizard limbs, to swell the wind-brushed lake,
> to repel the little pushing waves,
> pressing, pressing, infinitesimal and sure,
> to cover any landmarks ...

This is Miss Coghill the musician rather than Miss Coghill the poet, and there is nothing to catch the eye and hold it over the poem. She is more successful in the Dunmore poem where the water-colours pick out definite articles that can wear-and-tear before the gaze, yachts, birds, the rising moon, those inhabitants of the seaside day. What I miss in this slender volume is the trapped person finding personal release through Eliot's objective correlative. There is not enough contact with the underlying emotive fragments that come flying into one in authentic poetry. In other words, there is nothing here to tell us if the poems are really necessary.

*

Poems, by Elizabeth Bishop, come many-recommended, and critics like Richard Eberhart in America and Walter Allen in England have hailed her as something more interesting. I suppose once again, it all depends on what you require from a poet. In the poem she calls 'The Map', for instance, language is used with the delicate imagination that is beyond mere precision, but it seems to me that the language has overawed the person. It is six of one and not half a dozen of the other:

> The shadow of Newfoundland lies flat and still.
> Labrador's yellow, where the moony Eskimo
> has oiled it. We can stroke these lovely bays,
> under a glass as if they were expected to blossom,
> or as if to provide a clean cage for invisible fish.

This is fancy giving itself a pictorial content and being elegant if not significant, but then comes a line that lifts the reverie and which, too, does more than charm us:

> The names of seashore towns run out to sea.

What goes on, though, is a kind of poetic analysis in which the object seems to reduce the whole to its constituent parts while putting the picture together again. And picture, I think, is the operative and descriptive word. This poet is a still-lifer.

> The iceberg cuts its facets from within.

Like jewellery from a grave
It saves itself perpetually …

Daring felicities such as those keep the work alive, but the main reaction I feel is that there is always a large and careful lens of fancy lifted between this poet and her material. She has the blood-group of a standing mirror, an astonishingly embellished accuracy, but I can pass from her unmoved, since in the process of making poetry she herself seems to be unmoved.

'Night Thoughts' by David Gascoyne, on the other hand, is a dramatic poem in three parts, made definitely with the object of moving us to consider the human predicament. It was a Third Programme piece and produced with music and what I would call descriptive voices, since there is no dialogue of the usual kind, and much is in prose form. In its way it is poetic analysis at its best, and yet it moves beyond the realms allotted to the poetic form of apprehension. A philosophical discourse might fit it, or fit the form, were it not for the fervent feeling and the disillusionment and the hope, finally, that inform the poem—

'Man has become above all the most indefatigable mimic of all the ways of being man that have ever been thought striking,' says this poet in a cry out of the night. 'Men imitate, and I am imitating them. I say "man" and "men" and invest abstractions with all my own deficiencies and think I somehow thus may be absolved of the whole failure to be truly man. I cry out of my darkness. I could not cry if I were in complete despair.'

It is a great city night this, peopled not with giant despairs but the left-overs of the day, the tired feelings and the numb that seek some objective that is beyond the appetite. It is natural religion, indeed, seeking with that innate human thirst that has created all creeds, for the simplifying miracle that makes all men one inside it.

I confess it gives back to poetry its primal object. Mr Gascoyne has broken out the garden walls, and if the gods on the sheltered walks behind him have turned into conventional plaster-casts, the poet at any rate is walking naked and alive. 'To cry out is not to despair.'
—*Dublin Magazine*, January–March 1957

Verse Chronicle V

POEMS by Thomas Kinsella (Dolmen Press, Dublin)

THE INHERITORS by Richard Church
(Heinemann, London)

THE BURNING TREE Selected and translated from the
Welsh by Gwyn Williams (Faber & Faber, London)

A MORTAL PITCH by Vernon Scannell
(Villiers Publications)

A WINTER HARVEST: A FOLIO OF NEW POEMS FROM
THE NORTH OF IRELAND, edited Andrew Molloy Carson
(The Emerald Press, Belfast)

THE TRUE MYSTERY OF THE NATIVITY
by James Kirkup (Oxford University Press)

POETRY: A MAGAZINE (Chicago)

THOMAS KINSELLA is on the way to establish himself
as the best of the younger Irish poets, and in this new
book from the enterprising Dolmen Press he sustains
the promise of earlier work. I find, however, some slackening
of the general tension overall, and specifically as in such poems
as 'Dusk Music', where a fairly usual background gives no
poetic habitation. I quote:

> In hospital, where windows meet
> With sunlight in a pleasing feat
>   Of airy architecture,
> My love has sweets and grapes to eat,

> The air is like a laundered sheet,
> The world's a varnished picture.

I could put a penny-plain hand on the faults here, for they are too apparent, but in other and better stanzas there is a voice that is not the writer's own:

> For obvious reasons we ignore
> The leaping season out-of-door,
>   Light lively as a ferret,
> Woodland walks, a crocused shore,
> The transcendental birds that soar
>   And tumble in high spirit.

The total effect indeed, is pseudo-Auden, and as in Auden the cerebral pull is towards the general, not the particular; which is quite all right for the elder professor who, at his best, is a gigantic systematiser, but for this poet, whose gift is a daring imagery of his own, I think it is altogether the wrong road. Auden can give to an auctioneer's catalogue the necessary metaphysical kick that turns it into a work of art; Mr Kinsella is not deadpan enough for such specifically English and discreet craftsmanship. In the poem called 'Ulysses' the gesture is rhetorical, but more suited to him:

> To lie in the dark like a lover,
> His wrist gripped and scalding,
> His body strained as an arrow,
> Rooted in need, dementing
> His reason: Lo, she is there,
> My dear target, standing!

The poetry of a life is always the most difficult, for it is the essential auto-biography, and I feel that in most of those new poems, the poet is not in definite touch with himself. This makes the poems less interesting than they ought to be, but in an odd way enhances the poet's actual promise, since where the struggle is slow the material eventually proves the larger and the person bigger.

Mr Richard Church's new volume is in the direct line of all the poetry gone before, gentle, reasonably taut, and simply put together. If I say that he writes solid and economical verse, I must not be taken as denigrating a polished artist who reserves for verse that trimming of those emotional ballast tanks that keep his world serenely afloat. I do, personally, find it humdrum where I find a man like Mr Kinsella excites me, but I must admit that here is a real pictorial world as definite as a Dutch interior. And that has its advantages.

*

The Burning Tree, an anthology of Welsh poetry (in Welsh with English translation) covers the vast period of a thousand years, so all the well-known names are to the fore. To range over this, even by introduction, in one volume is truly to keep the straight line, so I am not surprised that Gwyn Williams leaves, for the most part, the backgrounds of the poems unexposed. In 'The Woodland Mass' of Dafydd Ap Gwilym, for instance, where the poet employs a Christian terminology, there is an obvious undercurrent of the elder religion which Mr Williams is silent about in his note to the poem, and which is nothing less than a laudation of the older God, whose symbol is the ash-tree. The merry-man Dafydd, indeed, with all the light learning of the true poet of the time, wrote here a cloaked but pungent satire on Welsh church-going:

> There was here, by the great God,
> Nothing but gold in the altar's canopy.
> I heard, in polished language,
> A long and faultless chanting,
> An unhesitant reading to the people
> Of a gospel without mumbling;
>
> The elevation, on the hill of ashtrees,
> Of the holy wafer from the good leaf.
> Then the slim eloquent nightingale
> From the corner of a grove nearby
> Poetess of the valley, sings to the many
> The Sanctus bell in lively whistling.
> The sacrifice is raised
> Up to the sky above the bush,

> Devotion to God the Father,
> The chalice of ecstasy and love.
> The psalmody contents me;
> It was bred of a birch-grove in the sweet woods.

The birch, it may be recalled, is the first tree in the Dolmen-alphabet, and symbolises the beginning of life, as it also is a symbol of the first month of the Dolmen-year.

There is a wholesomeness about this selection that makes our times seem thin, and it seems to me that we should return to the roots more than occasionally, if the human thing in the poet is not to decay. Here, there is praise and laudation, satire, sin and love, and above all an appetite for round living. I think this book should be a part of every shelf.

A lovely Ironic, Vernon Scannell's verse has the expertise of the wisecrack and the scalding wisdom of the social sooth-sayer; one eye is lidded low and the other has such a brazen stare that all his mauls are won before the bell. This is the true K.O. Those poems are attitudes rather than the verbal acoustic that goes out like radar and comes home with the picture. They are fixed mime, with limited but very specified objectives, and if nothing high and ranting of human glory seems possible to them, the medium has its human compensations. I admit I am taken by the scruff, and I admit I like it.

Authentic voices are rare in any place, and the North of Ireland is no worse off than anywhere else. This little collection certainly has two strong men, and one at least, in John Hewitt, who goes from strength to strength. Him we can be certain of, with his cult of the simple and his certainty of those overtones without which there is no poetry. 'The Spectacle of Truth' is a fine poem, 'The Municipal Gallery Revisited' even better, since it makes out of prosaic material and a casual every-day approach a solid bit of vision that encompasses also the fabulous dimensions of true art.

> O'Leary brooding in his long bronze beard
> Out of the saga now, a king remote;
> And the faun, Shaw, by Rodin's marble spared
> the pitiful declension of his thought;
> James Stephens, memory of a voice once heard

billowed on ether, solemnly afloat,
A small grimacing creature, urchin-lost,
too various to chill into a ghost.

George Russell then, my fellow-countryman,
a lad here as of seventy years ago;
you could not tell from this slight beardless one
that it was he who in the sunset glow
saw timeless spirits in their traffic run,
for there's no printed label left to show
what scale of man this stripling promised us;
the modelling hand, too, is anonymous.

Roy McFadden I always expect to hit the grandeurs. Here
he is muted to the ironic and I think his 'Postscript to Ulster
Regionalism' cannot escape being an anthology piece.

What of other contributors? Maurice Irvine doesn't give
much away and has no truck with the spellbound thing. He
writes as steadfastly as a good proseman. Andrew Molloy Carson is legendary-lost and contains himself in a mild Tennysonian warble. *Cuchulainn*, a long poem, reads like a sustaining
diet of milk and water. Edmund Gordon is finding a service-
able idiom of his own, and—thank God—has a right good
kick in his hindlegs.

*

The True Mystery of the Nativity is an adapted version from
the French mediaeval mystery cycle of Arnoul and Simon Gre-
ban. There is great simplification and additional carols, so the
play should act as if there were a church choir upstairs and a
Minister of Religion in the background. Maybe I'm not the
man to review this at all, considering, as I do, the mighty and
metaphysical mountain that has burgeoned about and above
this single mystery, and the Doctors of Law at their priest-like
task of pure ablution—but definitely, my reactions are so neu-
tral as to be unimportant. I don't think you can play down anything, however, on which a gigantic civilisation hangs, and one
just can't go back into time to rescue a faith that depends on a
couple of wooden figures such as this play produces. It is in the

tradition, certainly, but time must add or subtract, and this play diminishes and smells worm-eaten like any other mediaeval wood. If you can take that, here it is.

Three volumes of *Poetry* magazine complete my survey, all up to the high mark of this noble long-liver. Not an outstanding quarter for poetry, but I have seen worse.

—*Dublin Magazine*, April–June 1957

Verse Chronicle VI

POEMS 1943–1956 by Richard Wilbur (Faber, London)

THE SENSE OF MOVEMENT by Thom Gunn (Faber)

THE BODY'S IMPERFECTIONS by L.A.G. Strong
(Methuen, London)

THE ENEMY IN THE HEARTH by T.H. Jones
(Rupert Hart-Davis, London)

POETRY: A MAGAZINE (Chicago)

THE POET'S WAY OF KNOWLEDGE: AN ESSAY BY
C. DAY-LEWIS (Cambridge University Press)

*M*R RICHARD WILBUR has attracted attention since the publication of his first book of verse in 1947, and this present volume is a selection, culled from that early book and two others since published. He writes with an immense attractiveness, and really has an ingenious turn for the amplifying phrase which is the wit of poetry, and is all in all a very considerable poet. Acknowledging this with humility, I am left wondering why the reader in myself witholds the final qualification, that last word that acknowledges achievement in another. Is there something important lacking in the stuff, stuff that is both solid and lyrical, that can sing and still say, that concerns itself with the normal world as we see it and yet seem to make the generalisation that covers all worlds? I do not know. But having a small narking doubt is in itself, I suppose, some kind of windsock to one's final judgment.

Perhaps it is because so many of the poems gathered here are occasional in theme, or inspired by bits of painting or other art. Poems can rise out of anything, we know, and it is the poet that matters. I know minor masterpieces that have come out of the contemplation of a picture, but in essence those substitute an experience that is pro rata not as dense as that which first made the picture. They are not a complete organisation after the manner of nature. They are the thoughts that follow after.

I do not, however, wish it to be inferred that Mr Wilbur's verse is the embroidery of the occasion. What he does say is first-hand, as in a poem like 'Beasts'—

> Meantime at high windows
> Far from thicket and padfall, suitors of excellence
> Sigh and turn from their work to construe again
>   the painful
> Beauty of heaven, the lucid moon
> And the risen hunter,
>
> Making such dreams for men
> As told will break their hearts as always, bringing
> Monsters into the city, crows on the public statues,
> Navies fed to the fish in the dark
> Unbridled waters.

I fall for that greatly, but am still curiously seeking to remember where I heard it before. Some reminiscence? And is it rhythm or image? And questioning it, W.H. Auden crops into mind, perhaps quite wrongly.

A poem like 'Still, Citizen Sparrow', however, has authentic incantation;

> Still, citizen sparrow, this vulture which you call
> Unnatural, let him but lumber again to air
> Over the rotten office, let him bear
> The carrion ballast up, and at the tall
>
> Tip of the sky lie cruising. Then you'll see
> That no more beautiful bird is in heaven's height,
> No wider more placid wings, no watchfuller flight;
> He shoulders nature there, the frightfully free,
>
> The naked-headed one. Pardon him, you

Who dart in the orchard aisles, for it is he
Devours death, mocks mutability,
Has heart to make an end, keeps nature new.

Thinking of Noah, childheart, try to forget
How for so many bedlam hours his saw
Soured the song of birds with its wheezy gnaw,
And the slam of his hammer all the day beset

The people's ears. Forget that he could bear
To see the towns like coral under his keel,
And the fields so dismal deep. Try rather to feel
How high and weary it was, on the waters where

He rocked his only world, and everyone's.
Forgive the hero, you who would have died
Gladly with all you knew; he rode that tide
To Ararat; all men are Noah's sons.

Here for more than a while are all the felicities. Daring, too, with its veiled dichotomy—as if in the subconscious there was building up while he made the poem an almost vocal opposition.

Mr Thom Gunn creates opposition, and in thesis and antithesis the yea and nay that makes up his poetic method. For this he has discovered his appropriate language, a plain speech that finds its edges as it goes along through his thoughts.

> Although the narrow corridor appears
> So short, the journey took me twenty years.
>
> Each gesture that my habit taught me fell
> Down on the boards and made an obstacle.
>
> I paused to watch the flymarks on a shelf,
> And found the great obstruction of myself.

Here we are more conscious of the sense than of the writing, in contrast to Mr Wilbur's method; yet the writing is visual, carrying as it does the complex image that turns a nowise novel fancy into poetry. Mr Gunn goes for this clear-water effect all along the line, as if, indeed, he were exacting from the eye a kind of poetry of comment—

> On motorcycles, up the road, they come:
> Small, black as flies hanging in heat, the Boys,
> Until the distance throws them forth, their hum
> Bulges to thunder held by calf and thigh.
> In goggles, donned impersonality,
> In gleaming jackets trophied with the dust,
> They strap in doubt by hiding it, robust
> And almost hear a meaning in their noise.

This is one stanza out of five to a poem called 'On the Move', and personally I think the other four add little or nothing to the last line I have quoted. Mr Gunn, indeed, moves in a kind of step-by-step logic to an end that seems apparent to all but himself, as if it were not the end in itself that were important but the movement, the conclusions of heel and toe after each step forward—

> The street lamps, visible,
> Drop no light on the ground,
> But press beams painfully
> In a yard of fog around.
> I am condemned to be
> An individual ...
>
> Particular, I must
> Find out the limitation
> Of mind and universe,
> To pick thought and sensation
> And turn to my own use,
> Disordered hate or lust.
>
> Much is unknowable.
> No problem shall be faced
> Until the problem is;
> I, born to fog, to waste,
> Walk through hypothesis,
> An individual.

As statements of quandary, those are admirable and have the pithiness of axioms. Strangely enough, I think this is the larger side of Mr Gunn.

Mr L.A.G. Strong has been writing for a long time, but it comes as a surprise to me that so much of it is verse. A lot of turbulence has flown through the Psyche in forty years, and with it the bridges have altered and the traffic of fashions changed. Mr Strong's manners were made in Georgian days, which means that his approach to poetry is simple and dramatically effective. It means, too, that he leaves nothing in the air. Whether his poems will mean much to the present generation of readers is another thing. My own opinion is that this book could, with effect, have come to us in half the measure. Mr Jones is a Welsh poet who has appeared occasionally in this magazine. Like another Welshman, Mr Thomas, his best work comes out of his country—

> Back to the loved sky, and the humped hills,
> The night-infested woods, the fishcold brooks,
> Pride of the fox and buzzard, all lonely terror
> Of empty winds over Wales.
> My fronded boyhood breaking like a tide
> Flung up all contraries, the five gay kingdoms
> Of sense, and, dominant as a cloud,
> The obsolete map of chapels.
> God, a crabbed shepherd on a misty path,
> Whistled a thunderclap of truth.

Where Mr Thomas, however, uses a muted vocabulary, this other Welsh poet does not trim the edges. The sense falls out beyond the phrase and the exact thing does not come through in its full impact. Words are a sort of exchange and any little exaggeration effects the poetic current rate; and while, for instance, Dylan Thomas got away with his special inflation in some poems, the majority of them never reach the convincing conclusions of major poetry. Mr Wilbur and Mr Thom Gunn in their different ways have wrenched out of words that particular plainness which is good poetry, simply because they confide their experience to a visual language and do not expect from language more than they give. Mr Jones seems to expect language to enlarge for him the usual vision of life and to increase passion and feeling accordingly, but you've got to feed the brute first, give grist to the mill, and so on, never inverting the process by expecting language to do your thinking for you or your feeling.

A couple of issues of *Poetry*, that very fecund monthly, complete my survey, if we except an essay by Mr C. Day Lewis on 'The Poet's Way of Knowledge'. This, as might be expected from such a distinguished practitioner, has much to recommend it.

—*Dublin Magazine*, July–September 1957

*V*erse *C*hronicle VII

COLLECTED POEMS OF GEORGE BARKER
(Faber & Faber, London)

THE MAGIC FLUTE by W. H. Auden and Chester Kallman
(Faber & Faber)

LIKE A BULWARK by Marianne Moore (Faber & Faber)

THE HAWK IN THE RAIN by Ted Hughes
(Faber & Faber)

OXFORD POETRY 1957 (Fantasy Press)

ON POETRY AND POETS by T.S. Eliot (Faber & Faber)

A COLLECTED edition of the poems of George Barker, 1930–35, brings a quarter of a century's work into easy perspective, not only the work of this particular poet himself but of English poetry as a whole, from the time when Auden was a power and Mr Eliot the ruler of a waste land.

Auden, poker-faced or deadpan, needs another, different kind of poet to supply the opposite pole, and whether this almost major role will be thrown on the late Dylan Thomas or on George Barker remains to be seen. Dionysos has his share in the creation of all poetry of importance, the Corybantic dance is a response to the body rhythms that make up the releasing levers in man, and the flesh and the devil seem to be necessary to the process of lying down with the lamb. So the work of any major poet must acknowledge this dualism, not merely through the head, and in the cerebral agony of Mr Eliot, or in the dedicated understatement of Auden where the common affairs of the heart seem always to be side-stepped, or rather where the emotions are kept under remote control in the English manner.

Mr Barker, it seems to me, has much more head than Dylan Thomas, and just as heady a rhetoric, so as he has no qualms about large speech, many of the poems in this book seem to me to come off greatly. Just as many fail, of course, but ninety in any hundred poems written by any poet come to as much grief, and the one that wins out pays for the trouble.

How many winners in this book is another question. And another is, has the poet progressed from the very promising beginning of 1935—that is, if a poet ever progresses? To me, it seems that the early faults of the too-glib congruity, the flashy image that seems right on the first reading but moves—on the second reading—against the burden of the poem, are all there only more so in the later work. The poet is as susceptible to surfaces as ever, and seems as ever to be in search of the line rather than the poem. He is one that has his own meanings thrust upon him. And this, while it makes for an immediate sparkle and irridescence, leaves the major and underlying form of things obscured. Where Auden is black-and-white, an iceberg on a black north sea, Mr Barker is spendthrift summer in a squander of misty hills. It is in the lines we find him, little turns of the road, a gape of miniatures, rather than in the resultant plastic of the whole.

Mr Auden, harnessed by choice to Mr Chester Kallman, comes on the stage this time with a new version of the libretto of Mozart's *Magic Flute*. He is accordingly hogtied as a poet in more ways than one. Indeed, this playing to a musical score has as much character as a child playing with marbles and is not even as necessary. A commissioned job, of course, for dispersal over as many wavelengths as there are people and kinds of people, so we cannot expect him to add any personal meaning to the thing. Not that the opera did not require a revised libretto. Dent's version has all the silly bravura of a fat soprano, and I think the Auden-Kallman rearrangement, if it is singable, would bring the opera a new lease of life for people who require sense in libretti. Usually people don't. They find their classics emotionally in their teens and, blindspots and all, hold on to them for all they're worth. Libretti anyway are just old hooks to hold up an opera cloak, an excuse to make music visible.

Miss Marianne Moore is an exquisite verbalist. Her stuff is the still life that takes the painter's pattern. At its best it has a kind of wiseacre patter too, which is attractive, and being an observer she has a tourist quality of newness when she comes to make her summing up. I do not denigrate all this. I read her with vast enjoyment and I have found always in her rhythmical tricks more than much technical interest. (Does she or does she not evolve from Gertrude Stein technically? A Stein without the same again?)

In this little book the tone's the one she had in the beginning, and there are one or two silly poems in which only the prose keeps the bombast down. Inflation, I mean, not bombast. She needs the visual to build her communings on, something already in the picture on which she can count and recreate in her own inimitable manner. Without it, there is, alas, only manner—

THE WEB ONE WEAVES IN ITALY

grows till it is not what but which,
blurred by too much. The very blasé alone could
    choose the contest or fair to which to go.
    The crossbow tournament at Gubbio?

For quiet excitement, canoe-ers
Or peach fairs? or near Perugia, the mule-show;
if not the Palio, slaying the Saracen,
One salutes—on reviewing again
this modern mythologica
esopica—its nonchalance of the mind,
    that 'fount by which enchanting gems are spilt'.
    And are we not charmed by the result?—
    quite different from what goes on
    at the Sorbonne; but not entirely, since flowering
in more than mere talent for spectacle.
Because the heart is in it all as well.

A couple of postcards would say that better. And recipients would have the stamps for their albums.

Mr Ted Hughes's approach to the magic of image-making rings simple as the truth—

> O lady, when the sea caressed you
> You were a marble of foam—

And large speech too, with the large things coming through;

> O lady, consider when I shall have lost you
> The moon's full hands, scattering waste,
> The sea's hands, dark from the world's breast,
> The world's decay where the sea's hands have passed,
> And my head, worn out with love, at rest
> In my hands, and my hands full of dust,
>   O my lady.

There is a marvelous rightness in nearly all the poems in this book—

> But who runs like the rest past these rivers
> At a cage where the crowd stands, stares, mesmerised,
> As a child at a dream, at a jaguar hurrying enraged
> Through prison darkness after the drills of his eyes
>
> On a short fierce fuse. Not in boredom—
> The eye satisfied to be blind in fire,
> By the bang of blood in the brain deaf the ear—
> He spins from the bars, but there's no cage for him.
>
> More than to the visionary his cell:
> His stride is wildernesses of freedom:
> The world rolls under the long thrust of his heel.
> Over the cage floor the horizons come.

Some felicities do not make a poet. Here are plenty, enough for any major poet in the making if that were all that was required—

> I climbed through woods in the hour-before-dawn dark.
> Evil air, a frost-making stillness,
> Not a leaf, not a bird—
> A world cast in frost ....

There is a real person here, at any rate, who can set wit

growling and rare violence showing its teeth. This is a poem,
raw as a hawthorn in its maybloom;

> Whenever I am got under my gravestone,
> Sending my flowers up to stare at the church-tower,
> Gritting my teeth in the chill from the church-floor,
> I shall praise God heartily to see gone,

> As I look around at old acquaintance there,
> Complacency from the smirk of every man,
> And every attitude showing its bone,
> And every mouth confessing its crude shire;

> But I shall thank God thrice heartily
> To be lying beside women who grimace
> Under the commitments of their flesh,
> And not out of spite or vanity.

I am enlarging on this talent, and what I quote has been
almost at random. There is so much technique that one forgets
the art, so much art we take the technique for granted. Everything reads easily, as if words were born to their fate and their
fates were to fall into just such places as this poet makes for
them. I think I can safely hail a name that will be known in
times to come. If I am wrong it will be for one reason alone,
that the poet might miss what may be the major theme of his
time where the common language grows raw and televisionary
and communication comes in gasps and grunts. This work is
both virile and civilised, it may just miss the off-beat of something yet untold. I really can't guess, but I put down my shilling
on him with a certain vast complacency. This is a winner.

Oxford Poetry 1956 is bent upon a literary trend, and
seems set upon the too-chiselled past. What are we to do if
sons stand pat upon their fathers? Here is excellent verse, with
various and varying small touches to enliven all that went
before, as if the musician's business was to be concerned
entirely with grace-notes. It's not enough to be conservative if
the original must go into the discard. A blitzkrieg, not a book,
should be the aim of every young man. The only thing to consolidate is one's own very personal vision.

And now to prose a little, Mr T.S. Eliot's new book of

Essays, *On Poetry and Poets*. This reprints the first essay on Milton (1936) that scourged the classic-mongers, side by side with the 1947 essay that re-engaged the reconciling gears. I'd rather have the first one, though I'm enamoured of none. Those essays, indeed, I find thoroughly slow and much too academic for an established writer who made his name as a rebel. Now the Lares and Penates are back on the shelf, and Mr Eliot seems doubtful himself of what he has to say. There is much needless hedging too, and frankly I find this kind of thing unnerving:

When a man is engaged in work of abstract thought—if there is such a thing as wholly abstract thought outside of the mathematical and physical sciences—his mind can mature, while his emotions either remain the same or only a trophy, and it will not matter ...

Apart from this odd lack of the illuminating phrase which one is entitled to expect from a practising poet, it must be said that in matters which really affect him as a poet, Mr Eliot continues to be sound, if not enterprising. The essay on Yeats is beyond fairness fair, especially where the drama is concerned. Indeed, when he praises the play *Purgatory*, his only quibble is divinity, mistaking the whole Yeats doctrine— Eastern in origin—of natural purgation, in which the sinner after death plays out the sin till passion vanishes from it and it bleeds its way into nothingness.

From the point of view of the Eliot workshop, 'Poetry and Drama' is the most interesting essay in the book to me. Having seen all the plays of Mr Eliot down to *The Confidential Clerk*, I follow the reasons for his change of practice with more than the ordinary lust for information. In both *The Cocktail Party* and *The Confidential Clerk* I found the poet, as he suspects himself, failed as a poet verbally, for there is no getting away from this—a poet's business is words, and the right and proper words for a poet have a more than prose content. 'The beautiful line for its own sake is a luxury dangerous even for the poet who has made himself a virtuoso of the technique of the theatre,' he says in the Yeats essay. 'What is necessary is a beauty which shall not be in the line or the isolable passage, but woven into the dramatic texture itself ...' And I think what he means is a 'pretty' line. Yet if a stage writer is too much afraid of the purple, it will go to the moths and we all talk West-End, the bitten end of the English language, and worse than anything else lose the word-play that illuminates the motives of action. Certainly, the sleep-walking scene in *Macbeth* goes on the barest footsoles, but then it is a scene that could almost mime itself in silence and be effective. Contrast it with Cleopatra's last moments, where language is at its very highest, both dramatically and poetically—both having coalesced, so to speak. Shakespeare, indeed, has left us a large legacy of great lines; and I think the end of the poet's theatre will arrive when poets begin to write down to prose level.

It is something else to assert that the blank verse line has had its day, simply because it cannot use the ordinary speech rhythms of 1957. It depends, I suppose, on the individual poet; but it seems to me that a varied iambic can take most everyday speech into its orbit. Take the second scene of *A Winter's Tale* and see the marvellous cramming of the five-beat line. And take all those Shakespearian speeches which somehow come down to us in prose form, note how the beat of the iambic keeps recurring, exactly as if the actors had diluted the verse in their practice and the printers had taken their text off a wire-recorder. There is no monotony in this line as there is in *The Cocktail Party* or *The Confidential Clerk*, which sound exactly as prose on the stage.

—*Dublin Magazine*, October–December 1957

Verse Chronicle VIII

BRUTUS' ORCHARD by Roy Fuller
(André Deutsch, London)

HEART OF GRACE by Patrick Galvin (Linden Press, Cork)

ENGLISH LOVE POEMS edited by John Betjeman
and Geoffrey Taylor (Faber & Faber, London)

PENINSULA, AN ANTHOLOGY OF VERSE FROM THE
WEST COUNTRY edited by Charles Causley
(McDonald, London)

TEN POEMS by Padraic Colum (Dolmen Press, Dublin)

THE LAST quarter of 1957 did not arrive with the expected Christmas bang. The selection before me is not inspiring, and indeed outside a book from Roy Fuller, a well-established poet, I find none of the irrational relief that is the fruit of any reasonably poetic speech. Patrick Galvin, for instance, tries fancy to the limits and the poor jade stalls at the load—

> I beat the four walls with my heart
> And with a pin I scratched them
> But it made no mark at all
> Though I tried one day after another.
> My soul burnt itself up
> And a terrible ice grew round my breast
> Then four men with strong faces
> Tied me to a tree made of iron ...

What's wrong with this? Too much García Lorca—with-

332

out the black iron—and the castanets of gipsy tradition and the Spanish language. This, now, is a muted country and the violences, such as they are, need their own humdrum garb; above all, they require a casual everyday handling which allows of undertones and gives them room to come through the recording. A poem like 'My Little Red Knife' for instance, is a vulgarity in its present form; it is fancy without art—purpose, a bodiless thing that needs surrealistic flesh and riper vocabulary. Frankly, I find no world in any of the poems, even in those that hint of Gaelic originals.

Roy Fuller goes from strength to strength. Here is sincerity at any rate; and through a normal vocabulary an intensity, that puts the modern world in a truly personal focus. A poem like 'Ambiguities' makes a day's reading bright with concealed energies.

> A blackbird, rather worn about the eyes,
> Flaps down beside me as I clip the grass.
> From its clenched bill protrudes a withered mass
> Which with a sickened pity I surmise ...
> To be the fronds of some malignancy
> That drives the bird to human company.
> But it contrives to take a garish moon
> Of caterpillar in that beak, and flies
> Away before the ambiguities
> Of greed and pain can be resolved ...

I quote this because it is poetry of normal human range, not great but tenderly sensitive to the great human predicament in which man hangs under the bomb. It is speech, too, from a special time and a definite place, an ordering into one minute cry of the whole psychology of unavailing protest.

In some poems, almost without reason, there is an Austen skeleton, 'Summer' for instance. Yeats, great Maker, is here too, and for the good, since Mr Fuller's talent needs a ground-planning of comment when his themes are everyday. But I like best the 'Mythological Sonnets' in which the poet loses the tethers and moves into his own well-wishing. These actually, if I remember right, won the Guinness award for the best series of poems—or one long poem—for 1956, and I must say my judgement goes in glove with the assessors.

Two anthologies this quarter, *English Love Poems*, edited by two old poetry-lovers and practising poets, John Betjeman and Geoffrey Taylor, from Chaucer to Richard Murphy, a young Irishman. 'This Anthology', says the introduction, 'has been compiled by two married men in their middle years. Each thinks he knows the joys of love fulfilled and the sorrows of love unrequited. Each believes his, like no other art, can crystallise by using the right words in the right order those thoughts and emotions which love provokes ...' Which is as lovely and lordly a confession of faith as one may hope from anybody, and let me say at once that it has been beautifully carried out.

Omissions there are. Valentin Iremonger has been represented with a delicately ominous snapshot in which the time suddenly doffs its mask:

Her teeth were hedges of dense white sloe-blossom,
Her hair a development of black. Down the afternoon
From the rare peak of love, too, we are going, to the valley
Of age, lurching and stumbling dawn its gothic alleys
And grotesque approaches. ' I'm going down.' The gossip
Of the wind in her hair will be stopped much too soon.

But there are good poems from other poets that have not been used, from Seumus O'Sullivan, Patrick MacDonogh, Austin Clarke, Blanaid Salkeld to name some. Perhaps one of the most appealing—if one can use such a word—is 'Lines on a Young Lady's Photograph Album' by a young poet, Philip Larkin:

My swivel eye hungers from pose to pose—
In pigtails, clutching a reluctant cat;
Or furred yourself, a sweet girl-graduate;
Or lifting a heavy-headed rose
Beneath a trellis, or in a trilby hat.

Oddly, from William Empson comes a disappointing Villanelle. Even the master can do little with this form, which still wears its Dowson aura. The literary nineties have tethered it to vine-leaves and melancholy. Day-Lewis also comes up with another album poem which unfortunately for him cannot stand side by side with Philip Larkin's—

Then I turn the page
To a girl who stands like a questioning iris
By the waterside, at an age
That asks every mirror to tell what the heart's desire is ...

The rhyme here is frivolous. The last stanza, too, disturbs in another way. It is snug and smug, too open-vowelled in its benignity.

Charles Causley's anthology is a different kettle of fish. His terms of reference, broadly, confine him not alone to poets born in the West Country of England, the seven counties of Gloucestershire, Wiltshire, Hampshire, Somerset, Dorset, Devonshire and Cornwall, but to those who have shown any interest in it, since 'the western peninsula has always exerted a strong pull over creative artists of many kinds'. In other words, this is just another anthology of modern poets, with an excuse to represent some that are almost entirely unknown to us, and that's as good a reason as any other for gathering it together. In fact I know no better.

I renew an old love in meeting two poems from John Cowper Powys—

I never pass a sleeper's head
But another head I see;
And Christ—or Christ's own Mother—dead
Lies there in front of me.
O double life, O double death,
When will these spells confused
Dissolve 'neath some tremendous breath
Or be forever fused?
When will the house, the road, the shrine,
No more their secret keep,
And the human face seem as divine
Awake, as in its sleep?

Not oddly there are a couple of poems on Thomas Hardy, a chill comment by Siegfried Sassoon—Old Mr Hardy upright in his chair ...

Head propped on hand, he sat with me alone,
Silent, the log fire flickering on his face.
Here was the seer whose words the world had known.
Someone had taken Mr Hardy's place.

Which, as you might say, is something derogatory; Mr Sassoon shouldn't expect a masterpiece at a sitting. The tribute of a younger poet, Mr Day-Lewis—cousinly, fatherly, brotherly?—is on the contrary a little too pat.

Represented favourably are Laurie Lee, whose work is always filled with the fresh air, Geoffrey Grigson, and standing out in ire and grandeur two large poems of George Barker's. John Betjeman is represented by some typical poems and Terence Tiller by two not very much in his kind. The better known poets, indeed, are here the stalwarts who carry the whole.

And now a little note on a new booklet by Padraic Colum, beautifully produced by the Dolmen Press. One can say nothing new about Colum; I seem myself to have said it all over and over again, yet here I touch the old magic once again as when I first read him in late boyhood. There are ten poems here, and all the things that have charmed him to his life which in a way is also the life of Ireland. I am glad to see that he has dedicated the book to another poet, 'once my mentor, always my friend', Seumus O'Sullivan. I can recommend it to anybody.

—*Dublin Magazine*, January–March 1958